Notes from the Third European Urban Summer School

Architecture & Planning in Times of Scarcity
Reclaiming the Possibility of Making

Edited by Deljana Iossifova

THE EUROPEAN URBAN SUMMER SCHOOL (EUSS) AND YOUNG PLANNING PROFESSIONALS AWARDS (YPPA)

Izabela Mironowicz (AESOP) and Derek Martin (IFHP)

In 2010, the Association of European Schools of Planning (AESOP) launched a new annual event: the European Urban Summer School (EUSS) for young planning professionals. AESOP wanted to bring together young professionals and experienced academics and practitioners across Europe to discuss spatial issues.

AESOP's aim was to facilitate a better trans-European understanding of planning issues, promote an exchange of ideas and foster a debate on the most important planning topics. These aims corresponded with AESOP objectives set out in the AESOP Charter.

AESOP offers its teaching resources at EUSSs. Members of AESOP – European universities teaching planning – host the event. The EUSS is not a commercial venture. It is meant as a platform of debate and should be run on as low as possible fee for participants. Tutors do not get any fee for their work.

How it all began...

UN-Habitat, represented by its Central European Office in cooperation AESOP in September 2010 organized the 1st European Urban Summer School (EUSS) for young planning professionals. The host was the Wrocław University of Technology, Poland. The topic of the EUSS was *Heritage and Sustainability*. Izabela Mironowicz was the head of the school while Krzysztof Mularczyk acted as UN Habitat Coordinator.

The 2010 EUSS took as its starting point the fact that urbanisation is a global process, yet it has left a particular legacy in European cities. Students and tutors with diverse backgrounds congregated from all over Europe and beyond in a central European city to gain a better understanding of urban change. Reconciling heritage with development was the challenge to achieve a more sustainable urban future. 'Sustainability' was conceived here as a balance between historic legacy, regeneration and citywide urban transformation. Wroclaw, the host city generously provided the empirical setting to test these assumptions, to verify their validity through international comparisons, and to offer young professionals the opportunity to elaborate interventions towards a more sustainable urban future.

The outcome of EUSS 2010 has been published in *Urban Change. The Prospect of Transformation*, edited by Izabela Mironowicz and Judth Ryser (ISBN 978-83-7493-570-8). The book is also available for download from the AESOP website. Soon it will be ready for comments on the AESOP Digital Platform InPlanning.

AESOP asked other European partners from planning organisations, the European Council of Spatial Planners-Conseil Européen des Urbanistes (ECTP-CEU), European Urban Research Association (EURA), International Federation for Housing and Planning (IFHP) and International Society of City and Regional Planners (ISOCARP) to be involved in the 2nd European Urban Summer School (EUSS) in Lisbon, hosted by Lusófona University. Diogo Mateus was the head of the school and the topic was: *Quality of Space – Quality of Life*.

During the EUSS 2011, participants and tutors explored the definition and meaning of quality of urban space and its relation to the quality of life. Analysing carefully selected cases, they asked numerous questions: did these places lack quality? what was quality itself? how it did relate to urban space? what was essential about quality of urban space? were there components increasing quality of space? what kind of mechanism affected quality of space? But description and analysis were not the goals. They helped with understanding but they did not deliver the answer.

Therefore, the EUSS 2011 also looked for the methods for evaluation, monitoring and improving quality of urban space. Participants tried to compose the guidelines for assessment quality of urban space and comprising the set of tools for refining it. Young planners wanted to offer a solution not only ask the questions.

In 2012, within the framework of the so-called 'Decade of Planning', AESOP decided to invite ECTP-CEU, IFHP and ISOCARP to officially join EUSS. They were therefore active partners in this 3rd EUSS organised by the University of Westminster.

At this last EUSS, an initiative from the Netherlands was integrated into the summer school and challenged young planners with contemporary spatial problems: the *Young Planning Professionals Award (YPPA)*. This is an annual, 3-year international competition (2012-2014) funded by the Directorate responsible for planning at the *Dutch Ministry of Infrastructure and Environment (mI&M)*. Its aim is to stimulate thinking and promote innovative ideas on how spatial planning in Europe can adapt its form and methodologies to take on the present-day challenges and transformations facing our human settlements. The underlying thinking is that it is largely the younger generation (< 35) of planning professionals who will have to come up with the answers, as it is they who will have the responsibility to plan and develop those settlements in the near future.

The ministry asked IFHP and ISOCARP– both then with secretariats in The Hague - to organise the Awards. They decided to bring in AESOP and organise the Award within the framework of the jointly run EUSS. The theme of the Award is related to the theme of the EUSS. The winners get free participation at the EUSS and present their papers at a special session. The papers form part of the EUSS publication which is also generously supported by the mI&M grant.

The theme in 2012 was *Adapting cities to scarcity: new ideas for action. Trends, perspectives and challenges of spatial development in a phase of de-growth an decline in Europe*, in close realtion to the theme of EUSS 2012 *Times of Scarcity – Reclaiming the Possibility of Making*.

This year's award went to Clenn Kustermans for the paper *Shrinkage is Sexy: a New Strategy to Make a Shrinking Urban Area the Most Vital Part of Town* and Sebastian Seyfarth for the paper *Costa de la Ruina: Neglected Places at the Costa des Sol All the Way from Malaga to Manilve*. You will find their papers in this publication along with papers from the runners up and those deserving of an honourable mention.

All partners aim to continue with the EUSS and YPPA and establish it as the platform for young planning professionals for presenting their ideas on major planning issues to equip the profession with new ideas to meet contemporary and future challenges. We are particularly delighted to see the development and improvement of the European Urban Summer School becoming more and more a robust environment of planning ideas and concepts.

Wroclaw and The Hague, December 2013

CONTENTS

INTRODUCTION

REGENERATION

ADAPTATION

INNOVATION

SENSITISATION

PROGNOSTICATION

DIRECTION

APPENDIX

INSURGENCE! RECLAIMING THE POSSIBILITY OF MAKING THE CITY

Deljana Iossifova

In September 2012, almost 100 young planning professionals, post-graduate students, established academics and experienced practitioners came together in London to develop new approaches to issues around scarcity in architecture, planning and design. The Third European Urban Summer School (EUSS) – Times of Scarcity: reclaiming the possibility of making – was hosted in London by the University of Westminster, School of Architecture and the Built Environment, in collaboration with the Association of European Schools of Planning (AESOP), the International Federation for Housing and Planning (IFHP), the European Council of Spatial Planners (ECTP-CEU) and the International Society for City and Regional Planners (ISOCARP). The main partner in facilitating the EUSS was the London team behind the research project Scarcity and Creativity in the Built Environment (SCIBE). To coincide with the third EUSS, the Dutch Ministry of Infrastructure and Environment announced the International Award for Young Planning Professionals to encourage ideas with innovation potential on the topic of 'Adapting Cities to Scarcity: new ideas for action'. The award-winning entries are included in this publication.

Following the first Summer School in collaboration with UN-Habitat in Wroclaw, Poland (2010), and the second in Lisbon, Portugal (2011), we developed the third EUSS as an invitation – a call to arms – for young design and planning professionals to find new ways of thinking about and new tools in response to emerging questions around scarcity. This seemed a particularly timely task in a London marked by the legacy of the Olympic Games and recent austerity measures, just beginning to show their impact on the ground; most explicitly, on the Olympic Fringes. Applications from prospective EUSS participants and tutors were invited in the form of proposed physical or process-based interventions in response to previously identified specific scarcities in the built environment. Selected participants came together in east London to explore a charged territory located in-between central London, the Canary Wharf Estate and the Olympic site and surrounded by highways and railway lines: Bromley-by-Bow.

Six teams were formed and challenged to identify one mode of scarcity in this particular context through on-site explorations and fieldwork exercises; and to propose how to address this creatively through a physical intervention or through a change in the way in which things are done.

To supplement work on their group projects, participants were exposed to a large number of lectures and workshops delivered by devoted speakers and tutors throughout the duration of the EUSS. Every day of the Summer School had its own theme: a thorough introduction to planning in London and the concept and context of scarcity; sensitisation to the subtle nuances and facets of certain notions; awakening creative imagination; considering aspects of renovation; approaches to adaptation; methods of prognostication; pathways to the popularisation of planning; possibilities for outreach and the articulation of new ideas; and finally: the demonstration of projects developed by participants. In the spirit of the Summer School's theme (Times of Scarcity), participants had to adapt to very different working environments, ranging from the splendid surroundings of central London over University premises undergoing refurbishment to the cold- and wetness of Sugarhouse Studios, an old factory building on site which is currently used as an architecture studio, local cinema and pizzeria.

The questions we set out to explore together focused on approaches to architecture, planning and design under conditions of both operational and contextual scarcity. Operational, in that we, as design and planning professionals, increasingly see ourselves forced to work with less, with limited or depleting resources of all sorts: financial, social, natural. Contextual, in that the conditions within which we are asked to intervene are increasingly marked by resource scarcities that seem to encompass all domains of urban life.

It is difficult to produce a valid definition of a notion as multi- faceted as scarcity. Of course, scarcity is when demand outstrips supply. Natural scarcity could be defined as the scarcity of resources which are rare – rare earth, for instance, or precious metals. However, natural scarcity only becomes real through human interaction with a natural condition. All natural phenomena experienced by human beings are directed or at least influenced by human activity. Thus, scarcity is sociomaterial. It is always relational and reveals how resources within society are handled. Scarcity is artificial when it is the result of misdistribution: when the supply of a resource could be large enough to respond to demand – but when demand and supply are tweaked by decisions based on vested interest. Scarcity is engineered when it serves an interest: increased demand for a resource in limited supply will lead to a higher prize and thus more profit; the hoarding of a resource for the in-group will lead to scarcity for the out-group; etc... It is a systemic condition. Scarcity in one place, time or scale can trigger scarcity in another place, time or scale through human – non-human relations and feedback mechanisms. The process of becoming aware of scarcity is the process of social construction. Regardless of the factors that trigger scarcity, it is always perceived and experienced as a real condition. When used on the grounds of political or economic motivation, the idea (and fear) of scarcity may result in real actions with real consequences.

The 'final projects' delivered by the teams were impressive: many went through a lot of effort to discover on the ground what local residents wanted for their neighbourhood; others developed a 'scarcity toolkit', hoping to address the complexity around scarcity in planning; others again proposed new ways of looking at available resources in the area and how to re-use them without adding more infrastructure, money or material. In retrospect, however, what seems worth noting is the very particular process of transformation that participants (and tutors) seemed to undergo during and after the EUSS. Challenged to scrutinise the relevance and value of established design and planning approaches, initially, many participants began to see their possibilities (their 'toolkit') shrink in view of complicated sociopolitical and economic systems that seemed beyond their control; they felt left with just one option: to play along, to become complicit in the further spread and establishment of what they began to view as social, environmental and economic injustice. What are we, as planning and design professionals, to do? After this initial feeling of help- and powerlessness, however, a shared experience of new-found purpose began to emerge, the re-discovery of creativity and the possibility of doing otherwise. So what if scarcities are about more than simple resource depletion? So what if they are embedded in political, social and ecological systems? What are we going to do about it?

Some initial answers to these questions, I hope, will shine through in the material presented on the following pages. They relate clearly to issues of personal and professional integrity; to our ability to exercise our freedom and choose our role within – or outside – the system. They build on our willingness to redefine our profession and to reclaim the possibility of making within and beyond the limits of the city. Most of all, they all require a brave and decisive move: away from complicity and towards insurgence.

London, May 2013

INTRODUCTION

THE CITY

The focus area in context. Source: Google Maps and SCIBE.

Image © 2011 Bluesky

OLYMPICS
2012

BROMLEY-BY-BOW

CANARY
WHARF

©2010 Googl

18

Bromley-by-Bow: administrative ward boundaries. Source: Google Maps and SCIBE.

THE CONTEXT OF SCARCITY: A VERY BRIEF INTRODUCTION TO BROMLEY-BY-BOW

Deljana Iossifova

Scarcity and Creativity in the Built Environment (SCIBE) is a 3-year collaborative research project with teams in London, Vienna, Reykjavik and Oslo. In London, the project looks at the potential of creativity to intervene in the processes that trigger, maintain and reproduce scarcity with a special focus on Bromley-by-Bow, east London, one of the UK's most 'deprived' communities. Instead of inventing or appropriating pre-defined issues around scarcity, we designed our research to bring out what kinds of scarcities are experienced by people in 'deprived' areas, where, we assumed, scarcities of all sorts should certainly be present. Our aim was to develop a non-instrumental 'design brief' which should serve as the basis for work with selected designers (architects) and other creative design and planning professionals. In the hope to understand what scarcity means in the context of a 'deprived' east London ward, we photographed and observed, asked 105 residents to take part in a survey and more than 30 to contribute their own photographs and to tell the stories behind them.

UNCERTAIN FUTURES

When we first began our investigation, Bromley-by-Bow offered reason for hope and for concern. For concern, in that the ward's population was expected to double within the current decade, further impoverished by the Government's recent funding cuts and newly introduced policy reforms. For hope, in that an astonishing amount of cosmetic work was underway or had recently been completed; however, the on-going aggressive commodification of former Council housing in the area was blatantly apparent. When speaking to residents and business owners in the area, we encountered a ubiquitous fear of the future, especially in view of changing planning regulations and public policies: 'What happens when our lease runs out, now that the housing association has taken over? Can we afford the new lease? What will happen to our livelihoods?' These were the questions raised by local shop keepers and business operators; seeing the 'middle class' march in, not one of them seemed confident.

About one third of our participants were college or university graduates, whilst more than ten per cent had only attended primary school. Many were unemployed, but two fifths of our respondents were employed, whilst another fifth consisted of students and pensioners. We found that 46% of our respondents lived on less than £10,000 a year. Three quarters of the people we interviewed lived in flats, followed by those who lived in terraced houses (21.2%). More than eighty-five per cent rented their homes – mostly from the Council or a Housing Association. Less than 15% owned or leased their homes. Seventy three per cent of homeowners felt that they had to restrict their energy use because they were afraid they would not be able to afford it. In total, however, 'only' less than half of all of our respondents were worried about their energy bills. About 40% of all respondents received housing benefits.

'Only' 10.6% stated that they lived under overcrowded conditions. Our interviews revealed how housing standards and occupation rates mean little in a context of constant and continuous 'overcrowding' and when public policy, Council and Housing Associations alike fail to deliver to actual need and instead cater to the wants of another, parallel middle-class. Council attempts to tackle overcrowding and the scarcity of large family homes by offering incentives to move to those under-occupying are met with disdain and resentment: many of these under-occupiers are senior citizens, they have lived their lives in these flats and have watched their children grow, they are attached to these flats and wish to hold on to their memories.

There were the mixed feelings and perceptions of having to wait for the council to provide services, on the one hand; and of being entitled to these services, on the other. Living in council flats, it seemed, discourages agency: alterations are not allowed; thus prohibiting the appropriation of space; thus prohibiting the identification with space; thus prohibiting attachment to space; thus prohibiting agency. Once strong, the sense of community – built on the experience of shared facilities in walking distance: corner shops, dental office, and related facilities were once available in walking distance and neighbours made use of them, thus meeting and bonding with others – has been transformed into a sense of loss as developers moved in to replace the familiar with centralised facilities further away.

There was a shared sense of being invaded as former neighbours were displaced and unknown individuals or developers began to invest in refurbished and new-built flats that then sit empty for years in the face of acute shortage of homes for real people. The show flats, we heard, are routinely bigger than the ones that people end up buying; many were on interest only mortgages, getting nowhere close to their dream of ownership, the promise of profit.

THE NOTION OF COMMUNITY

Only about one quarter of our interviewees were born in the UK; almost two thirds were born in Bangladesh, the majority of them in Sylhet, to be precise. The majority were married and had children. Our in-depth interviews began to reveal complex histories of engineered and inherited scarcities: tracing the triggers of migration leads on to scarcities within entirely different time periods and geographical contexts, histories of occupation and intentional impoverishment as practiced by the British Empire; of exclusion and marginalisation based on place of origin in the own country; of hope and sacrifice upon arrival in Britain; of struggles to survive and struggles to adapt; of dreams and hopes for better futures back 'home'; of the impact of foreign remittances on the conditions of food and water scarcity in the home country, where building and construction activities contribute to the fast decline of the environment; of value systems transformed by the impact of the 'dominant group' in the UK and lost to the logics of the prevailing market systems; of family relations becoming difficult as individuals try to make space for themselves; of journeys back and forth, between Britain and Bangladesh; of feeling torn between the feeling of responsibility for the members of their family and the desire to do better for themselves; of negotiated existences and of real need – not only of the material means to survive, but also of instructions: how does one navigate the system?

'I was better off in Bangladesh' – a frequently encountered statement, revealing the constant awareness, and sometimes regret, that there is an alternative, another place waiting to become home, again; the continuous knowledge that being in the UK was and is a choice: 'You know how it is... You don't know what happens next in Bangladesh'.

On average, people in our sample had lived 8.5 years in their current accommodation. They had moved to Bromley-by-Bow because the Council had given them a flat in the area; whoever had come 'voluntarily' had done so because of the good transportation links or the established Bengali community and the advantages this brings in terms of proximity to relatives, friends and mosques. Despite these motivations, more than half of our informants stated that they never took part in community events. An astonishing 25% of the people we spoke with did not know of a community centre nearby, despite the proximity of the famous Bromley-by-Bow Centre. The fact that a large proportion of residents in the area are of Bangladeshi origin seemed to contribute to the invisibility of any potentially existing communal self-help network (i.e., 'community', as we understand it, is both gendered and hidden; it does not happen in 'public' space).

In fact, we encountered not one, but many communities in Bromley-by-Bow, all intertwined. Each of the existing faith-, ethnicity- or class-based communities worked in their respective own interest, claiming their own space and protecting the assets available to them. The competition for available community spaces between the remaining 'white' population in the area and the Bangladeshi newcomers is large, contributing to moments of hostility between groups as well as individual members.

REGARDING PLANNING AND DESIGN

The architects we spoke with complained about the difficulty of achieving the promises that Councils and Housing Associations have made: decanting decrepit housing blocks is complex, making sure families are moved directly into their new long-term homes, avoiding temporary accommodation, designing for maximum flat number, maximum profit, minimum space... Repeated accounts on the struggle to meet the developer's needs, on the expense of the needs of future residents. Can we assume that commodification of a 'natural' talent or skill, such as creativity, places it on the market – in this case, in the form of 'design'? Does the commodification of creativity have potentially dangerous consequences? If creativity is triggered in response to external challenges to the system – such as, of course, the emergence of scarcities – is design, as commodified creativity, the appropriate skill to assure a resilient response? Creativity may respond to needs. Design responds to wants. Would creativity elsewhere, outside of a capitalist context, serve the evolutionary goals of adaptation and survival – within the capitalist context, as design, it serves first and foremost the accumulation of capital. What, then, are we, as designers, to do under conditions of scarcity?

TEAM 5: PILOTS, PLOTS, PLOYS & PLANS FOR AN ALTERNATE EAST ENDERS

Students: Alessandra Lualdi, Christine Oluwole, Huanqing Li, Marina Sapunova, Sebastian Seyfarth

Tutor: Steven Chodoriwsky

Footage available for viewing here: http://goo.gl/20KZGC

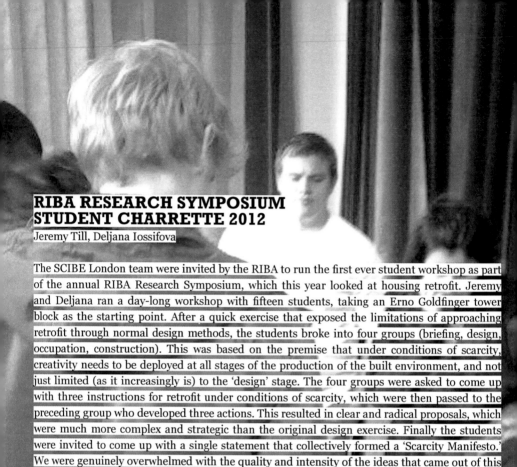

RIBA RESEARCH SYMPOSIUM
STUDENT CHARRETTE 2012
Jeremy Till, Deljana Iossifova

The SCIBE London team were invited by the RIBA to run the first ever student workshop as part of the annual RIBA Research Symposium, which this year looked at housing retrofit. Jeremy and Deljana ran a day-long workshop with fifteen students, taking an Erno Goldfinger tower block as the starting point. After a quick exercise that exposed the limitations of approaching retrofit through normal design methods, the students broke into four groups (briefing, design, occupation, construction). This was based on the premise that under conditions of scarcity, creativity needs to be deployed at all stages of the production of the built environment, and not just limited (as it increasingly is) to the 'design' stage. The four groups were asked to come up with three instructions for retrofit under conditions of scarcity, which were then passed to the preceding group who developed three actions. This resulted in clear and radical proposals, which were much more complex and strategic than the original design exercise. Finally the students were invited to come up with a single statement that collectively formed a 'Scarcity Manifesto.' We were genuinely overwhelmed with the quality and intensity of the ideas that came out of this short exercise, suggesting that scarcity thinking has wide implications for architectural education. The day is summarised in the presentation Jeremy made to the RIBA: http://goo.gl/6ehbtw.

MIND THE GAP: FACTS ABOUT SCARCITY? A CONFRONTATION OF GOVERNMENTAL AND USERS' PERSPECTIVES OF OVERCROWDING IN BRITISH HOUSING

Michael Klein, Barbara Elisabeth Ascher, Isis Nunez Ferrera

Scarcity can be understood as an attempt to state a condition of lack or a limit of availability of something. What and when we consider something to be scarce relates to large extents to the motivation and the respective standpoint from where the claim scarcity is raised. The contextual forces, which range from the material conditions and its use to the cultural practices, norms and values expressed by people living in those specific environments, can be considered a decisive factor for the differences from what one considers as scarce to the other. Ultimately, it is a matter for what purpose we raise the question about scarcity: from a historical distance, from the perspective of the directly affected, as a designer, policy maker or from a critical theoretical perspective. It is, however, as well a question of the limits referred to and a matter of distribution, i.e. who gets what share.

In order to discuss the challenges of scarcity in the discourses in planning and architecture, we look at the specific case of overcrowding in housing. Overcrowding can be considered a specific, 'actual' scarcity, as opposed to the theoretic abstraction of the concept of scarcity. Indeed, we are aware that any form of scarcity is constructed. Our aim is to discuss a dualism which arises from the attempt of separating abstract concepts from praxis within the realm of planning. Because of the relational character of scarcity, the dualism of the abstract category and the everyday experience and practices also affects our understanding of overcrowding. What we consider scarce, does not only relate to the respective context, but, in its relational nature, it shifts and alters with the changing context, which raises the question of how to define or determine scarcity. 25

This is the case in the setting of a standard and an example in the built environment provides the overcrowding standard. Even though overcrowding is not equal to scarcity, it presupposes scarcity: scarcity is underlying overcrowding, for the argument goes 'too many persons' for 'too little' space. Overcrowding – we are referring to the British case here – has been a 'consistent worry'[1] in this country. It could be described as well documented – as a concern of defining the 'problematic living conditions' indeed; the other side of those affected however often goes unheard. The goal of this text is to shed light onto the circumstances and methods in 'defining' the problem of overcrowding through occupancy rates by policy-makers and researchers and, by doing so also helped to 'construct' the problem and to confront it with perceptions of the other

---

1   So Former Housing Minister Keith Hill in a parliamentary debate, see HC Deb 20 January 2004 c26

side, of the concerned.

A designative line of scarcity, so it exists, should be identifiable by following various methodical paths. The conduct of research by detour of more than one approach, sometimes termed triangulation in qualitative research methods should help to validate findings by more than one source and a surplus of knowledge. Moreover, multiple viewpoints and methodical approaches further enrich the knowledge by the various epistemological potentials (cf. Flick 2009, p.444). For our purpose here, triangulation is taken up not for validating (a truth of scarcity) by dual evidence, but instead for discussing scarcity as a contingent category in relation to its background, as we can assume that scarcity will differ from one time to another, from one place and perspective to another. Investigation thus the position of the administrative body of the state concerning overcrowding on the one hand and contrasting it with the experience of overcrowding of dwellers on the other should help to elaborate the difficulties and risks of (necessary) standardisation as well as it should create awareness for planners to pay regard to the ambiguity and relativity of the issue of scarcity.

Overcrowding, 'the too small accommodation for your household' as British housing organization Shelter explains it[2] has been a particular a is one thing state interventions into housing have sought to eliminate. To do so, the body of administration draws upon the level of occupancy, a second-order concept based on two - more or less unchallenged- concepts: the one of household and the one of dwelling.[3] Both of them, the count of dwellers and the physical configuration, i.e. size and rooms, determine housing according to their standards and together form the basis for measuring occupancy. The exceeding of a rate of occupancy - which often accompanies 'poverty' - has been tackled by welfare states. By doing so, the states have re-inscribed their power into housing markets countering over-occupancy by defining a 'truth' of overcrowding:

> 'To ensure that dwellings do not exceed this [level of occupancy], an overcrowding norm is set. The level is in part determined by what housing administrators and politicians believe to be acceptable minimum standards, but naturally there is a potential disagreement about where the line should be drawn' (Kemeny 1992, p.28).

The history of shifts of the perception of overcrowding does not only hint at the contingency of such standards, but they also reference the problem to generalize the implications on housing on a universal level. Various actors have tried to frame overcrowding differently at different times. What was considered a decent standard of living entailed long-lasting debates in the field in policy-making. It diverges even more when looking at different cultures of living together.

The following sections on the historical discourse related to overcrowding in Britain and the interviews from a case-study on the perceptions of scarcity by the local residents in the London Bromley-by-Bow, the area of study of the EUSS 2012 summer school, illustrates different routes of investigation and their implication on the establishment of the definition of overcrowding.

THE STANDARDISATION OF OVERCROWDING

The standard of overcrowding was first introduced into the British legal system by The Housing

---

2   As described by Shelter. See: http://england.shelter.org.uk
3   Against this schemes much housing research draws upon, Jim Kemeny(1992, p.10) argues for the use of 'residence', referring to dwelling as a home in its locational context.

Act from 1935. This standard, set out in part 10 of the act, measures overcrowding by basically two factors. The first, 'sexual overcrowding' is reached if two persons of opposite sexes have to share one room (with the exception of married couples) including living rooms and kitchens. The second is a count of the people - each dweller counting as one, only children below ten years of age are counted as a half – and set in proportion to the number of rooms the accommodation provides. This is measured against a nominal standard scheme (1 room for 2 persons; 2 rooms for 3 persons; etc.). Everything that is not conform to the scheme is overcrowded. [4]

The statutory standard of overcrowding in the 1935 housing act was accompanied by a large-scale survey in the years 1935- 36, measuring the extents of overcrowding and, implicitly, what would be necessary to counter it. In its relation to the survey and beyond, the intended policy for decent living conditions, the standard obtains full meaning. The measurability of overcrowding in housing entered the sphere of law through a policy package and it did so for the purpose of public utility. By means of law, the state sought to establish a standard below which housing was no longer tolerable. Neither should people live in unsanitary nor in overcrowded conditions for reasons of endangerment - of the public health on the one hand and of morality of the people on the other. To be more precise, thus, doing away with overcrowding and the negative epiphenomena, rather than a decent living was the motivation for the housing act.

The setting of the standard of overcrowding gave a measure of scarcity, to determine an almost 'technical truth' of scarcity. This meaning is not present in the object of housing itself or in the living conditions, but it is constructed within the discursive formation as a relation between the institution of the state-government, the practice and means of law and the concern of the occupancy of the built objects[5]. Because of their relational nature, the understanding of scarcity and overcrowding heavily rely to the contextual forces that determine them on a legal basis. In doing so, the management of overcrowding by means of standardization and regulation becomes an instrument of power. As the standard signifies the line that separates what is tolerable from what is not, it also marks and defines scarcity in the occupancy of living space as well as it regulates supply and demand. By the setting of the standard and the policing of an area on base of particular knowledge and practices, the scope of the governmental body and its power extends into new domains. Here, discursive formations re-establish and re-inscribe the power of the state authority in the realm of housing through the new standard, below which the living conditions must not remain.

Once the survey had been conducted and the standard been established as a norm, renting out under conditions of overcrowding meant an offense against the law and resulted in a penalty for the landlord and the eviction of the tenants. The survey was conducted by the Health Department, yet the authority and avengement lied in the scope of the local government, which also allocate social housing to tackle overcrowding.

The discursive formation of power and the standard of overcrowding further imply that, for power is created within, the standard cannot be considered as absolute and set in stone, but it is a possible subject to hegemonic struggles. For the overcrowding standard, this was the case from the onset and the implementation of the Housing Act through the national government. Already at the time of implementation, the Labour party heavily criticised the standard for it implicitly

---

4   See Housing Act 1935
5   See e.g. Hall (Hall 1997, p.44): 'Meaning is constructed within discourse (...) and nothing which is meaningful exists outside discourse.' The discursive formation exists as a relationship between the involved institutions, practices and more; they are 'are not present in the object'. (Foucault 2002, p.49)

involved the acceptance of everything above standard. With 3.8% of the total households, the number of overcrowded appeared rather low; the standard, so the assumption was to become the legitimization of everything slightly above overcrowding.

Even though the standard was not considered as an ideal and the intention of the government was that its low level should become obsolete and be updated according to respective requirements[6], it was neither touched nor changed. The housing acts of 1957 and of 1985, in spite of several requests and claims[7] saw the overcrowding standard from 1935 continued in consolidated forms. Only in course of the Housing Act 2004 the (Labour) Government put effort to amend the overcrowding standard by a new form of measuring, for the one used up until that date was 'no longer defensible in a modern society'. One major reason for that discussion is that overcrowding, as mentioned, is the base drawn on for allocating social housing in determining priorities[8]. Yet because overcrowding is higher amongst social renters, allocation and also necessary re-allocation has to relate to the standard.

The New Labour Government subsequently published several papers on the behalf of the effects of overcrowding and the issue of a change in defining the standard. [9] The housing health and safety rating system was considered to tackle overcrowding for a while [10], yet ultimately, a statutory standard of overcrowding was to remain as a 'fall-back'. The proposition therefore was to follow the Bedroom Standard developed in the 1960s and used in the Survey on English Housing since 1993/94. The Bedroom Standard regards composition of the household, age and sex when contrasting a target standard model of allocation of bedrooms[11] to the factual number of bedrooms that the apartment provides (convertible spaces such as kitchens are no longer counted). It is complemented by the Space Standard(including a referencing breakdown of floor area) with the Overcrowding Bill as amendments of the statutory 1985 (1936) definition. This bill was presented as a secondary legislation in 2004to be tested by pathfinder authorities, which favoured to adopt the new standardand from then on formed also the basis for strategy documents. The amendment was projected for 2009, underlining a phased and manageable move. In 2011, the new Coalition Government again posed the question whether the 1985 overcrowding definition was eligible to describe acceptable living conditions anew. A majority of respondents said that it was no longer fit for purpose. The respondents' suggestion was to use the bedroom standard.

The change and its relating debates are interesting for the issues that have been risen along. The Labour Government has repeatedly underlined not to defend the existing standard, yet refused 'symbolic gestures'. In the debate, the governments promoted the bedroom standard, but they shifted to focus on strategies to tackle overcrowding, to differentiate social housing supply and adapt it to urgent needs, to delivering more affordable homes and on strategies how to re-allocate 'under-occupied' housing. The 'hesitant' implementation of a new statutory standard lies in its enormous impact. Raising the standard would ultimately increase the demand for housing. Instead, one rather favoured improving the housing supply. Furthermore, a new standard could fall back on the local authorities and the respective allocation schemes for social housing, because

---

6   See HC Deb 30 January 1935 c364
7   For example:: later example: HC Deb 29 January 1996 vol 270 cc647-750
8   Housing Act 1996
9   See: (Office of the Deputy Prime Minister 2004)(Dep. for Communities and Local Government 2006)
10   The proposal of a New HousingFitness Standard to tackle overcrowding
11   The Bill schedules a bedroom for each person over 21 years of age, for cohabitating couples, for two of the same sex between 10 and 20, for two persons under ten, two of same sex if one is between 10 and 20 and the other under 10, for any person not fitting to this standard. Cf. Overcrowding Bill 2004 , p.2

housing issues still is a public concern. Ultimately, the debate on the overcrowding standard raises the question of standards in general - not only in the efforts needed for amendment, but also who is benefitting from it.

The bedrooms standard addresses a rather low level of overcrowding as the British Housing Condition Survey after the implementation shows: approximately 3 % of the total households are overcrowded in the 2008-09 survey. It varies by tenure, highest among social renters (6.7%) and above average among private renters (5.4%) [12] and by ethnicity and it is higher in urban areas headed by London. Already in 2010, however, the NHF prognosticated a drastic rise of overcrowding as an effect of the crisis and recent notes seem to confirm this expectancy and recent austerity cuts have also hit the housing sector particularly on the side of low income.

THE PERCEPTION OF OVERCROWDING

'We have two singles and two doubles here, and seven people altogether. My husband and my son have the singles. Myself and the baby boy, we have a double. The other double, my mother-in-law shares with the two girls. She is here permanently [...]' [13]

This account of a 36 year old married woman with four kids on their bed-room situation in a council flat in London, depicts the gap between the legal definition of overcrowding and the perception of the described condition as a state of being filled with more people or things than is desirable. [14] Using the survey on housing conditions in Bromley-by-Bow that was conducted by the London-team of the SCIBE research group between autumn 2010 and spring 2012 as a source, the following findings reveal a different notion of overcrowding than the official statistics are able to uncover. [15]

The selected interviews as summarized in the brief for the 'Scarce times: alternatives futures' competition in May 2012 and in the brief for the EUSS in September 2012, are based on 105 semi-structured interviews with local residents in Bromley-by-Bow, supported by diaries and photographic essays by some of the inhabitants of the area. The following examples are not meant to deliver a complete picture of all possible impacts of overcrowding, but they take advantage of the social situatedness of the research data: 'Know that the human meaning of public issues must be revealed by relating them to personal troubles- and to the problems of the individual life.' (Mills 2000, p.226) The qualitative material hence emphasizes the local dimension of overcrowding and the impact it has on everyday-life of the affected residents. [16] The empirical material of the case-study on Bromley-by-Bow shows that only 10% of the interviewed residents lived under conditions

---

12 See (Communities and Local Government 2010)
13 Here and in the following: SCIBE and The Architecture Foundation (SCIBE & The Architectural Foundation 2012)
14 Collins English Dictionary
15 The increasing use of ethnographic material within interdisciplinary spatial practice is noteworthy. See Jane Rendell (2010, p.175)'...the ways in which disciplines foreground and value certain patterns of enquiry and knowledge production, and ignore, marginalize and even repress others. Perhaps the very interest that architecture currently has in ethnographic practice is present precisely because these methodologies contain qualities and activities that have been and are currently cast aside and devalued in architecture...'
16 The open-ended approach towards an investigation based on personal encounters has obvious weaknesses looking at the possibility to validate and universalize findings, especially if the standpoint and intentions of the interviewer does not become obvious. A certain doubt about biases of the research has to remain, especially when the theoretical backgrounds, power-relations between actors and the context of the interview situation are not made sufficiently transparent.

considering the legal definition (SCIBE & The Architectural Foundation 2012, p.27), based on the Bedroom Standard[17].

Fifteen per cent of the interviewed residents shared accommodation with persons they were not related to, not necessarily under conditions of overcrowding. According to the documentation of selected interviews, we can assume, that there might be a larger number of men than women, who share accommodation with non-relatives. Most of them are either renting a place together as a group or are subletting from a private owner, who lives in the flat. All female interviewees sharing accommodation had some kind of family relation to the other members within the same household. Although it might seem as if only a minority experiences overcrowding themselves, a larger community reports being affected, especially by the misuse of public and semi-private space for private purposes such as laundry and storage.

Overcrowding and the quality of the accommodation are treated as two separate issues in the survey, with a separate account on the building standard and comfort level of the apartments. This important link between those issues is inflicted by the fact, that not all rooms of an apartment could be used for permanent habitation in the most extreme cases due to their health-hazardous conditions or certain day-activities due to poor thermal insulation or lacking daylight, as the following example of Claire, a woman in her late 40ties, who lives in a 1-bedroom apartment in Bromley-by-Bow delineates:

'At the night she and her sister sleep together on a mattress on the floor of the sitting room. They both have problems breathing in the bedroom-the walls and ceiling have become overgrown with mould' [18]

Raising standards of living had and have impact both on the definition of overcrowding, but as well on the expectations connected to the availability of certain standards for everyone. As 31year-old mother of four Bahiya´s following statement of illustrates

'You know what makes us have take-out food? That kitchen! I don´t want to cook here. A big kitchen to cook; not like my box! A bigger kitchen, more storage, an additional toilet- that would be good! A nice dining room- that´s what makes you happy and lead a healthy life!' [19]

Notions of desirable apartment standards often influenced by an ideal of residence that represents spatial equality relative to others:

'Where I come from, sharing is good. But here, I am waiting for me to have my own room!' [20]

It may be noted at this point, that there is some indication that the perception of overcrowding either as a 'choice of living' or a 'denied better' situation seems to influence the way people talk about these issues, although their living situation might be clearly defined as overcrowded according to the given standard. In Phillipa´s case, a 48year old married woman with one child

---

17 The following definition based on the Bedroom Standard has been given: 1 room = 2 people, 2 rooms = 3 people, 3 rooms = 5 people, 4 rooms = 7.5 people, 5 rooms or more = 2 people per room, and did not take into account room sizes
18 (SCIBE & The Architectural Foundation 2012, p.41)
19 i.b.d. , p.81
20 i.b.d. , p.81

that lives in a one bedroom Council flat, she chooses to take in family members on a temporary basis:

'Two nieces stay with her often, and so a lot of space in her sitting room is occupied by the bunk bed they sleep in. Phillipa cannot find anything to complain about with regards to her flat and thinks of it being in a very good condition.' [21]

This positive attitude towards overcrowding may be especially true for homeowners that are subletting parts of their apartments in order to finance the down payment of their mortgages. This becomes evident in the case of separated 47 year old home-owner Ahmed:

'Inspired by the Chinese couple next door-who let out their bedroom and added a partition wall between the originally open-plan kitchen and the sitting-room Ahmed found a Bangladeshi flatmate. He charges him 750 Pound a month and is happy to have found a way to ease his financial burdens- and someone to keep him company when he comes home from work in the evenings. Even, if that means sacrificing his only bedroom. 'The siting room looks quite cramped now, as I am using it as my bedroom. There is not enough space to hang clothes my flatmate is using the back of the door." [22]

In which regard the provided dwellings are capable of providing multiple activities simultaneously or asynchronous in a night-day rhythm seems crucial on how residents could adapt spaces, when facing a housing crisis due to financial distress, or relocation, or other conditions that trigger overcrowding for example hosting a long-term visitors from abroad.Statements as the following from Jhuma and Ziaul, a married couple with two children that live temporarily in a two bedroom flat assigned by Poplar HARCA, the local Housing and Regeneration Community Association, are thus not uncommon in a multi-cultural community as Bromley-by-Bow:

'My mother-in-law is here to visit right now. She can only bear to stay with us a few weeks at a time, because she misses the company, the community back home. It´s like jail here she says.' [23]

The significance of the home as a gathering space becomes increasingly relevant when the financial means of a family do not allow them to participate in social, cultural or commercial life in the same extend as others. This maybe especially true for children, whose needs vary widely according to their age: 'Our flat is overcrowded. I mean, it´s alright now, but when the kids grow older it will be difficult.' [24] Bahiya, a 31year old single mother of four kids living in a 2 bedroom flat worries.As she continues:

'There are just buildings, nothing more. It will be too many people in one place soon. No freedom for the kids! If you put them in the house, they will be frustrated. They won´t get self-confidence. You can´t let them play on the balcony-there are people who need to take a

31

21   i.b.d. , p.96
22   i.b.d. , p.46-59
23   i.b.d. , p.75
24   i.b.d. , p.72

rest, who need to go to work. They will complain about the kids.' [25]

Widening the scope of the understanding of overcrowding to a local and regional context, it becomes obvious that measuring persons accommodated per apartment only measures one scale of the problem, while neglecting for instance the scale of dwelling densities – number of residents per km² - as a crucial factor for the living conditions of larger areas.

FROM OVERCROWDING TO SCARCITY?

The residents´ perspective on issues of overcrowding contrasts and/or complements the understanding of overcrowding as described and defined in official standards. In such a way, taking into account the substantial information the material provides has capacities to fulfil a substantial role: First, it would contribute to a more nuanced understanding of overcrowding. With the collected information, overcrowding can no longer be broken down to a simple persons-per-rooms ratio. The material of interviews assembles multiple experiences of residents that accounts for an ordinary knowledge about overcrowding and the perceived scarcity and the everyday tactics to cope with these conditions of scarcity. In doing so, this added perspective could also serve as an empowerment strategy directed towards overcoming the hegemony of interpretation and the definition of what is scarce by official institutions within an established political system as the basis for housing policies. Research thus can be understood as a tool, which underlines the relativity of the hegemonic practices in defining as well as it creates opportunities for alternative interpretations and possible future interventions. Doing so, the 'critical theoretical perspective aims at producing knowledge and understanding that has the potential to change the world for the better' (Soja 2010, p.192).

Regarding the research on scarcity and the built environment, the complementary investigation of the official perspective and one considering the knowledge of residents and users could contribute to a deeper understanding of the issue. None of them is actually able to map the whole field of processes or impacts that contribute to a 'multi-perspective' picture of the problem that takes into account various positions.

Scarcity is shaped by complex local and global social and political processes, historical determinations, respective time frames of investigation and ambitions for future scope of action. The framework of how to go about when researching on scarcity is therefore crucial, as it will establish certain relationships of factors and emphasize certain aspects over others. Due to the complex, interdisciplinary and abstract nature of scarcity, no one single method would guarantee a research result of a complete overview over scarcity. It is therefore necessary to ask ourselves which kind of information we need in order to make more informed decisions within housing policies, urban-planning and architecture and how this could be translated into non-reductionist research strategies, supporting the idea, that a complex problem is more than an account of its different constituents. A complementary approach does, however, not need to remain limited to the field of research. Particularly the field housing, architecture and the built environment that shows gradual transitions from research activity to implementation and policy would provide manifold aspects of applying different methodical approaches.

While such perspectives will not easily come up with consensual solutions for the possible disagreement of the respective interests, they provide the necessary stable foundation of

---

25   i.b.d. , p.76

definitions that would prepare the common ground for fruitful dialogues. The implied potential for disagreement destabilized especially second-order concepts, such as overcrowding or scarcity. For the governmental perspective of planning authority this implies partially abandoning holding a single truth of scarcity and overcrowding. Moreover, this would entail the potential for a truly different conception of what policy can be: Shifting from the order of a top-down perspective in the very sense of policing towards a 'weak' and open understanding of non-pre-determined policy as a social process of negotiation.

References

Communities and Local Government, 2010. English Housing Survey Headline Report 2008-09, London.

Dep. for Communities and Local Government, 2006. Tackling Overcrowding in England.

Flick, U., 2009.An Introduction to Qualitative Research, London: SAGE.

Foucault, M., 2002.The Archaeology of Knowledge, Abingdon England ; New York, NY: Routledge.

Hall, S., 1997. Representation: Cultural Representations and Signifying Practices, London: SAGE.

Kemeny, J., 1992. Housing and Social Theory, London - New York: Routledge.

Mills, C.W., 2000. The Sociological Imagination, Oxford University Press.

Office of the Deputy Prime Minister, 2004.The Impact of Overcrowding on Health and Education: A Review of the evidence and Literature, London.

Rendell, J., 2010. Afterword: working through the field. In S. Ewing et al., eds. Architecture and Field/Work. Abington: Taylor & Francis.

SCIBE & The Architectural Foundation, 2012. Scarce Times: Alternative Futures. London, University of Westminster, London: University of Westminster.

Shelter, Available at: http://england.shelter.org.uk.

Soja, E.W., 2010. Seeking Spatial Justice, UnivOf Minnesota Press.

Figure 1-2 Sugarhouse Studios when Assemble moved in. Source: Assemble.

Figure 1-3 Event evening at Sugarhouse Studios. Source: Assemble.

SCARCITY IN PRACTICE: ASSEMBLE AND SUGARHOUSE STUDIOS

If scarcity is the disjunction between wants/ambitions and the resources at hand, our work has been a process of prioritizing things, or the process of finding alternative means to fulfil ambitions. It is worth saying that what brought us together to work independently and in an undefined/continuously evolving way [as Assemble, a design and architecture collective], was our previous experience working in offices. The scarcity could be described as the lack of integrated design, or an understanding of how a task relates to the overall project ambition; how a CAD drawing relates to the act of casting concrete.

As our practice grows, more 'scarcities' creep up, such as financial resources in relation to growing ambition, our experience in relation to a desire to maintain a democratic management, etc... Sometimes the realization of the 'scarcity' in a project, or in a situation, is what frames subsequent problem solving. Ignoring the 'scarcity', i.e. not taking a step back, has always had a detrimental effect on the work – for example not working out the budget/sustainability of a thing; relying too much on the power of on-site instinct; or vice versa. Similarly allowing the scarcity to lead the design has produced unexpected results. For Cineroleum for example, the desire to recreate the luxury of the picture palace combined with the need to find the cheapest, most durable materials. Similarly much consideration was invested into the details of the foyer, as well as the programming of the films – from popcorn holders to staff uniforms, car noise friendly films, everything was important. Not to mention the importance of making profit on the bar, as a way of covering our overheads.

SUGARHOUSE STUDIOS

Sugarhouse Studios is a project which gradually developed in collaboration with the LLDC. It all began with our scarcity of storage space for all the Cineroleum materials which we have inherited after completion of the project (mainly chairs and curtains). Calling up our local councils to find an abandoned room for all our stuff led us to Unit A2 on 107 High Street in Stratford – a light industrial building, owned in 2011 by the LDA property, then the LLDC and now LandProp Holding. We initially agreed to retrofit the property, to accommodate and programme a fortnightly community film club in return for rent and a place to work. Prior to this Assemble existed in each other's living rooms and pubs or via lengthy email threads. This building was in a state of disrepair, full of previous tenants' things; it has been squatted for a few years since the Griffin Signs business went bankrupt.

Now the whole Sugarhouse Lane area is earmarked for development - the 13 acre residential mixed use development Strand East. The certainty of our building's demolition and the initial short term lease (our first agreement was only for one year) had a direct impact on construction of the space. Gradually the project grew, a pizza oven was installed, local organisations got involved in our public programme, our office gradually set up in the back of the building, forming more of a residency. With the public events programme, we tried to focus on issues related to development of east London, got people involved in making things as well as just having fun in this big light industrial building. Casting concrete with school children via Groundwork; celebrating the new Young Mayor with Newham Youth Council; running across the A11 with Run Dem Crew; or watching Utopia London followed by Q&A with the director.

Although Sugarhouse Studios has worked as a destination, or venue for conferences and special events such as the Summer School, general footfall has proven difficult on daily basis. However, it was the recognition of our place in the Sugarhouse Yard and the wider Stratford High Street business community, which became a significant part of our residency. Making the connections to our neighbours, such as the two music schools and building equipment suppliers, or the residents across the road, is gradually shaping our ambitions for the space. Gaining popularity with students as a place to buy food and play ping pong, we secured a contract with Access to Music to become their official canteen. Similarly, the popularity of events and the benefit of 'creative' enterprise in what could otherwise be a semi-demolition site have helped us gain a lease extension with LandProp as the new landlord of the site. With at least another two years ahead, potentially longer (depending on the speed of Strand East), we hope to take part in the rapid and particular development of this part of Stratford High Street.

Figure 1-4 The Cineroleum - one of Assemble's projects - transformed a disused gas station into a cinema.
Source: Assemble.

Figure 1-5 The Cineroleum: a self-made cinema! Source: Assemble.

REGENERATION

The A12 cutting through Bromley-by-Bow. Source: Deljana Iossifova/SCIBE.

STRATEGIC PLANNING IN LONDON IN AN AGE OF SCARCITY

Duncan Bowie

As one of the leading 'world cities', the governance and planning of London generates considerable international interest. London's hosting of the 2012 Olympics focused significant attention on the city, but it is important to study the development of London as a whole as well as the delivery of a single mega-event.

In the last decade, London has changed dramatically, the most visible change being the London skyline, with a new host of high-rise buildings – with the recently completed Shard building being, at least for the time being, the highest building in Western Europe. But it is important to look beyond the most visible change and to understand both the successes and failures of London's governance and spatial planning regimes; to understand the interaction of the recession, representing scarcity of public and private resources, and the scarcity of land imposed by historic but intentionally created spatial planning policies. In 2000, London chose its first directly elected Mayor. For the previous 14 years, London did not have its own directly elected administration and with the abolition of the Greater London Council in 1986, was directly managed by Central Government. The 33 lower tier authorities – the 32 London boroughs and the Corporation of the City of London continued to provide local services, but were not in practice strategic authorities. Central Government was responsible for strategic planning guidance and ran some investment programmes directly (for example the Housing Investment Programme through its agency, the Housing Corporation) or allocated capital and revenue resources to the boroughs. The borough-controlled London Planning Advisory Committee could advise the Government but had no statutory basis to publish plans. The establishment of the Mayoralty in 2000 created a new regional executive authority, together with an elected London assembly to act as scrutiny body. The Mayor became the strategic planning authority for London and was also given powers to intervene in specific new developments. The Mayor was also given control of London's bus and underground network, though not of its surface rail network, and part control of the London Development Agency, the Government's regional regeneration organisation.

London's history of strategic planning is not a narrative of continuous progression. The Abercrombie plans of 1943 and 1944 (the County of London Plan and the Greater London Plan) are rightly famous. The London Plan produced by the Mayor in 2004 was only the third region-wide plan for London. The County of London 1960 review was limited to inner London. The Greater London Development plan was not adopted until 1976 and the amendments proposed by the Labour controlled Greater London Council in 1986 fell with the abolition of the GLC. The London Plan drew on the European tradition of spatial planning and its focus on economic, environment and social sustainability reflected the approach set out in the European Spatial Development Perspective This was later to be reflected in the relatively short lived provisions on regional planning in the 2004 Planning and Compulsory Purchase Act.

London planning has faced a number of challenges in the last decade. The first challenge has been the impact of globalisation, with the growth of the financial services sector and London's increasingly critical role within world financial markets and its pre-eminent role in relation to relative to other financial centres such as New York and Tokyo.

The second has been a significant growth in population, an increased diversity of population and significant levels of both in-migration and out-migration, with an increasingly mobile labour market, but also with a growing reputation as a relatively safe haven, both for business in terms of its attractive labour market and tax regime and for those fleeing from other countries in terms of a relative high level of security and tolerance. London has become the most ethnically and linguistically diverse city in the world – a true world metropolis, and a city which largely tolerates and even welcomes its diversity, though this does not mean that the city is completely free of racism and ethnic discrimination. London has its attractions and opportunities for young skilled professionals from across the world.

The third challenge was the change of governance arrangements which impacted on spatial planning and its implementation. The 1999 Greater London Authority Act, piloted through parliament by the Minister for London, Nick Raynsford, intentionally established the mayoralty as a small executive authority without direct service delivery functions. In the 2007 Greater London Act, as a result of effective lobbying by the first Mayor, Ken Livingstone, the Mayor's powers were extended to include responsibility for the London housing strategy, and then in 2012 direct control of the Government housing investment budget. The 2007 Act also strengthened the Mayor's planning powers. These changes reflected on the growing success of Livingstone and his successor Boris Johnson, who were seen as strong advocates for London. While both mayors at times challenged central government – Livingstone for example over the issue of the private financing agreement for improvements to the underground railway network and Johnson over airport strategy, both Labour and Coalition governments were prepared to devolve further powers to the Mayor. The onset of the localism agenda under the post 2010 Government shifted the balance of power more in favour of the mayor, without strengthening the ability of the London boroughs, or for that matter, the elected London Assembly, to challenge the mayor.

The fourth challenge was the recession of 2008, with the weakening of both the financial services sector on which London's economy largely depended and the stagnation of the housing market, not just in terms of transactions in the second hand homes market, but in terms of the slowing down of the new development programme. London however recovered relatively quickly from the recession. By mid-2012 housing prices had reached and in some cases significantly exceeded pre-recession levels. While some major development schemes were on hold, the prime central London property market, with significant investment in new residential and commercial development. Money flowed to London from the Middle East and the Gulf States, South and East Asia, while the Eurozone crisis led to investment from some European countries moving to London. With new tax regimes being introduced in some European countries, most recently France, London is seen as wealth friendly and tax light. Within the UK, there has been an increasing differentiation between the economic strength of London and the stagnant or even declining economies of provincial centres. The focus on London as an island of prosperity has not only revived the historic North/South debate but also diverted attention on the increasing inequities within London.

The spatial planning model that was adopted by Ken Livingstone as Mayor was that of the 'compact city'. Influenced by both urban designers and architects such as Richard Rogers, who led on the study 'Towards an Urban Renaissance' for the central government, and under pressure from both environmentalists and city business interests, Livingstone adopted the view that

London should seek to contain both its population and employment growth within the existing London boundary. With a rigid policy on the protection of the Green Belt and other open space, this meant building at much higher densities – upwards rather than outwards. This alliance of economic and environmentalist pressures did however lead to the falling off of the social planning agenda, as new homes became smaller and more expensive, involving vertical social segregation.

The decade saw a significant reduction not just in the supply of existing social housing for lower income groups, but a falling off of the proportion of social rented family sized homes in the new development programme. Significant reductions in government investment in new homes was a critical factor, and by 2012 the Government had stopped all funding for social rented homes, preferring instead to focus on the provision of sub market rented homes by the private and housing association sectors, with low income households being supported through increased welfare payments including housing benefit. London has seen further social polarisation, which is increasingly taking a spatial form as central London becomes dominated by the very wealthy from around the world, while low income Londoners get pushed to the periphery and beyond. Yet despite these trends and a population growth nearly twice the previous rate, the belief in the compact city is largely unchallenged – and the Johnson 2011 London Plan only includes relatively minor changes from the Livingstone 2004 and 2008 versions, though under the Johnson regime, following the lead of the national Coalition government of David Cameron, there has been a further move away from the provision of genuinely affordable social rented housing.

There has not been any fundamental rethink, nor has there been sufficient analysis by academics or practitioners of the outcomes of spatial planning in London - of the failures as well as the successes. The focus on the 2012 Olympics has perhaps diverted attention away from the study of wider issues and it is only in recent months that there has been a public recognition of the extent of London's housing crisis. The compact city/sprawl debate also needs to be revisited and a proper debate held as to the most sustainable form of development to meet London's future needs.

It is important to recognise that in the context of analysing spatial planning and housing policies, *scarcity results from choices and is not an inevitable paradigm*. Scarcity of public resources is the consequence of a decision by Government not to introduce a more progressive taxation policy which would have generated significant additional receipts for government reinvestment. Scarcity of private resources in the post-recession period was a temporary consequence of the mismanagement of financial and housing markets, as the availability of private finance for both development and home purchase through mortgages was constrained, without sufficient counterbalancing public sector intervention to fill the financing gap. However, it only had a relatively short term impact and today international investment is generating a new property boom in London which has significant negative as well as positive effects as homes are developed for the needs of the international investment market rather than for the needs of Londoners.

Perceived scarcity of land partly reflects a Government decision at both national and Mayoral level not to develop on undeveloped land. As referred to above this policy has had a significant negative impact in terms of social planning objectives. The use of the terms 'scarcity' and 'austerity' in the UK context are of course relative. Scarcity can be a consequence of Government policy as well as the limitations on natural resources such as the availability of land. Austerity can also be a consequence of Government decisions – a Government decision to raise tax leads to limitations on the availability of public funding for investment. Compared with many other countries, investment resources, land, and development capacity in London and the UK are plentiful. We do not have any excuses for not meeting the housing and wider quality of life aspirations of all the population of our capital city and our country. The position we are in reflects explicit political choices as well as external economic factors and we should not forget that economic factors are to a large extent a consequence of political decisions and ideologies.

The planning system in England remains highly centralised in terms of governance but remains market driven in practice. The current rhetoric on localism and neighbourhood planning has not as yet had significant impact on that position. While local authorities may have slightly greater powers than previously, the financial constraints remain tight with local authorities having little financial autonomy. For the position to be improved, local authorities and, in London, the Mayor as the regional authority, need powers and resources if a fundamental shift in development outputs is to be delivered. Ownership of land and the power to acquire land is a central issue. Without this fundamental shift in powers, resources and land ownership, even the most progressive plan making authority can only react to the market rather than actually take the leadership in determining that its plans come into effect.

SUSTAINABLE COMMUNITIES
Mat Proctor

The planning and construction of 'ideal' urban forms in the modern era dates to the 19th century, and Ebenezer Howard's Garden City concept. The advent of the environmental/sustainability agenda since the 1970s, and the imperative to reinvent many cities in a post-industrial age, has revived the debate, and it is within these parameters that the concept of 'sustainable communities' exists.

Sustainability has been subject to multiple definitions - in general terms 'sustainable development' has meant pursuing growth economic strategies that 'put greater value on environmental resources, extend the time horizons in which actors think and operate, and promote greater equity between different social groups and communities, primarily through new forms of democratic governance' (Raco, 2005). Perhaps more specifically to urban planning and urban design, Owens & Cowell (2002) describe sustainable development and communities as the prioritising of 3 inter-related objectives in city design – environmental protection (reducing resource consumption, waste, and pollution); social development (equity and justice), and the pursuit of economic growth. In his polemic Cities for a Small Planet, the architect Lord Richard Rogers defines the 'sustainable city' as:

* A Just City where resources, education, and justice are fairly distributed, and in which all feel enfranchised;
* A Beautiful City, where physical surroundings fire the imagination;
* A Creative City, where people are encouraged to experiment, solve problems, and fulfil their potential;
* An Ecological City with minimal environmental impact and optimal resource efficiency;
* A City of Easy Contact, where the public realm is valued and information is freely exchanged, virtually and face-to-face;
* A Compact and Polycentric City, which respects surrounding countryside and focuses on neighbourhoods;
* A Diverse City, in which activities overlap to generate animation and inspiration.

This definition shows how the concept of the 'sustainable city' or 'sustainable community' can be implemented at different scales – regional/metropolitan, city, neighbourhood and individual building. A truly sustainable community must combine physical and socio-economic factors to pursue more equitable societies as *'poverty, unemployment, ill-health, poor education, conflict – in short, social injustice in all its forms – undermine a city's capacity to be environmentally sustainable'* (Rogers, 1995). This relationship between socio-economic status and environmental degradation is multi-faceted, but a key issue is the movement of populations in unsustainable ways. In the developed world, people with money and choices migrate from inner cities to suburban or semi-rural areas, necessitating the loss of open countryside, road building, increased car use, congestion, and pollution. Those communities which do not have such choices are left to suffer the phenomenon of social exclusion, which was described by the Labour government's Social Exclusion Unit as *'what can happen when people or areas suffer from a combination of linked problems such as unemployment, poor skills, low incomes, poor housing, high crime, bad health, and family breakdown'* (Social Exclusion Unit, 2001, para. 12). It is not sustainable in the long-term for a society to allow significant sections of its population to live in these conditions if serious civil unrest is to be avoided. The events of August 2011 were perhaps evidence of the significant challenge facing England's cities in these terms.

Williams &Dair (2006) identified 2 tiers of sustainability, with communities designed and built to be *technically sustainable* (i.e. in terms of materials, construction methods, morphology), whilst residents are supported to adopt behavioural sustainability (i.e. recycling waste, utilising resource-efficient modes of transport). It is therefore necessary to regulate and monitor construction and design of new developments to ensure technical sustainability is reflected, which can be achieved through the statutory planning and building regulation systems, and also to nurture and support a socio-economic climate that encourages and rewards sustainable lifestyles, through notions of citizenship and accountability. Under these terms, it is therefore not possible to achieve 'sustainable communities' solely achieved through physical plan making, though physical planning at various scales does play a crucial role.

PHYSICAL PLANNING AND SUSTAINABLE COMMUNITIES

Since the mid-1990s, there have been numerous central government initiatives aimed at creating 'sustainable communities', making buildings more energy efficient, promoting sustainable building materials, and increasing levels of awareness in the advantages (and necessity) of adopting sustainable construction methods (Sustainable Buildings Task Force Group, 2004). These efforts have spanned both Conservative and Labour administrations, suggesting something of a consensus on the need to at least be seen to be facilitating sustainable growth. However, research has shown that there has been little success in meeting these aims, to the extent that little of England's housing stock can be seen as sustainable, in terms of construction, design, or performance in use (Williams & Lindsay, 2005). Williams &Dair (2006) identified 8 sustainable behaviours that could be 'enabled by design features in neighbourhood developments':

* use less energy in the home;
* use less water in the home;
* recycle waste;
* maintain and encourage biodiversity and ecologically important habitats;
* make fewer and shorter journeys by fuel inefficient modes of transport, especially by car;
* make essential journeys by fuel efficient modes of transport such as bicycle, public transport, or on foot;
* taking part in local community groups, local decision making, and formal and informal social activities; and
* using local services, amenities, and businesses.

A 2006 study by Williams &Dair into the reasons for failing to include sustainable technology in new mixed-use and residential developments between 2001-2004, found that though many socio-economic aspects of the sustainability agenda, such as accessibility, economic viability, response to the townscape context, and mix of housing and tenure types, are frequently considered and included in new developments, technological aspects of sustainability, such as the design and siting of buildings to promote efficiency in resource use, was almost wholly ignored. Stakeholders interviewed as part of the study stated that they aimed to meet, but rarely exceed, statutory requirements in these areas. This would suggest that the statutory planning system has a role to play in specifying higher standards of sustainable design.

Williams &Dair identified twelve barriers to better sustainable urban development, with the most frequently observed being a lack of relevant skills and knowledge amongst stakeholders in a regulatory role, such as local authority planners and planning committee councillors. As many were unaware of how developments could be designed and constructed in a more efficient manner, they did not suggest or insist upon alternative proposals, and opportunities for design improvement were consequently lost. Efforts were made by the Commission for Architecture and the Built Environment (CABE) and the Department for Trade and Industry (DTI) to address these shortcomings, in the shape of the 'Constructing Excellence in the Built Environment' and 'Urban Renaissance Institute' initiatives, but these programs have since lapsed into history with the advent of the Coalition government and the new economic reality of austerity and a decimated public sector.

Perhaps the most revealing discovery of the Williams &Dair study is that 'end users', namely residents of new homes and occupants of commercial buildings, showed very little evidence of any interest in occupying a sustainable built environment. This is highly significant as end users effect demand directly, and a failure to request 'sustainable communities' will, and does, result in developers arguing that they are not economically viable (Williams &Dair, 2006). In terms of proposing how sustainable communities might be pursued in the future, it would therefore appear to be important that stakeholders at every level of the development process are exposed to information on the wide-ranging, and potentially life and death nature, of building in a sustainable manner in the future.

THE STRATEGIC REGENERATION FRAMEWORK
AND SUSTAINABLE COMMUNITIES

The Strategic Regeneration Framework (SRF) developed for the Olympic 'host boroughs' of Hackney, Waltham Forest, Greenwich, Tower Hamlets, Newham is a 20 year strategy aimed at improving the lives of resident communities so that they have 'the same social and economic chances as their neighbours across London'. The host boroughs house some of the most deprived communities in England, with generations of residents having experienced chronic levels of poverty, poor health, high crime, overcrowding, unemployment, and squalid public realm since at least the late 19th century. Government agencies at all levels appear to believe that the 2012 Olympic Games represent an historic opportunity to finally correct this hidden aspect of Europe's richest city.

The policy objective of the SRF is termed the convergence principle, and is to be embedded in relevant policy at all government levels, and is required to be addressed in all applications for planning consent in relevant areas. The creation and maintenance of sustainable communities is one of the SRF's critical actions to 2015, with the aim 'to create well designed, successful and sustainable places that attract new business, create mixed communities, and enhance existing neighbourhoods' (SRF, October 2009, pg. 6). The current combined population of the host boroughs is estimated at 1.25 million, with Greater London Authority (GLA) projections suggesting that the host boroughs may have to accommodate up to 250,000 additional residents over 20 years as much needed housing at regional level is concentrated in east London.

One of the challenges that host boroughs have traditionally faced is a high degree of population 'churn'. This means that the host boroughs attract poor migrants willing to accept cheap, though often substandard, rented accommodation until they are able to move away. The SRF states that 'the constant flow of transient populations does not assist in the creation of sustainable communities, and tackling this problem on a pan-London basis will be a significant factor in achieving the reductions in deprivation that are at the core of the SRF'. In simple terms, this would suggest that improving the environment in the host boroughs sufficiently so that they become places where people want to stay once they have the option to leave. This is a huge task which is distilled into 7 key indicators where efforts should be concentrated:

1   Raising results at Key Stage 4 (GCSE);
2   Improving results at Key Stage 2 (11 year olds);
3   Increasing employment rates;
4   Increased mean incomes in the bottom 2/5 of earners;
5   Reducing the number of families in receipt of benefits;
6   Reducing the rate of violent crime; and
7   Increasing life expectancy.

Physical planning has a role to play in the stated 'outcomes' contained within the SRF of: creating a coherent and high quality city within a world city region; homes for all; enhancing health and well-being; reducing serious crime rates and anti-social behaviour; and maximising the sports legacy (of the 2012 Olympic Games) and increasing participation.

A COHERENT, HIGH QUALITY CITY REGION

The SRF wants to see 275,500 additional residents of the host boroughs 'satisfied' with their local area as a place to live, and aims to achieve this through better connections across the locality, enhanced social infrastructure, and physical development providing for local economic growth. It is the aim of the host boroughs that the SRF area is seen as a single 'city within a city', with all elements of the existing planning system aligned to meet these objectives, albeit 'that the system is already too complex and (we) wish to see simplification rather than the creation of further additional separate plans' (SRF, 2009, pg. 22).

Section 106 contributions will be used to generate and enhance social infrastructure (no specific definition of this is provided, beyond 'the other ingredients that make a community'), whilst physical infrastructure will be provided via the Olympic Park, Crossrail, and Stratford City (which is now Europe's largest retail and leisure destination). This would suggest that significant private sector development will be required to generate the necessary Section 106 funding streams for infrastructure and public realm enhancements. Though subject to assessment as part of the convergence concept, the 2006 Williams &Dair study would suggest that it is unlikely that this aspect of new development will actually be sustainable. In addition, the SRF acknowledges that the large developments that already are taking place at Wood Wharf, Silvertown Quays, and Greenwich Peninsula are unlikely to accrue Section 106 financial contributions of pre-2008 levels, and that 'significant' public investment will be required. In the new economic paradigm, this is very unlikely to materialise, suggesting that the propositional physical planning capabilities of the SRF are, in reality, severely limited.

HOMES FOR ALL

The SRF aims to provide for 50,000 more homes, of which 12,000 will be 'affordable', as well as reducing overcrowding, encouraging residents to remain in the borough as their economic circumstances change, and securing 'the highest quality of housing, inside the homes and in the neighbourhoods'. The reality, acknowledged within the SRF, is that host boroughs will be reliant on the private sector to provide this additional housing, so that 'in the short term we are dealing with the impact of the credit crunch and the potentially serious slowdown in delivery of new homes...a key part of the response to this is public investment' (SRF, pg. 33). As new housing completions are at historic lows, with little sign of revival, the SRF and the statutory planning system would appear to be powerless to meet its objectives in this area.

The London Mayor's Housing Design Guide contains standards that would ensure new homes would be marginally larger than those previously developed in the private sector (and which would remain amongst the smallest in Europe), and it is a stated objective in the London Plan 2011 that better efficiency is achieved in housing completions to meet targets of a 60% reduction in carbon emissions by 2025. These factors all point towards 'more' sustainable communities in the host boroughs, but it is debatable whether 'enough' is being done.

CONCLUSION

Sustainable communities have been subject to numerous definitions, with language used to justify both neo-liberal policy (e.g. many of the divisive out-of-town and docklands developments of the 1980s were 'brownfield') and retrograde 'deep green' thinking advocating reduced levels of consumption and therefore economic growth. However, it is possible to view the Olympic host boroughs SRF as an attempt to create the balanced, connected, citizen focused, resource-efficient, humane places described by Lord Rogers in Cities for a Small Planet. These are places where people are both able and happy to remain in irrespective of their economic situation, in which pedestrians and cyclists have priority over cars, and where businesses and innovation flourish.

However, Raco's 2005 critique of New Labour's 2003 interpretation of sustainable communities remains salient in this analysis of coalition era, Great Recession realities. Raco argues that while it should be welcomed that there is now recognition of the structural imbalances in the English/London economies, there remains a denial that the overarching architecture of urban development and economic 'growth' could be divisive and by definition unsustainable. The SRF is, in Raco's words *'a light green manifestation of sustainable development...with economic growth characterised as the means and ends of policy'*. Whilst there remains a market-driven solution to spatial planning challenges, like the creation of sustainable communities for historically disadvantaged communities, with the emphasis placed on facilitating the supply-side requirements of potential investors to generate new housing and a humane public realm, there is little hope for sustainable communities in the host boroughs.

Bibliography
Sustainable Development, Rolled-out Neoliberalism and Sustainable Communities: Raco; Antipode; 2005
Sustainable Urban Forms: Jabareen; Journal of Planning Education and research, 26:38-52; 2006
A Framework of Sustainable Behaviours: Williams and Dair; Sustainable Development; 15: 160-173; 2007
What is Stopping Sustainable Building in England?: Williams and Dair; Sustainable Development; 15: 135-147; 2007
Cities for a Small Planet: Rogers; Faber & Faber; 1997
Strategic Regeneration Framework: LB Greenwich, LB Hackney, LB Newham; LB Tower Hamlets, LB Waltham Forest; October 2009

GENTRIFICATION OR LOCAL GAIN?
SPATIAL DEVELOPMENT UNDER AUSTERITY: THE CASE OF EAST LONDON
Judith Ryser

CONTEXT OF THE BROMLEY-BY-BOW STUDY AREA
Any long term scenario for future spatial development benefits from a long view into the past to discover the 'archaeology of spatial memory'. Recovery from the Second World War with its devastating destruction is chosen to trace London's regeneration strategies and efforts to rebalance London's East and West.

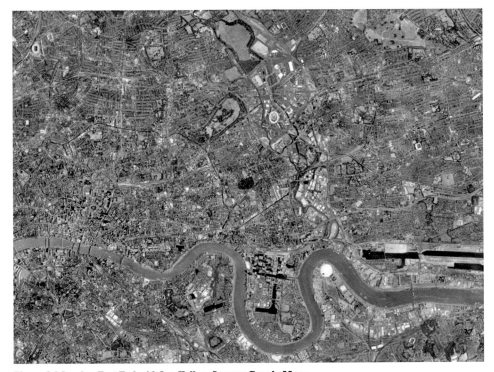

53

Figure 2-1 London East End with Lea Valley. Source: Google Maps.

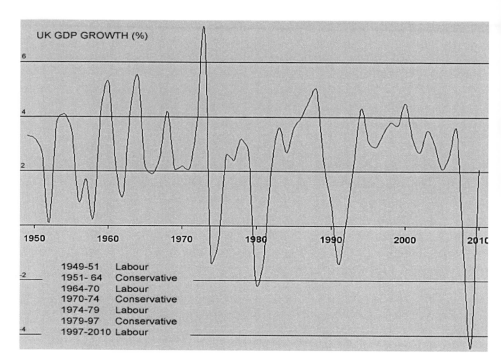

Figure 2-2 Economic context, UK GDP growth since 1950 and corresponding governments. Source: http:// blogs.channel4.com/factcheck/factcheck-do-we-only-vote-labour-when-times-are-good/9026

Patrick Abercrombie included rebalancing East and West in the 1944 London County Council (LCC) 'Greater London Plan', based on 'social studies' in the Charles Booth tradition,[1] aimed to establish balanced local neighbourhoods[2] and to decongest London into eight self-contained new towns beyond a newly established green belt to contain London's growth. However, London's population of 8.6 million in 1939 had shrunk by about half a million [3] and there was a great need to regenerate London's destroyed fabric.

Post war period of growth

The Town and Country Planning Act 1947 provided the new post-war framework for a balance between public interest and development led planning which, arguably including spatial and social redressing of imbalanced development.

Britain's economy took a long time to recover from the war and was only expanding in the 1960s. In 1963, The London Government Act [4] enlarged London's administrative boundary by setting up the Greater London Council (GLC) with strategic planning powers and wide ranging executive functions. The GLC led an expansionist period of large scale urban renewal involving slum clearance and blanket destruction of existing buildings without special attention to East

---

1   http://booth.lse.ac.uk/cgi-bin/do.pl?sub=view_booth_and_barth&args=531000,180400,6,large
    ,5. Charles Booth Online Archive, with Booth Poverty maps of London from 1889.
2   County of London Plan of 1943; Greater London plan of 1944, published by the London County Council; archives of the British Library.
3   There was no census data during the war.
4   London Government Act 1963, HMSO

London, where the Lee Valley Regional Park Authority [5] (LVRPA) was set up in 1966 to regenerate derelict and neglected land into high quality public open spaces and wildlife habitats and to preserve the region's historic value.

The nineteen-seventies oil shock

The most promising area for regeneration in East London was Docklands. In 1973, the conservative Heath government and the conservative GLC commissioned Travers Morgan to devise scenarios for the five Labour controlled London Boroughs in Docklands. In 'Docklands, Redevelopment Proposals for East London', [6] they proposed five main plan-led scenarios for Docklands [7] despite being asked to involve the private sector. Due to the recession no plan was implemented and the plans were abandoned by the incoming labour government.

In 1974, the Docklands Joint Committee, (DJC), was set up by the incoming Wilson labour government with five labour Docklands London Boroughs to devise a development strategy for Docklands with emphasis on public housing and industry. The then labour GLC was also adverse to private investment. The DJC produced the 'London Docklands Strategic Plan' in 1976,[8] the only Dockland plan ever approved by parliament. In 1977, the Dockland Forum was created to involve local residents [9] and ease antagonisms. [10]

In 1976, the GLC published the Greater London Development Plan [11](GLDP) which took up ideas from these studies with the aim to rebalance East and West London. It was approved by the government but never implemented, as the conservative Prime Minister Thatcher aimed to abolish the Greater London Council achieved in 1986.

1980s: development led strategy (state initiated, state subsidised)

Meanwhile, the Thatcher government set up the London Docklands Development Corporation (LDDC) in 1980 [12] during a recession to kick start development-led action in the Docklands after decades of stalemate. The LDDC benefited from large land endowments and public funding and imposed a 'market-led' real estate driven development policy.

Despite considerable state interventions, take-off was slow. An Enterprise Zone [13] was instated from 1982-1992 which 'freed' development from all planning constraints and provided favourable fiscal conditions, as well as direct and indirect public subsidies. Up to three buildings were built and demolished on some sites in the EZ while the hinterland, such as Bromley-by-Bow was excluded from that Bonanza. Aesthetics prevailed over social concerns for the local population

5   http://www.visitleevalley.org.uk/en/content/cms/outdoors/walks-walking/ Lee Valley Park
     Authority, London
6   Travers Morgan. 1973. Docklands, Redevelopment Proposals for East London. HMSO
7   'East End Consolidated' (business as usual with industry); 'City New Town' (mark 2 mixed use of residential and employment); 'Waterside' (more green in East London, leisure and residential for high-tech society); 'Thames Park' (leisure and regional recreation); and 'Europa' (responded to the entry of the UK into the European Community in 1973 when the conservatives were pro-Europe; the scenario included international road networks, a cargo terminal, the channel tunnel, a freeport, a new airport in the Estuary, Disneyland and rapid transit to City).
8   Docklands Development Team. 1986. London Docklands Strategic Plan. Docklands Joint Committee. HMSO
9   Joint Dockland Action Group. Activities: Publication:1982. Private housing: the key to the Docklands Regeneration. People's Plan, for the Royal Docks; Docklands Community Poster Project 1981-1991. http://www.cspace.org.uk/cspace/archive/docklands/dock_arch.htm
10 Sue Brownhill. 1990. Developing London's Docklands: Another Great Planning Disaster? Sue Brownhill, Paul Chapman Publishing. Lawrence Susskind and Michael Elliott et al, Paternalism, conflict and co-production, learning from citizen action and citizen participation in Western Europe, 1983, Plenum Press NY
11 http://www.lddc-history.org.uk
12 Under the Local Government, Land and Planning Act 1980
13 Enterprise Zones were also enabled in the 1980 Act, op.cit.

and the LDDC commissioned Gordon Cullen to devise a Development and Design Guide for the Isle of Dogs [14] with little impact though.

Lessons (to be) learnt from this shrinking period

An expansionist vision free from a planned overall conception is not attracting private sector leverage without substantial state incentives. Moreover, implementation of any such large development requires a long term timeframe of a generation or two.

Interestingly, the initial attempts to change the approach to development, making planning more development-led and opening development up to the private sector, resulted in development proposals conceived within a conventional planning framework (Travers Morgan). Conversely, the mission of the Dockland Joint Committee to return to 'state-led' planning produced a strategy which sought private development initiatives.

Expansionist period with intermittent recession: 1986 - 2008

In 1986, the 'Big Bang', the liberalisation of the financial sector, opened up the potential for a second financial city in the East End besides the 'square mile' City of London Corporation. Reg Ward (LDDC) installed secure fibre optic connections to enable banks to displace their back offices to cheaper Docklands premises. Despite opposition from the City, the Dockland Light Railway and the Jubilee line underground extension were built to service by now some 80,000 new jobs in Canary Wharf. Significantly, it took a quarter of a century with a phase of receivership [15] in 1992 and outstanding incentives for the developers to build one million m2 of offices. The abolition of the Greater London Council in 1986 was also considered to assist planning liberation, as the London Planning Advisory Committee (LPAC) which took over some strategic planning functions had no political clout.

Neither then, nor later did the deprived surrounding areas such as Bromley-be-Bow benefit from this massive development investment, while the local authorities were stripped of their planning powers but remained liable for public services. The A12 road which constitutes the northern LDDC boundary acts as a deep barrier to the hinterland. The financial jobs were mainly imported without easing East End unemployment, thus creating an ever increasing gulf with surrounding areas. Not surprisingly, the enormous wealth generated on the doorstep of among the poorest communities in East London provoked resentment and protests. [16] However, their exclusion from the Docklands bonanza was a learning process which served them well when they were bargaining better benefits from the next large influx of development on their doorstep, the Olympic Games.

When the LDDC was wound up in 1998, it left a lot of land undeveloped, including in the Royal Docks. The London Borough of Tower Hamlets had regained planning powers and produced the Millennium Quarter Masterplan to put some order into this development-led chaos. The Greater London Authority (GLA) was instated in 2000 with a directly elected Mayor for London with executive powers. [17] The First London Plan published in 2004 included an urban renaissance for Docklands which was a permissive approach by a labour mayor to private development. The

14   Christian Salvesen, Hollamby E, Gosling D and Cullen G, Isle of Dogs: A Guide to Design and Development Opportunities, 1982, LDDC
15   read bankruptcy
16   For the relation between the LDDC and the local community see, e.g. the work of Bob Colenutt, 1994, City Capital and Water, Docklands and the State, TechnologieNetzwerk; Bob Colenutt, 2011, Community action, Docklands and future prospects. UEL; Sue Brownill 1990.Developing London's Dockland.Another Great Planning Disaster?Sage; Sue Brownill and Neil McInroy. 2009. Urban Regeneration, a critical perspective. Spon; Sue Brownill.2013 (forthcoming). London Docklands, reflections on regeneration. Routledge.
17   Greater London Authority Act 1999.The Stationary Office. www.legislation.gov.uk/ukpga

Canary Wharf Group Plc., created in 1993 [18], took over Canary Wharf and acquired more land. More public money is being invested in Docklands, e.g. Crossrail which will have a station on the Isle of Dogs. Expansion continues there and the current London Plan 2011 of the conservative mayor retains the growth corridor in East London which includes Bromley-by-Bow.

New institutions such as the London Thames Gateway Development Corporation (LTGDC), set up in 2004 did not have a land endowment like the LDDC but obtained public subsidies for the Thames Gateway (TGW) to attract £43b private sector money over 20 years. [19] Terry Farrell proposed an alternative blue-green development strategy, the Thames Gateway Parklands Vision. The third initiative reverted to public works projects, but thwarted by the economic crisis after 2008 the LTGDC was abolished in 2012. Regarding efforts to shift growth to East London, the TGW initiative amounted to the third iteration of development. Started by Peter Hall under Michael Heseltine in the 1990s as 'linear city', it was followed in the early 2000 by the labour Deputy Prime Minister to generate half a million affordable dwellings in the South East.

When London won its bid for the Olympic Games in 2005 it shifted real development to the Olympic site, the adjacent Stratford town centre, and the Lower and Upper Lea Valley and the Upper Lea Valley situated in a London Plan development corridor. 'Wow architecture' was the hall mark of the Olympic site, alien to the surrounding East End which may benefit from improved public transport but not from speculative tower blocks with luxury flats which have emerged in the vicinity, a sure sign of gentrification. These many development initiatives in East London have created a bewildering number of agencies [20], many of them short lived, and most of them to the detriment of democratic accountability.

Lessons to be learnt from the expansionist period
Lack of coordinated or integrated vision has led to a proliferation of institutions and development initiatives, many of them abandoned soon after their creation or replaced by other organisations and groupings of agencies, amounting to considerable waste and confusion. The quadrupling of the Olympic budget from £2.3b to some estimated £9.6-12b [21] is just one sign of unfettered profligacy. During a period of economic expansion, with salaries in the city going through the roof, such increase of public expenditure was taken in the stride of the growth whirlwind, but after the financial crash, attitudes tended to change.

The expansionist strategies may have yielded some macro-economic gains during economic growth. They have generated some leverage from the private sector, but nowhere near expectation, and it remains doubtful whether any or how much of this will accrue to the local population.

Expansion and unplanned development - be it London Docklands, the Olympic site, the Thames Gateway or Mile End Road - has been displacing local residents and businesses from these development sites [22] and little points to the possibility that the legacy programme may redress their losses. The same goes for the 'foot-holders', artists, social entrepreneurs and creative place-makers who tend to be pushed out once their actions have added value to sites and run down

57

18 Canary Wharf group plc is a 'Phoenix' risen from the ashes with newly formed O&Y Properties Corporation owned by the Reichman brothers, who constituted a consortium in 1995 with George Soros, Lawrence Tisch, Michael Price and other investors, e.g. Saudi Prince Al-Waleed.
19 In reality this amounts to a small leverage: 1.15b/y = 3.45b/3y = 1/3 leverage as regards the public investment of £9b for 2008-11). According to Michael Edwards, it is likely that this will lead to some speculative housing and retail parks, but no public infrastructure or social equipment. www.michaeledwards.org.uk
20 The Olympic Development Agency (ODA) was in charge of developing the site with the Olympic buildings and a park in cooperation with the Local Organising Committee of the Olympic Games (LOCOG). The London Development Agency (LDA) was previously involved in land holdings and development operations in that area.
21 Creative accounting and commercial secrets will ensure that the exact figure will never be known.
22 see Games Monitor for example. www.gamesmonitor.org.uk

premises they are occupying and upgrading. Greater equity in the yields of expansion should be envisaged for these groups, without whom the development industry would not have stepped in.

Global financial crisis 2008 – austerity period from 2010 under new coalition government (development led with scarce private investment)

The crisis hit many developments in mid-air, while the Olympic Games were ring fenced. Public sector intervention, a remedy during recession, preserved public transport projects such as Crossrail, but progress of the Olympic legacy is less certain and the new Enterprise Zone in the Royal Docks may diffuse investment.

From 2004 to 2013 planning legislation has shifted towards development-led presumption [23] reflected in continuous development in Docklands. The London Legacy Development Corporation (LLDC), created in 2012, is taking over responsibility for private sector led development of the Olympic Games site and adjacent land. How much that will benefit the more deprived population of London's East End is an open question.

Lessons to be learnt from development under scarcity and austerity

In times of austerity, squandering scarce resources should encounter stern objections, but they seem to be confined to niche groups, while the majority remains seduced by the spectacles of the Queen's Jubilee and the Olympic games. The main area affected by austerity measures seems to be sustainability goals, such as mitigation and adjustment to climate change which are gradually displaced by austerity programmes. Targets are no longer mentioned and cuts are gaining priority over preventive measures.

'Necessity is the mother of invention'. This motto may be a useful guide for a new departure from both state-led and development-led spatial strategies, applied and often failed over the recent past. Perhaps a new combination of top-down and bottom-up development models could lead to more harmonious and less disruptive development processes. A revival of a 'third way' perhaps? Experimenting with such alternatives could be a challenge for young planning professionals. The chances are though that 'business as usual' will prevail, although it may do considerable damage - economic as well as environmental - under conditions of scarcity.

TWO CONTRASTING DEVELOPMENT MODELS

Many different development models exist and have been discussed widely. In his analysis of London Docklands Matthew Carmona, for example, distinguishes between four types of approaches: plan led – market led – plan based – opportunity based. [24] As he himself argues, none of these categories are mutually exclusive and tend to overlap. Nevertheless, development models have contrasting features. Two opposing typologies of development are considered here: top-down and bottom-up in the London East End encompassing Docklands, the Olympic site and the Bromley-by-Bow area.

'Development Industry' model

The top-down model explored here a quango with corporate culture. Quangos can be para-

---

23 Already under labour and during economic growth the 2004 Planning and Compulsory Purchase Act has 'alleviated' planning constraints in favour of development. This has been reinforced in the 2008 Planning Act, the 2011 Localism Act, and the 2012 National Planning Policy Framework (NPPF). The government has announced further planning relaxation for 2013, not least the abandonment of the quota for affordable housing imposed on development plans by labour.

24 Matthew Carmona. The Isle of Dogs revisited. In: Urban Design, Issue 112, 2009.

Figure 2-3 Site with surrounding areas of influence. Source: Design for London, GLA

public authorities, [25] or development corporations. [26] They have often monopolistic powers, may squander resources [27] and their accountability is weak, rarely to existing local populations and businesses. This model thrives on the public purse directly or indirectly [28] and benefits from a favourable administrative context, either through contextual institutions or from 'industry-own' institutional arrangements. Some development industry friendly examples follow.

LDDC, para-public development-led driver
The London Docklands Development Corporation was a pro-development quango acting as a de facto plan-less authority with strong compulsory purchase powers but weak public accountability.

---

25   e.g. Port of London Authority, Thames Water Authority
26   e.g. LDDC, ODA, LLDC, LTGDC, etc.
27   e.g. land left idle for decades, and environmental neglect.
28   e.g. borrowed capital, tax relief, other fiscal advantages, subsidies or planning concessions, etc.

It was entrusted with an enormous amount of public land. [29] It was dispensing high direct and indirect public sector subsidies to the development industry, contributing up-front environmental improvements [30] and providing some infrastructure [31] without providing increasing energy efficiency. [32]

BIDs, business-led driver
Business Improvement Districts are another example of top-down, market-led development. BIDs are set up by private businesses to capture market opportunities in their area. They are substituting for local public sector planning powers, while collecting a levy from business participants to finance capital investment and possibly running costs of area-based physical regeneration. [33] BIDs are supposed to enable business 'localism', although it is not uncommon that BIDs consist of a limited number of large businesses and exclude local SMEs which oppose them and object to the loss of diversity and fine grain urban fabric. [34]

Government initiated, development-led drivers
The government driven legacy in and around the Olympic site was entrusted into various quangos [35] with some input from the Mayor of London and the 'Olympic London Boroughs'. Other development industry consortia and public-private partnerships were created around the Olympic Games site to facilitate development.

Success of the 'development industry' model?
The 'development industry' model was obviously successful on its own terms. LDDC managed to bring about a second financial city in the East of London. BIDs mobilised the business community to take over improvement and management of buildings and public realm with own financial contributions. Olympic game site quangos attracted the Westfield Group to build one of the largest shopping malls of London on the Olympic site, and brought about the acquisition of the Olympic village by private investors. [36]

Longer term legacy success of the 'development industry' model?
The bulk of the Olympic site is put into the hands of the LLDC, an independent corporation under the control of the mayor of London, with a land portfolio, compulsory purchase powers, estate management functions, selling and letting powers. It is not subjected to an implementation schedule or a timeframe for its own existence. Over and above these powers, the LLDC claims local 'legacy and moral ownership' of areas surrounding the Olympic site where it substitutes local authority planning powers. This includes the Three Mills Island, [37] Hackney Wick [38] and the Lower Lea Valley, but its complete portfolio is not known. Whether such concentration of public land into the hands of the LLDC corresponds to the spirit of the Localism Act is another matter.

---

29 e.g. from the Port of London Authority and public utilities, such as electricity, gas and waste disposal, etc.
30 e.g. land and water decontamination and reclamation, landscaping of public realm to attract inward investment
31 public transport such as the Dockland Light Railway (DLR), but as an afterthought with insufficient capacity and the Jubilee underground extension which was undertaken post hoc at greatly increased costs.
32 For example using the large water planes to install heat pumps ex ante for the whole area.
33 Examples in London are: Marylebone, Regent's Street, Victoria Station, Fitzrovia, etc.
34 e.g. Fitzrovia
35 LDA, LTGDC, ODA, LOCOG, OPLA, LLDC, op cit.
36 Triathlon Homes, Delancy and Qatari Diar, the latter a global investor, to take over development, sales and management of its housing, commercial real estate and public realm.
37 Initially acquired by the LDA
38 inherited from the London Thames Gateway Development Corporation

Success of the 'development industry model' regarding the local community?
The LLDC continues to cooperate with several community groups which have been created during the development of the Olympic Games site. [39] There is no great enthusiasm though for setting up Community Land Trusts, something the local inhabitants are keen about; or a formal consultative forum at which local groups would have a guaranteed voice.

Lessons
The ultimate test of whether the 'development industry' is a 'success' from the point of view of the existing population would be to achieve regeneration without gentrification, or at least that some parts of the area would escape displacement and pricing out the local population and local businesses.

'Community based' development model
The bottom-up 'community based' model favours local inhabitants and businesses in the development process. It gives them a voice, opportunities to take active part in development initiatives and a share of the value added by such development in both the short and the longer term. They would also have some assurances against unwanted displacement and compensation mechanisms for loss or uprooting of local homes, businesses and recreational spaces.

The Bromley-by-Bow Centre
The aim of the Bromley-by-Bow Centre (BBBC) was to adopt 'new ways of thinking about urban revival, and devising new tools in response to (endemic) issues of scarcity'. [40]

The Bromley-by-Bow centre originates in the appointment of Andrew Mawson to rescue the abandoned and derelict reform church in Bruce Street in Bromley-by-Bow. Although hired by the church, Mawson had a perspective of a social entrepreneur from the outset. Opposition by parts of the local community and the local authority did not discourage Mawson from refurbishing the church building with a team he built up among local residents, immigrants, artists and activists. He transformed it to accommodate several functions besides Sunday services, including a crèche, a ballet school and festive events for different ethnic and faith communities, ranging from the pearly queens and kings to the Ede festival. He refurbished outbuildings and let them cheaply to artists and artisans in return for some of their services to the local community. These activities expanded organically. Meals which were prepared by people from different local ethnic groups expanded into a self-financing and self-managed cosmopolitan café. This inclusive approach engaged elderly and mentally disturbed people in gardening around the buildings, art therapy and soft gymnastics.

Mawson mobilised support from Lord Ennals and other humanists, was able to build a better relation with the local authority, entered social housing functions and managed to build a health centre which was focused on catering for local cultural needs. He transformed an adjacent derelict open space into a communal garden with an allotment area engaging local children to learn about plants and food. In turn, local food was used in what had become a restaurant with emphasis on healthy eating. Many other community support services were offered, such as English language tuition, and enabling women from various backgrounds to set up and run their own micro-businesses. His objective was aiming at high quality in every undertaking of the Bromley-by-Bow centre aimed to help local people to help themselves.

Clearly, structural changes were needed when the centre expanded geographically as well as

61

39   www.londonlegacy.co.uk/community e.g. Youth Panel, faith communities for outreach work, etc.
40   www.bbbc.org.uk

functionally and became a multi-million enterprise. This was not an easy ride for the team and not all the locals subscribed to the entrepreneurial approach.

Other community-led bottom-up organisations

Many other bottom-up groups are operating in the East End. Some were formed in protest against development, including the Olympic site where their housing was demolished, their businesses closed down and they were chased from their allotments and displaced altogether. These groups included local leaders [41] but also artists and marginal communities. [42] Some are connected with local teaching institutions. [43] Faith communities are also active, together with other interest groups, community architects, self-builders, urban agriculture enthusiasts and others. Some were more transient, for example artists who were pushed further out eastwards in their pursuit to find cheap premises in derelict areas. They, together with a substantial immigrant population play a significant part in the socio-cultural fabric of this area and its transformation.

Bromley-by-Bow 'extra'

Engaged in CAN, [44] Mawson kept in touch with local people in Bromley-by-Bow. Driven by his expansionist ambitions he started to cooperate with both other voluntary and mainstream institutions. [45] Knighted for his efforts, Mawson moved towards the establishment. He joined the Water City [46] initiative with Richard Rogers as architect and Leaside Regeneration Ltd, set up his own company and is currently a board member of the newly created LLDC.

Success of the bottom-up community-led development model?

Without a doubt, the Bromley-by-Bow centre has become a much liked social institution in Bromley-by-Bow. This is also reflected in the SCIBE interviews. [47] The Centre is often a first port of call where people seek assistance or just a social life and has become a role model for bottom-up social entrepreneurship. It is a rather rare long term success of bottom-up community-led development.

Many alternative initiatives have failed after a short time of protest, or after some temporary but limited success. Contrary to the top-down development model the bottom-up development model lacks material resources and tends to operate on the margin of mainstream values and customs. Often groups are constituted in opposition to concrete threats from the outside. Once the threat has vanished, for example when individuals have taken up offers to move elsewhere, the 'raison d'etre' of such resistance groups is diminishing and they tend to decline below the threshold of critical mass. Constituted ad hoc such activist or resistance groups tend to lack cohesion, organisational capacity, common purpose, sustained energy and drive. After a while of intense involvement and dedication, they succumb to burn-out or exhaustion, a little researched phenomenon. There are numerous accounts of occupations by artists, student revolts, political protest movements like the '68 events and their inability to achieve concrete lasting social change or spatial justice.

To come back to the London situation, residents and businesses have been displaced from the

---

41   e.g. teachers or managers of tenant associations,
42   including travellers who had been present in the East End for a long time.
43   including Queen Mary University, UEL, local colleges, academies and schools
44   CAN: Community Action Network, aimed to disseminate social entrepreneurship more widely
45   The adjacent primary school, local housing associations such as HACA, a mental health care charity, etc. He was involved in the refurbishment of Poplar Town Hall, Tower Hamlets public library, refurbishment of social housing and public realm in various adjacent neighbourhoods.

46   amawsonpartnerships.com/help/water-city
47   SCIBE and Architectural Foundation.Scarce Times: Alternative Futures. 15 May 2012.

Figure 2-4 Bromley-by-Bow Centre. Source: Judith Ryser.

Olympic site with little compensation and those in surrounding areas seem to be next in line for having to make way to gentrification. The student protests have not managed to halt fee increases, the riots have not brought about social change in the deprived areas where they took place, and 'Occupy'[48] has all but disappeared from the radar.

Questions
Can a bottom-up community-led development model succeed in the long term, in what circumstances, with which means, over what period of time? Does it stand a better chance in times of scarcity, as it is accustomed to operating under permanent scarcity and is well versed in austerity measures, as well as dealing with scarcity in an innovative and creative way?

63

Blurring boundaries in times of scarcity
The development process described above has followed the typical business cycles of growth and decline: 1973 oil shock, 1986 Big Bang, 2008 global economic and financial crisis. Usually, the state steers its way out of recession, either by adopting a Keynesian model of public infrastructure investment, or by means of fiscal or monetary manipulations. The period after 2008 seems to differ from this pattern as the state in the UK and elsewhere resorts to prolonged austerity measures to exit the economic depression and reduce the irresponsible debt mountain accumulated by both the state and consumers over an unsustainable boom period. What impact does this have on the two contrasting models of urban regeneration? Early signs are that the state is resorting to measures which may entail irreversible damages, not least regarding climate change mitigation

Figure 2-5 Bromley-by-Bow Centre entrance with health clinic in background. Source: Judith Ryser.

and adaptation. In policies and deeds 'sustainability' tends to make way to 'scarcity', 'resilience' and 'austerity'. The adaptation of the London Plan to the National Planning Policy Framework (NPPF), takes advantage to relax 'public interest' or redistribution targets, including affordable housing. 'Localism' may be taken up mainly by vocal neighbourhoods, but it is also appropriated by the 'development industry' in carrying out higher density urban transformations under the guise of 'regeneration'.

Rapprochement between development-led and community-based development models?

Which of the two development models explored here – top-down and bottom-up - is better equipped to cope with recession? Averse to austerity, market-led models function best either under conditions of economic growth and/or with large scale, up front public investment, subsidies and tax relief. Self-regulated and self-reliant community-led models operate well under conditions of scarcity as it is one of their inherent features. Often secretive and with little public accountability, top-down models incessantly demand removal of 'red tape', but they welcome regulations to protect their own added value. They expect state subsidies to act and state bail-out when they have overreached themselves. The current ease of shedding corporate debt and recuperating undervalued assets under new management contrasts with the treatment of insolvency of social and voluntary organisations. Both models have to adapt to change all the time, but the top-down model tends to hold on to its tried and tested formula while the bottom-up model has an internal dynamic which tends to create instability due to inherent precariousness, heterogeneity, weakness of checks and balances, and being prone to take overs by vocal minorities. Most importantly, the top-down model has a material base, albeit sometimes precarious, while the bottom-up model is subjected to a relentless pursuit of scarce resources which may lead to exhaustion.

Alternative adaptation processes are needed for the survival of both models in times of internal or external crisis. The top-down model may shift its targets and ease its constraints, while the bottom-up model may relax its sometimes rigid value system. Opinions differ over whether the top-down model of the Olympic Development Authority (ODA) in charge of developing the Olympic Games site has delivered in time and to budget. Its activity fell mainly into a growth period while its ring-fenced budget tripled during the ensuing austerity period. Conversely, it could be argued that the Bromley-by-Bow Centre which started as a bottom-up model aiming at inclusion, equality and self-reliance has transformed itself into social entrepreneurship, akin to capitalist enterprise, at least for its outreach undertakings. Has more stringent austerity moved it toward a more neo-capitalist mode of operating? Is it a transient period of greater expediency or will its internal transformations become permanent? Most importantly, how do these changes affect its initial objective of achieving greater social and spatial inclusion?

Impact of austerity on regeneration and gentrification

Should austerity be seen as a negative impact on current pursuits and modes of operating, or an opportunity for adaptation and new departures? Is the development-led model really softening up towards local conditions and local people and, paradoxically, is the community based model moving toward the majority model out of necessity?

Although it may have to compromise, the bottom-up model may have an advantage over the top-down model due to its experience with adapting to precarious and unforeseen situations under constant conditions of scarcity. When seeking rapprochement with the bottom-up model to cope with austerity the top-down development model may undergo internal structural changes by adopting more appropriate means, albeit alien to its habitual corporate culture. Is such rapprochement between the two types of models possible? In which way would such blurring of boundaries evolve? Could it lead to mutual compromise and cooperation on agreed terms which would facilitate equitable conditions of engagement, including sanctioning mechanism in case of non-compliance?

How would such adaptation processes impact on urban regeneration and gentrification? At the very least it would presuppose an agreed view of the purpose of urban regeneration and the role of gentrification during the current period of scarcity. A key challenge would be to set out general principles which would disconnect gentrification from urban regeneration and provide much broader access to the value added of development. Most importantly, it would have to establish rights to a more equitable share for the existing residents and businesses, including a return to the regenerated area with benefits of improved conditions. It would also mean that the 'place-makers', the transient occupiers of abandoned land and derelict premises whose foothold often triggers the regeneration process also gain access to an equitable share of their contribution to the turn-around of derelict and deprived areas. In times of scarcity, their temporary and often creative occupation could continue to contribute to the regeneration process in which they should have a voice.

Even the current period of austerity will come to an end in the evolution of economic cycles. Accelerated pace of change under economic expansion will eventually revive the development process of rapid capital accumulation and circulation and reinstate excess gains and greed until the cycle will have reached another unsustainable peak. The development industry is closely linked to the boom and bust of the economy in general and the chances are that such temporary rapprochement between the two development models would vanish and give way to past antagonisms, unless the process of cooperation would have brought about tangible benefits for both types of development models.

Scarcity is socially constructed. Clearly its interpretation differs between the protagonists of the two opposing development models discussed here, between politicians, the development industry, local communities and newcomers. A period of scarcity could provide an excellent opportunity to explore sustainability and resilience of urban regeneration with attention to the process of gentrification. Such a pursuit should also analyse current deficiencies of urban living, the power of the fear industry; state-sanctioned intrusion into citizen's privacy; the scarcity of affordable housing and risks of negative equity; the artificial creation of scarcity in the development process, including deliberate land hoarding and slowing down development to push up real estate prices; intentional dilapidation of existing buildings, asset stripping and generation of negative asset values; and the role of private mobility in the share of finite public ream. Importantly, it should include imaginative ways of providing greater access to indeterminate spaces for transitional activities, as well as recognition and material reward for the contribution of informal place makers.

In practice, scarcity is not just about lack of money, it also affects access to information, share of legacy spoils, provision of social amenities and public facilities. Scarcity can be generated deliberately by the development process itself. Not only should such a study focus on a more equitable distribution of the value added from regeneration for local residents and businesses and newcomers, but also on adequate care for the environment to achieve sustainable longer term economic development. In particular, it should examine the balance between property-led – real estate-led –capital investment-led development and its impact on its users, their activities, their chances of empowerment, their quality of life and their share of spatial and social justice. Such rebalancing could lead to progressive social change. Of interest to the professionals of the built environment is the role of design in this process.

Changing the political role of design

Not surprisingly, in times of scarcity, the development-led model focuses on the relationship of design with business. The Global Design Forum [49] asks 'how to convince people to have what they don't yet know they want'. Public participation takes the form of convincing local residents, businesses and visitors that they need urban change, in the direction of the producers, i.e. the development industry or large scale business occupiers. For this business community [50], the purpose of design is to 'maximise limited resources to solve social and human issues on a global scale and yet still entice people to consume'. [51]

This is a far cry from the objective of the Bromley-by-Bow centre to 'create meaningful alternatives to an all-pervading economic system that depends on infinite growth in a finite world'. [52] For a quarter of a century their purpose was to develop organically at a scale and pace which the local population can handle. This included an adequate site, new premises, inclusive activities on the site, outreach and networked cooperation with other like-minded mutual or cooperative initiatives in the wider neighbourhood. They want to devise 'new business and economic models that make sense for a future sustainable society', and this approach is also reflected in the type of design they have adopted for the activities of the centre.

Is there a need to invent design which suits the rapprochement of the two opposing development models, for example, a more interdependent relationship between capital investment and running cost; better use of land and premises between the end of traditional

---

49   The London Design Festival, Global Design Forum, first thought-leadership event of the London Design Festival, September 2012.Central St Martin's art school campus, Kings Cross.
50   E.g., developers, investors, financiers, landowners, estate managers, lawyers, etc.
51   London Design Festival Op.cit
52   Bromley-by-Bow Centre research and evaluation: integrated practice – focus on older people. 2004 BbB

use and regeneration; broader and equitable access to land by means of community land trusts; accountability for the sustainable use of resources form cradle to cradle, etc.? Would this involve rethinking the pecking order between property, private mobility and people? Or is it sufficient to adopt existing design philosophies and technologies to the period of austerity, regardless of which model is followed?

The 'Water City': convergence of development models over several business cycles
The Water City [53] is an example of an initial attempt to converge the two opposing development models. The Water City is situated in London's Lower Lea Valley, conceived initially by the LDA and the LTGDC on 1,218 ha of brown field land which included the 2012 Olympic Games site. Although the history of the Water City is very difficult to trace [54] it has stated aims. [55] The Water City [56] for which Richard Rogers produced an early scheme [57] wanted to be the overall East London hub capitalising on the fact that 'people start to like where they live'.However, the 2012 Olympics site [58] has become the main catalyst of regeneration, followed by the new Enterprise Zone in the Royal Docks and Silvertown Quay, although the Water City wants to remain part of this bigger picture. [59]

LESSONS TO BE LEARNT FROM SCARCITY VISION
'Necessity is the mother of invention'. In this sense, scarcity may do some good for the often unsustainable and profligate development industry. Some convergence between development-led and community-based models of development could bring some promising change, but the evolution of the Water City project may indicate that such convergence may not that easily transcend the current, market led and supply side driven development process.

What next? Longer term future 2065?
In the light of the many contrasting development strategies adopted and abandoned since the second world war in London, with development occurring often in a haphazard disjointed mode under economic phases of boom and bust, it is difficult to envisage a longer term development future, let alone expect it to occur under a prolonged period of austerity.

Instead of conceiving a sort of end state scenario for a particular moment in time for in the future, it may be more appropriate to envisage scenarios for diverse development processes which may lead in different directions but should be flexible enough to accommodate unforeseen contextual influences, notwithstanding the continuous pattern of economic fluctuations which

---

53 Mawson was an early supporter of the Water City and involved Leaside Regeneration, social entrepreneurs, of which he was a director. He has now shifted his directorship to The Legacy List, a charity founded by the LLDC and the Mayor of London.

54 References to Leaside Regeneration, Paul Brickell, chief executive, and Water City:

http://www.leasideregeneration.com/water-city

http://londonliving.at/water-city-east-londons-regeneration-wizards

http://www.londonmet.ac.uk/services/london-office/activity-by-the-london-office/leaside-regeneration-ltd.cfm

55 Water City project objectives: make use of east London's water heritage: ensure a high quality built environment; help build an entrepreneurial culture; engage local people and communities in practical, entrepreneurial ways; create a true legacy for east London, both physical and social.

56 www.leasideregeneration.com/water-city

57 www.richardrogers.co.uk/RSHP_A_JS_4220_L_E_MP.pdf

58 with its 45 miles of canals and 1450 ha of surrounding land ripe for regeneration

59 E.g., showcased at www.watercityfestival.org.uk The £20b budget for Lea Valley development in next 20 years constitutes the precondition for this global destination of raw talent, resources and space.

Figure 2-6 Urban area with potential for small scale infill development with local participation. Source: Judith Ryser.

are inherent in the capitalistic system. Scenarios for such long term process modes could only provide a loose framework for medium term development strategies, together with instruments to attempt to achieve them. This approach should not prevent short term, smaller scale development initiatives which may stand a chance of materialising because they may be more doable, less costly and would require less comprehensive institutional involvement. They do not have to be piecemeal as in the recent past and could benefit from such the longer term strategy envisaged here for a more balanced and inclusive development in London's East End.

CHANGING CONTEXTS AND VISIONS FOR PLANNING: THE CASE OF MADRID CENTRAL AREA

Teresa Franchini

How to cope with the concept of scarcity as an issue for planning? What does it imply for a traditional planning system based on a set of instruments aimed at guiding the city in the long term? To what extent does a master plan have the capacity to deal with the issue of scarcity? How can these plans be successful - or not - in this attempt? In which way does the changing economic and social context influence the type of planning pushed forward by the authorities in charge of the matter?

This article tries to give some answers to these questions by exploring the interplay which exists between the overall economic context, the dominant vision in planning, and the planning instruments produced for cities affected by changing circumstances, drawing on the master plans designed for Madrid during the last 30 years. The article is structured around these three key aspects, with the aim to extract some lessons from this experience. The laboratory used to explore these questions is the central district of the city. It is an urban realm to which all the approved planning instruments have given a special treatment to improve a traditionally deprived area, whatever their supportive vision.

A BRIEF VIEW ON THE CHANGING MADRILENIAN CONTEXTS AND THE ASSOCIATED PLANNING VISIONS

The past

Conversely to the rest of Europe, the effects of the 1973 oil crisis had a late impact in Spain, affecting its economy only at the end of the 1970's. As regards planning, this period coincides with the drawing up of the first master plan for the city under the democratic period. The critical economic situation led to the adoption of a shrinking vision in planning, according to which Madrid was facing a process of stagnation. By that time, the focus was placed on the need to complete the city edges and to attribute special care to the existing urban tissues, particularly its central area, characterised by strong urban decay.

The present

Immediately after the approval of the 1985 master plan the first symptoms of the end of the economic crisis emerged, a fact that gave place to a new planning vision, based on an expansive image of the city, open to unexpected opportunities. The mandatory review of the existing plan gave rise to the need to produce a new planning instrument for the city. The principles of the Master Plan approved in 1997 were quite the opposite of the previous one: the need to offer enough land to capture investment implied a renewed interest in focussing the planning action on

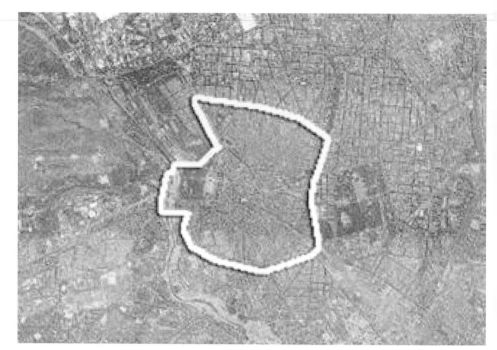

Figure 2-7 Historic Centre delimitation, 1885 master plan. Source: Area of Urbanism and Housing, Madrid City Council.

huge peripheral growth proposals.

The future

The global economic recession initiated in 2007 pushed the Spanish economy to the worst possible scenario due to, among other motives, its strong dependency on real estate investments promoted by the previous economic model and favoured by a planning practice adjusted to the principles of the expansive vision. The revision of the current master plan – in progress at present and estimated to be approved by 2014 – is being developed yet again under the scarcity vision. It includes new principles based not only on the recovery of the existing urban fabric and of the powerful dynamism of the central area expanding towards the periphery, but also on the need to move the existing local planning practice towards new ways of dealing with urban needs.

THE SHRINKING VISION: THE 1985 MASTER PLAN

Accordingly to the recession that led the country to economic stagnation, the professional team in charge of drawing up the master plan for Madrid adopted as the leading principle the no growth principle. It centred the attention on the existing city, mainly the Historic Centre, an area consisting of 350 hectares, 5,000 dwellings and 130,000 inhabitants. By that time, the urban state of this area deserved a profound treatment to improve its existing conditions (see Figure 2 7).

There were two planning objectives for the central area of the city:

* Recovery of underused space, such as the Railway Green Corridor project, a strip of almost 7 km at the fringe of the central area, aimed to enhance the living conditions of the deprived neighbourhoods settled along the railway track.

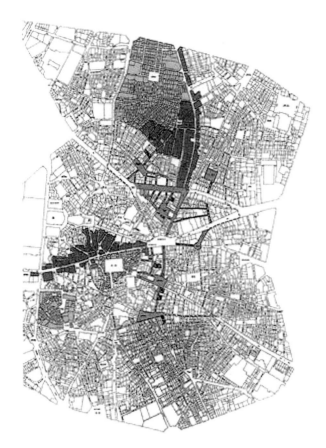

Figure 2-8 Areas of Preferential Rehabilitation and interventions with European Funds. Source: Area of Urbanism and Housing, Madrid City Council.

* Rehabilitation of the urban fabric, by means of launching special ordinances and of an ample catalogue of urban elements protected under the label of urban heritage.

Except for few actions, the outcomes of those proposals were scarce, in fact only few actions were undertaken, resulting in a progressive deterioration of the district. The cause behind this failure was obvious: the proposals implied too much economic effort for a single municipality in times of scarcity.

The 1990's gave a new opportunity for the historic centre, when two positive factors coincided in time and space. In the first place, an inter-administrative protocol of cooperation was signed by the three levels of administration - state, region and local – to finance the rehabilitation of the capital city central district, a fact that gave birth to a new approach to planning: the selection of specific target areas articulated by squares and streets operating as neighbourhood centres of urban activities, called Areas of Preferential Rehabilitation. Secondly, the City Council had the possibility to apply for some European funds, aimed at the regeneration of urban environments, which gave the opportunity to improve the most depressed neighbourhood of the central district, as well as some selected urban itineraries (see Figure 2 8). This experience was internationally

Figure 2-9 Urban improvements in residential and commercial areas. Source: Teresa Franchini.

recognised, in 1998 when it was ranked as Best in the Habitat Best Practices Award; and in 1999 when Europa Nostra recognised the value of the activities taken by the local administration for the recovery of the built heritage (see Figure 2 9 and Figure 2 10).

Some lessons to be learnt

Pros:

* Political decision: the alignment of multi-administrative levels to recover the dynamic of the capital city central area is a key factor in that matter
* Integrated instead of scattered actions: isolated rehabilitation is a slow process that does not prevent urban decay
* Strategic selection of the areas of intervention: the betterment and renewal of certain streets and squares is essential to trigger private investments in the surrounding areas
* Social and economic perception: the improvement of the urban scene, mainly the public realm, generates a highly satisfactory reaction from the citizenship.

Cons:

* Gentrification process: the lack of public initiatives to redress the economic logic of the owners of the dwellings affects the situation of tenants and users.
* Partial rehabilitation: except for those selected areas in which the administration has taken special care, not all dwellings of the central area were rehabilitated.

THE EXPANSIVE VISION: THE 1997 MASTER PLAN

Soon after the launch of the 1985 master plan, the Spanish productive structure started to show the first signs of expected recovery, changing progressively the previous shrinking vision towards

Figure 2-10 Urban improvements in residential and commercial areas. Source: Teresa Franchini.

a new one, based on the expectation of an unprecedented dynamism that later put the country among the leading European economies. At the beginning of the 1990´s the building activities, transformed into the leading productive sector of the country, found the proper conditions for its expansion, and demanded the greatest possible flexibility of the existing urban regulations, thus favouring the beginning of an important process of planning deregulation.

The master plan for Madrid adopted in 1997 followed the general tendency and concentrated its attention on the urban expansion. The new plan enlarged the central area to 523 hectares, 91,000 dwellings and 320,000 inhabitants - giving it a new denomination, the Central District (seeFigure 2 11).

For this area two lines of actions were proposed:

* New areas for Integrated Rehabilitation,following the positive results of the previous experience
* Strategic Plan for the Revitalisation of the Central District (2004), drawn upby an ad-hoc administrative body - the Central Area Office – in charge of promoting the dynamism of the central city district (see Figure 2 12).

Among the projects proposed to fulfil this aim, one is standing out. It is the mega undertaking called Manzanares River Project (2004-2011), launched with the aim to recover this unique and hidden natural element for the city, a narrow stream of water that crosses the city from north to south, flanked since the 1970´s by one of the inner rings road, which would provide a new urban axis to interconnect the adjoining neighbourhoods. Two objectives were set out for this purpose: the environmental restoration of the river banks, including the burying of some stretches of the ring road, the design of a linear park on the recovered land, and the urban renewal of the adjacent districts (seeFigure 2 13, Figure 2 14, Figure 2 15 and Figure 2 16).

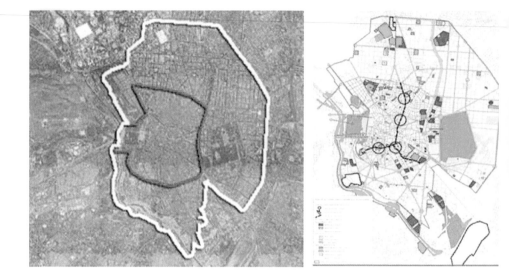

Figure 2-11 (left) Historic Centre, 1997 master plan. Source: Area of Urbanism and Housing, Madrid City Council. Figure 2-12 (right) Strategic Plan for the CD Revitalisation, 2004. Specific projects. Source: Area of Urbanism and Housing, Madrid City Council.

The project implied the burying of 8 km of highways, the treatment of 120 ha of urban land and the delivery of 50 ha for new green areas, all included in a budget of 4,100 million euros. The project was put in motion in spite of the heavy indebtedness it implied for the City Council, a situation that can only be understood in relation to the buoyant local economy existing at that time. It is expected that the citizenship will be paying this urban improvement over the next thirty years.

Some lessons to be learnt
Pros:
* City marketing: political decision to put the city on the international map through big urban projects
* Political leadership: importance of personal involvement of the political leaders, mainly the Mayor, in the developing of certain key urban projects
* Social and economic perception: the improvement of the urban quality of life as a highly positive factor for ordinary people and businesses, let alone the recognition of efforts by the local administration in the matter
* Ad-hoc administrative bodies: the establishment of working teams in charge of specific projects, outside the current administrative system, facilitates not only the decision making process but the political discourse around them.

Cons:
* Environmental, social and financial tensions generated by the project management: this is the case of Manzanares River Project, due to lack of environmental reports, political transparency and public participation to decide about the expected results and budgets committed
* Limited outcomes in dwellings rehabilitation: except for a few cases, the process is left to private initiative.

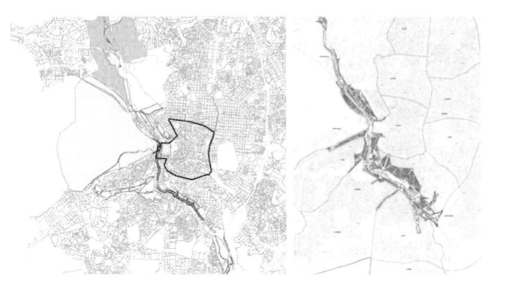

Figure 2-13 (left) and Figure 2-14 (right) Manzanares River Project, location and area of interventions.
Source: Area of Urbanism and Housing, Madrid City Council.

THE SCARCITY VISION: THE MASTER PLAN 2014

The 2008 global crisis strongly affected the Spanish economy, dragging the country into a depression that continues today. The national economic base, mainly supported by the strong building industry consolidated during the expansive period, has showed its incapacity to meet the present social and economic demands. In planning terms, the new reality wiped out the previous vision based on urban growth aimed to satisfy the speculative real estate market, to give room to a new approach based on the satisfaction of the urban needs in a scarcity period. Facing this situation and after almost 15 years of implementation, the City Council has begun the process of drafting a new master plan based on the principle of recycling the existing city according to criteria of flexibility and innovation. At present this process is at the stage of preliminary studies and proposals, intending to complete final version of the plan by 2014.

For the central area – known as the Central Almond, an enlarged area of 5,070 hectares, 530,000 dwellings and 1,075,000 inhabitants - the Central Area Office delivered a Strategic Project in 2011, putting forward a new conceptual approach for an area that is seen as the urban engine in times of scarcity. For this proposal three key aspects were treated: quality of public space - understood as the most effective level to act on city transformation -, energy efficiency and climate change awareness, and sustainability principles to underpin the evolution of the urban tissues (see Figure 2 17).

Being a strategic proposal based on the value of urban recycling, it includes several sectoral strategies. The most significant one from the planning point of view is the one that proposes a brand new vision for spatial organisation and managerial treatment of the Central Area. In contrast to the traditional way of dealing with the urban tissue, based on zoning and regulatory ordinances, the proposal contains three innovative instruments which require the same innovative attitude from the City Council for its implementation. The project has been awarded as Best Applied Research at the XVIII Ibero-American Biennale of Architecture and Planning, Cadiz, Spain, 2012

Figure 2-15 (left) and Figure 2-16 (right) Manzanares River Project: Linear Park and urban rehabilitation.
Source: Teresa Franchini

New areas for planning management
The Central Almond is divided into 24 Areas of Homogeneous Identity (AHI) that is, zones with similar physical, social and economic characteristics. The implementation of this proposal implies the removal of the current administrative division composed of 7 districts and 47 neighbourhoods (see Figure 2 18).

New way to describe the central area
In order to facilitate the understanding of this complex territory, the central area is divided into so called Urban Cells (UC), composed of several blocks that constitute the basic unit of urban articulation. Each cell acts as a reference of identity for residents, stressing thereby the sense of belonging of every particular piece within the city mosaic (see Figure 2 19 and Figure 2 20).

Apart from this, the UC intends to be a singular planning element and a place for the promotion of innovation in terms of normative, density and hybridisation of uses. Within the cell, the inner streets are transformed into channels of pedestrian movements while the public transport system runs along a grid of approximately 400 x 400 meters. The location of new uses is proposed within the existing blocks for the hybridisation of uses, opening the private areas to the public. Public facilities are located on the UC fringes, taking advantage of the existing public means of transportation in the external streets. The implementation of this new urban organization demands a progressive process of inner restructuration to be fulfilled in the long term.

New regulatory criteria
For the planning regulation, that is, the norms to be applied in each UC, the proposal contains two levels of intervention: the definition of global planning parameters for the entire AHI net, and detailed plans for every UC, intended to facilitate the administrative process of obtaining building permits. To put the whole regulatory system into practice, the implementation of the new criteria will imply the steady replacement of the existing ordinances and accordingly, the current bureaucratic process (see Figure 2-21).

Some lessons to be learnt
Pros:
* New approach to regulatory planning practice: the revision of a current planning instrument gives the opportunity to apply new visions for planning and a new culture for administrative practice

Figure 2-17 (left) The Central Almond: a new central area for planning. Source: Area of Urbanism and Housing, Madrid City Council. Figure 2-18 (right) Areas of Homogeneous Identity. Source: Madrid Centre Strategic Project, Area of Urbanism and Housing, Madrid City Council.

* Flexible regulation at the micro scale: the decomposition of an urban tissue into small areas facilitates the drawing up of detailed plans, adjusted to the specific conditions of the place
* International recognition: the transference of knowledge should be one of the leading principles that support this kind of urban proposals.

Cons:
* Difficulties derived from innovation: novelties are often hampered by the inertia of known and firmly established practices, especially when it involves taking major policy decisions
* Complexity in implementation: in operative terms, radical changes introduce considerable difficulties to integrate the proposals into the existing administrative structures, which are reluctant to modify the on-going processes
* Loss of political support: in the case of study, the demise of the Office of the Plan due to changes in the direction of the new master plan, meant the loss of interest in the project, leaving their proposals just as open ideas to chance or as possibilities, included in the new master plan.

SOME CONCLUSIONS ABOUT THE CHANGING CONTEXTS AND THE RESULTING VISIONS FOR PLANNING

Focusing the topic on reclaiming the 'possibility of making in times of scarcity' through planning, there is an obvious swinging movement that oscillates from one position to another, depending on the economic and social context within which cities operate. The analysis of this situation through the evolution of the visions that encouraged the drawing up of the master plans for Madrid during the last three decades, clearly exemplifies the effects of this changing situation that oscillated between scarcity and prosperity. The implementation of each plan has produced positive and negative outcomes, from which some lessons can be learnt.

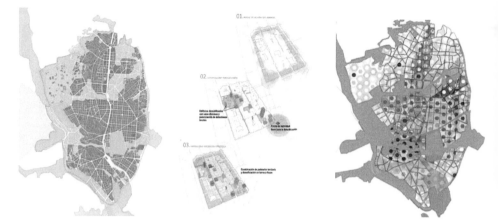

Figure 2-19 (left) Urban Cells net and cell conceptual inner organisation. Source: Madrid Centre Strategic Project, Area of Urbanism and Housing, Madrid City Council. Figure 2-20 (middle) Urban Cells net and cell conceptual inner organisation. Source: Madrid Centre Strategic Project, Area of Urbanism and Housing, Madrid City Council. Figure 2-21 (right) Areas of Homogeneous Identity, detailed planning. Source: Madrid Centre Strategic Project, Area of Urbanism and Housing, Madrid City Council.

It is obvious that during periods of affluence it is easy to promote urban projects, especially the big ones, but what matters in those cases is the understanding, on the part of the local political leaders, of the value of their implications in their implementation as a way to strengthening the position of their cities in the urban system.

However, even during scarcity times, when the 'possibilities of making' are reduced, it is possible to introduce innovation in the cities by using different strategies. The urban acupuncture is one of them, intended to produce small but effective actions, involving different levels of administration in the implementation process as a mean to obtaining the required investments. Another way is to envisage strategic actions not necessarily related to physical aspects but close to social and economic ones.

The last reflection with respect to the 'possibility of making' refers to the relationship between innovation and the contextual opportunities. The case of Madrid shows how a favourable situation fosters the construction of innovative planning visions aimed at promoting substantial changes in the traditional way of making the city. But this case also shows the high dependence that exists between new ideas and proposals and the political support that facilitates or hinders their application in practice. As a corollary to this situation, it is possible to conclude that innovations in planning find their limits in the existing administrative and political structures, strongly implanted in the local governments since the rationalist period.

References

Madrid City Council (1985) Madrid Master Plan

Madrid City Council (1997).Madrid Master Plan

Municipal Housing Company (1999). Areas of Preferential Rehabilitation,Interventions in the historical centre and peripheral neighbourhoods of Madrid (Spain), 1994-1999. Madrid City Council

Area of Urbanism and Housing (2009).Action Plan for the Central Area Rehabilitation, 2008-2011. Madrid City Council

78

Area of Urbanism and Housing (2011).Strategic Project for the Centre of Madrid, Madrid City Council

ADAPTATION

Figure 3-1 Skeleton structures in Manilva, Sabinillas. Source: Sebastian Seyfarth.

Ministry of Infrastructure and the
Environment of the Netherlands

INTERNATIONAL YOUNG PLANNING PROFESSIONALS AWARD 2012

The *Young Planning Professionals Award (YPPA)* is an annual, 3-year international competition (2012-2014) funded by the Directorate responsible for planning at the *Dutch Ministry of Infrastructure and Environment (mI&M)*. Its aim is to stimulate thinking and promote innovative ideas on how spatial planning in Europe can adapt its form and methodologies to take on the present-day challenges and transformations facing our human settlements. The underlying thinking is that it is largely the younger generation (< 35) of planning professionals who will have to come up with the answers, as it is they who will have the responsibility to plan and develop those settlements in the near future.

The ministry asked the International Federation of Housing and Planning (IFHP) and the International Society of City and Regional Planners (ISOCARP) – both then with secretariats in The Hague - to organise the Awards. They decided to bring in the Association of European School of Planning (AESOP) and organise the Award within the framework of the jointly run *European Urban Summer School (EUSS)*.

The theme of the Award is related to the theme of the EUSS. The winners receive free participation at the EUSS and present their papers at a special session. The papers form part of the EUSS publication which is also generously supported by the mI&M grant.

The theme in 2012 was '*Adaptive cities: new ideas for action. Trends, perspectives and challenges of spatial development in a phase of de-growth and decline in Europe*'. The winning entries can be found on the following pages.

SHRINKAGE IS SEXY: A NEW STRATEGY TO MAKE A SHRINKING URBAN AREA THE MOST VITAL PART OF TOWN

Clenn Kustermans

Shrinkage is globally considered as a negative phenomenon, and shrinking cities are seen as the opposite of growing, successful cities. Psychologically, there's strong coherence between this consideration and the development of our human body and mind. In our lives, shrinkage is the precursor of dying. But when city quarters dealing with a gradually declining population and an emptying housing stock are declared as Free States, these urban areas could become the most vital part of the body, err town. Within Free States, unused space could be exploited for the fulfilment of individual and collective living desires. Create whatever you want!

Because of declaring Free States and striking out several regulations, (local) governments and collective house-owners can focus their gained time and money on small scaled actions. Strict and rigorous interventions are sometimes necessary, especially when too many houses lack occupancy. Overall quality can be increased by effective, inexpensive and fast actions. The tristesse of the former over-regulated shrinking area can slowly disappear, and possibilities for a happy life will attract young people who tend to start their career as independents. In order to shape a socially sustainable space, the idea of all generations living together is implemented in a new concept of state-offered services. To achieve such a thing, keywords are trust, community, solidarity and action.

By showing the example of the post-socialist city of Chemnitz in Eastern Germany, I try to filter general principles that can be applied in other shrinking urban areas in Europe. Chemnitz, once an important industrial centre and the socialist model city Karl-Marx-Stadt, has been struggling with population decline and urban decay since the 1980s. Especially the 'Plattenbausiedlungen', or tower block areas, are in need of alternative answers. The potentials of the empty DDR blocks and the public space are huge.

HOW TO READ THIS PLEA

This article is meant to be a pleading story that should be read (chrono)logically. Therefore, I first introduce you to the city of Chemnitz. Secondly, I zoom in on Fritz Heckert, a tower block area with interesting spatial and social potentials. Then you will find a description of my suggestion and its motivation. After demonstrating you the innovative character of the proposed interventions, I will show you the applicability of the idea in other European contexts. A conclusion is terminus station. If you lose track, you can always return to this paragraph.

CHEMNITZ: A POEM

Chemnitz is a poem that could have been written by W.H. Auden or Dylan Thomas. Melancholic, tragic, but with sunny, hopeful streaks, changing its character in such unforgiving and relentless way that one can hardly identify its new image or remember its old image.

Other German cities alike, Chemnitz had its economic and demographic peaks in the 1930s. The city had become an important manufacturing centre in the 19th century as a concentration of textile industry. Chemnitz was known as 'Manchester of Saxony'. Later, when nationalism arose and war was inevitable, heavy machinery, locomotives, automobiles and other vehicles were produced in Chemnitz.

After the important stronghold of Panzer tank production had been bombed by allied air forces at the end of the second world war, 95% (!) of the city was demolished. Although the new era inspired many to recover the ancient inner city and surroundings, Chemnitz became part of the newly found Deutsche DemokratischeRepublik (DDR). Being renamed Karl-Marx-Stadt in 1953, the city was a laboratory; a test case for modernist architects and planners. Inspired by functionalist ideas and following the 'principles of planning and designing socialist city centres' the inner city was filled with high-rise apartment blocks. Street patterns were modern and functional, streets were wide and windy. Moreover, the city expanded by building the peripheral Fritz Heckert Area: a new city district with 31.000 model apartments for 90.000 inhabitants. The city was reordered to grow. Because when cities grow and develop, ideologies are justified.

But the heydays of socialism didn't last. When the 'two Germanys' reunited in 1990, a lot of (young) people moved to the west of Germany in search of jobs and a free or better life. However, Chemnitz had already been shrinking demographically since 1982. Today, Chemnitz has fewer inhabitants than in 1945 and the city is still shrinking, while neighbouring cities Leipzig and Dresden are growing steadily. Shrinkage is not just spread out over the city: some parts of the city are desolated places while other parts are inhabited and doing well. Former socialist 'Plattenbau' suburbs are specific desolated places nowadays. In these uncool urbs, average income and education are low, while average age and unemployment are high. Chemnitz is now known as the 'oldest city' in Germany - not for respectably being the first settlement, but for being the city with the highest average age.

Nevertheless, there are bright sides as well. The former image of city of industry has disappeared. Chemnitz has a well-known university of technology, which attracts talent and technology (two important T's, besides tolerance). Moreover, the university is an important employer. Many German students register at Eastern German universities because of their good reputation and affordable housing and living costs. Young couples move to specific parts of the city, because it is affordable compared to Leipzig or Dresden. Especially the areas built before 1918 are popular (Jugendstil and Gründerzeit architecture era) among youngsters with starters' income. These individual houses of several floors high are neatly designed and built in blocks, and there are communal gardens where kids can play safely. Except the houses, the attractiveness of the surroundings is considered too. The popular area has bars, restaurants and cultural places, and the inner city is within walking distance. Besides, the municipality is successfully funding the redevelopment of the inner city and the station area. There will be a direct connection between the main railway station and the university, which underlines the importance of the university.

Because of these attractive areas, the number of households in Chemnitz still remains quite steady. The steadiness of Chemnitz' households could mean that the city is not shrinking physically yet. In fact, the number of houses does not have to change. But as stated before, some areas in Chemnitz are popular and some not, which means that demands in the housing market shift geographically. Not the amount, but the location of the demanded houses has changed.

FRITZ HECKERT: A NOT SO OLD MAN WITH HIS INCONVENIENCES

In 1973 the Central Comity of the leading party SED declared a housing programme to satisfy demands and to maintain social harmony in the DDR. In order to offer housing and amenities rapidly, industrial technologies were applied. The ideology of standardized, prefab apartment blocks was used in socialist (and also capitalist) countries worldwide. In Chemnitz, socialist planners built the residential area Heckert five to nine kilometres southwest of the inner city. Why there? Because there was space! Comprising 31.000 units, Heckert became the second largest high-rise area in the DDR, after Berlin Marzahn-Hellersdorf.

The standardized model apartments, including the luxury of a bathroom and a private toilet, were designed for standardized model citizens (modern, progressive, collective). Under socialism, people were not just a consuming part of a consuming collective. You didn't own a garden, but there were parks and collective gardens nearby. Housing blocks were located in low-traffic streets. The peripheral location of the residential zones was no problem, because people could go to work via an extensive network of public transport.

The reunion of the 'two Germanys' lead to high vacancy levels in houses in Eastern German cities in general and areas like Heckert in particular. From 1998, the city of Chemnitz and collective house-owners have torn down buildings and parts of buildings in the city, especially in Heckert. Apartment blocks were demolished and either replaced by one-family houses and shopping centres or by nothing at all. Other blocks were 'decapitated': brought down to four stories. Some redevelopments (from apartments into one-family houses) took place too. From 31.000 units, 11.000 (or 35%) were gone in 2009. Housing vacancy is still 20 to 30%. Statistics in 2009 show that Heckert has 58% less inhabitants than in 1992. Birth rate is very low and mortality rate is high. The average age is 51, while Chemnitz is the oldest city in Germany with an average age of with 47. Unemployment is 12 to over 20%.

The tower blocks were produced fast, en masse and monotonously. In the 1970s grown-up baby boomers started to form families and settled down in the tower blocks collectively. Within the DDR, people didn't change their place of residence as often as today. Forty years later (today) the tower blocks still accommodate a large group of 'early residents'.

Furthermore, the image of model citizenship has changed. The ideology of the model apartment is diminished to the factual four walls and a roof. Heckert has become a place with a high concentration of socially fragile people. One could call it an internal clash between three main groups: a large group of old natives who have lived there ever since, a small minority of immigrants in search of cheap housing and lower educated youngsters. In places such as Heckert crime, political extremes and social instability aren't rare. Moreover, the peripheral location has turned into a problem. Because of not being an integral part of the city, Heckert can turn into a ghetto if not dealt with properly.

A vast majority of housing units is managed by collective land- and house-owning companies such as the Grundstücks- und Gebäudewirtschafts-Gesellschaft (or GGG). GGG, a fully owned subsidiary of the city of Chemnitz, has a quite simple concept: tenants rent apartments that are maintained by GGG. The formal owner is the city of Chemnitz. Apartments cannot be bought by private individuals or families. GGG only rents its housing stock. Regarding services and shops, Heckert is quite standard. There are kindergartens, primary schools, city services, clinics, sport grounds and chain supermarkets. As birth rate and children numbers are low, many schools have disappeared since 1990.

HOW HECKERT AND CHEMNITZ CAN BECOME ALIVE AND KICKING AGAIN

It should not be the city's ambition to become like Dresden or Leipzig. These cities are popular because of their cultural values. Dresden is beautifully restored and there are a lot of activities, and Leipzig is a cool, modern city with interesting historical artefacts. Chemnitz is not beautiful. Chemnitz is not classic or charming. Therefore, today's city's slogan 'City of Moderns' is right. It is modern, and it is different than anyone else.

Heckert and Chemnitz have certain potentials. Within its own region, the city can become popular again. Instead of trying to achieve the demographic peak from 1930, the ambition should be to offer a comfortable life quality with development possibilities in a safe environment. The university is an important starting point, because it annually attracts new talented youngsters. In addition, the oldest city in Germany can become a centre of old people's homes, social care, healthcare and other amenities. Chemnitz can become or stay a medium-sized, lively city, relatively cheap in its region, attractive for all generations. And more specifically, Heckert is just 40 years old... much too young to die.

A few interventions are needed though. My idea is built on a few suggestions: declaration of Free States, action-oriented government and collective house-owners, new ownership strategy and generation building.

DECLARATION OF FREE STATES

People or suburbs like Heckert were standardized from the moment they were born. Raised in a regulated society, there were procedures, rules, regulations, exemptions in specific cases within strict limiting conditions, etcetera for almost everything. You cannot paint your house red if all the houses next door are yellow. Your hedge can only be maximum 80 centimetres high and in some cases maximum 100 centimetres if transparent and if not thicker than 15 centimetres. Your roof may not be higher than 12 metres. You may not break down walls. These regulations demotivate (prospective) inhabitants. And this makes Heckert uncompetitive to other areas in Chemnitz or eastern Germany that are organized in a traditional Germanic way.

So let's forget about regulations! Let's break out, declare a Free State and make room for initiatives of the inhabitants, the real users of the houses and public space. Free states will attract liveliness. Regulations were made in a psychological context of fear. We need to trust people. We need to trust in people's capability and wish to build up a community.

Within Free States, that can be re-demarcated anytime, unused space could be used for the fulfilment of individual living desires. Except a few agreements on zones that must stay unbuilt, building and zoning regulations are lacking. You can remodel your tower block apartment, including the empty apartments next-door horizontally and vertically. The creative potential of the prefab apartments is huge: tear down walls, build stairways between floors, make an indoor garden... Do you want to open a shop? Please, go ahead. Make it a lively place. Build whatever you want, meet your neighbours and transform the public space inside and outside the way you want to. I hereby would like to note that these so-called Free States merely consist of building and rezoning creativity. These Free States are not party islands.

By introducing Free States, the tragic Plattenbauten become alive and attractive for people in search of a house in an urban and alternative environment. It is not the outlying ghetto anymore where you live when you don't have any other possibilities. Furthermore, the positive effect of ownership and taking care of the apartment and public space is introduced - instead of having standardized space without any (financial and emotional) ownership or responsibility. Especially this element is a huge potential within suburbs like Heckert.

The first Free State will be declared in one of the high-rise apartment blocks with many empty units, including the unused public space around it. This place will become a laboratory; a test case like the city was in the socialist era. If successful, the concept can be applied in other blocks too.

ACTION-ORIENTED GOVERNMENT AND COLLECTIVE HOUSE-OWNERS

Most cities today, Chemnitz included, tend to have overall policy coverage of their territory in order to keep order. On the other hand, all legislatures have focus areas. Currently, Chemnitz is successfully funding the redevelopment of the inner city by adding shopping malls in buildings designed by modernist architects Hans Kollhoff and Helmut Jahn, recovery of historical buildings, public transport, new public space etcetera. Moreover, the station area is redeveloped in order to make a straight connection to the university and to invite ICE-trains (high-speed trains connecting main cities). It can be an understandable choice to focus on inner cities and stations instead of outlying suburbs. But my proposal would then be to skip the regulations in the outlying suburbs and to forget about overall policy coverage! Uniformity is in my eyes a misinterpretation of constitutional equality.

Striking out building and zoning regulations seems to be an easy thing to do, but it is not. Most probably, the city will receive complaints of upset neighbours or pleads to financially compensate ownership rights. So, the city installs a contact person in the Free State. He/she will gain a lot of bottom-up experience and an extended social network within his/her working area. The contact person will try to find compromises within reasonable terms. The Free State lacks building regulations, but there are still common values agreed on by the residents. To build up a community, certain agreements will have to be made. But anchoring these agreements in regulations is highly unnecessary. It is about freedom and not limiting someone else's freedom. This plea has undoubtedly been done before, but in this era of scarcity, negativism and dogmatism it really might be the right thing to do.

Furthermore, the city can cooperate with the university, city-run housing associations and private companies to create a job and building programme to stimulate students to work and live in Chemnitz after their studies. The University of Chemnitz is known for its mechanical engineering, mathematics and computer science, as well as philosophy and social science. Linking study programmes and work together can make sure that talented graduates do not leave Chemnitz right away after their studies.

The campus is located south of the city centre. The city or university can buy units in Heckert to hire them to students. It is cheap, students have a lot of freedom in Heckert (compared to standardized model apartments somewhere else) and it is not far from the campus. During and as part of their studies, students can start rebuilding their apartment in the Free State into something of personal value.

An encouragement to set up local shops and services can be done too. For example, many independent merchants and entrepreneurs spend a lot of time and money on permit and tax regulations. The city can stimulate small business people by taking away administrative discomforts.

The city's main focus will be to encourage private developments. On the other hand, gained time and money can be used by the city and house-owners to redevelop parts of Heckert. If it turns out to be necessary to tear down (parts of) apartment blocks, the quality of space and the future function should be considered. It is a matter of balance: if there are too many buildings, the quality of the public space is endangered. If there are too few buildings, the place can become desolate, unattractive and unsafe. The local government and collective house-owners can react by punctual interventions: swift actions on a small scale in order to eliminate problems. Temporal use of space is possible if it does not obstruct future redevelopment.

GENERATION BUILDING

Heckert has demographic and spatial potentials to become 'senior city': a residential area for elderly people with their minds on stability and quietness. But this would not form a socially sustainable choice, because this would lead to isolation of individuals. Furthermore, a homogenous society does not exist and therefore it should not be aspired. In my eyes, social sustainability is driven by integration of generations, income classes, languages, races and nationalities. A melting pot, indeed. Therefore, a social and generational mix is intended. By implementing building freedom and taking the tristesse of the former over-regulated shrinking area away, young people who tend to start their career as independents can be attracted (students, young couples with or without kids). But trying to create a young trendy quarter is not a socially sustainable solution either. Many examples have shown that 'gentrification'27 has many negative sides that overshadow positive effects on the longer term. So: how to overcome a generation gap?

A simple answer would be to separate generations: Block A, Free State, is for youngsters, while B, still under building regulations, is for elderly. However, in order to shape a socially sustainable space, the idea of all people living together is implemented in a new concept of trust, community and solidarity. A Free State is a house of generations. Several generations living together is a positive condition for all inhabitants, because on the one hand people grow up fast and worldly while on the other hand people stay young longer. No isolation, but involvement and integration. Within a local economy of a Free State, senior care will be an important economic pillar in the near future. The Free States are small worlds in which a community can be formed. There are many non-disturbing activities such as shops, bars, restaurants and services. People know each other and there are common values. The anonymous life in the high-rise blocks can change into new social contacts on a human scale. And there's a lot of freedom to build or create what individuals or collectives want, elderly people included. This also means that people are free to refuse to use this freedom. But limiting someone else's creativity or desire is considered negative, and it therefore should not be possible. We live together on this planet, so let's live together!

It is like a dance floor. Space is limited, but people are free to dance. You can be timid and some basic steps, but you can also swing round boldly. The floor is made for people to communicate and play together, not to curtail someone else. It is a collective individual happening in search of some happiness. The spatial planner is a background musician, bringing the beat and defining the pace.

OWNERSHIP

Besides planning principles for a new strategy for shrinking urban zones, bringing together different kinds of ownership is an important question that should be answered to really realize ideas. Today the housing companies are shared corporations, and that seems to be a good start. The corporation/cooperation can keep housing affordable, because it can get relatively favourable mortgages. However, apartments are not sold to individuals yet. This leads to the classic gap between corporation (owner) and tenant (user). The lack of financial and emotional association with the apartment or public space leads to general disinterest by tenants. Public space is for everybody - and nobody. Therefore it would be an improvement if tenants can also buy shares or parts of houses and public space.

Indeed, if housing association/city sell apartments to individuals or collectives, it will be more difficult to break down a tower block if vacancy is too high. Private/collective development in Free States and strong government action form a combination of overlapping interventions. Both are possible at the same time and in the same space. As housing companies are subsidiaries of the city, it can be comprehensively involved in interventions by the local government. A small and effective intervention team can be formed to take away obstacles. Housing units can be used for other non-disturbing daytime and evening purposes too. If hope is really given up, a tower block can only be dismantled if housing company/city buy back the units or offer the owners an alternative unit. On the other hand, building and zoning freedom will lead to interconnected units, larger units, collective units, new purposes of units and less vacancy of units. Temporary student housing or other activities are possible too. If housing company/city are unsure about future occupancy, they can first try to sell parts of apartment blocks to people's collectives as they form a steadier base than individuals. If housing company/city persists on not selling apartments, more and more units will have to be broken down - and this would lead to a fatal decrease of finances as well.

INNOVATION AS KEY ANSWER TO OLD QUESTIONS

I believe that a concept of Free States, punctual government action, generation building and collective ownership is an innovative proposal, especially in former DDR Plattenbau areas. This statement is based on the following motivation.

* Total building liberalism in Free States is special and innovative within regulated Germany in general and overregulated Eastern Germany in particular. If more space is offered, Chemnitz can really make a difference and attract young people who tend to start their 'living career' in an alternative, urban environment.

* An active and light instead of a reactive and heavy city administration is new too. To solve problems and to maintain order, no overall policy coverage is needed. The local government can allow a lot more than today without getting complications. Instead of heavily regulating every square metre of its territory, the city can invest in punctual actions within a certain framework. After all, pure liberalism will not lead to an improvement of space.

* Community and generation building is an alternative to narrow individualism. After becoming part of the western, capitalist society, Eastern Germany quickly transformed and tried to catch up on the developments in the west. The new ideal was an old one: to own a detached house and a garden and to buy your goods in shopping centres and huge D.I.Y. markets. By doing this, the society followed mainstream - which is reasonable, but it does not distinguish itself from the grey mass. By building a community of different generations, classes and nationalities (combining old and young, foreign and native, poor and rich) it can become a special place.

* The positive elements of (partial) ownership aren't really implemented yet. In order to stimulate people's responsibility and financial and emotional bond with a certain space, people can be shares of houses (grow plan) and public, collective space. This too is innovative in Chemnitz, where the model apartments cannot be bought yet and where public space does

not belong to anyone.

Of course, this is why the proposal is innovative within its context. But the ideas itself are innovative too, in my eyes. I propose two extremes: on the one hand a far-going liberalism within unregulated Free States and on the other hand strong government intervention when the government announces it is required - if necessary also in Free States. I believe in a combination of these too extremes, instead of covering everything with the same, single coloured sauce. Too often we try to smooth innovative and rough (sides of) ideas until there is an agreement, or consensus. The pureness of ideas gets clouded when certain key brains need to be convinced. But to really enforce potentials of a certain space, the pureness needs to be kept.

IS THIS IDEA APPLICABLE TO OTHER EUROPEAN CITIES?

By showing the example of Chemnitz, my proposal might only seem applicable in relatively dense urban areas where ownership is limited to a few collectives. Shrinkage in for example rural France, Spain or Finland and towns in England or peripheral regions in the Netherlands and Belgium seems to be another story, because it is not city-like and there are many owners.

But on the other hand, collectives of ownership can be formed anywhere to buy vacant houses and land. The positive part of collectives is that they can get a mortgage cheaper and that people can buy shares and feel responsible for and proud of something. Free states can be declared on all scales (from regional level to a single house) and generation building can be done within all contexts (rural, townish, urban, metropolitan). If there is no initiative on the short term, the local government can start to use its network and motivate people by creating and communicating a lack of, for example, building regulations, and by stimulating private and collective initiatives.

TERMINUS

The tower block areas in the 1970s and 1980s were made to accommodate citizens in a growing city in a society characterized by mass production and employment programmes. Today's reality is that these specific areas are subject to demographic shrinkage. While on-going consumption is questioned by more and more people, alternatives are being sought. In times of financial scarcity political extremes can repossess people's minds. Populist politicians conceptualise totalitarian states with strong government influence. Another extreme reaction is total liberalism: to lower government costs, people are responsible for their own well-being. In my proposal I combine the positive elements of both extremes: on the one hand strong government intervention and on the other hand zoning and building liberalism. When we build communities and collectives, we can find an alternative to narrow (and expensive!) individualism. Local governments use their local knowledge and networks to take up a more lean and stimulating role. Private and collective development is stimulated to realize 'healthy growth' - without quantitative goals. Especially within the context of Chemnitz collective Free States and collective action can lead to improvement. Individual action can support reaching collective aims. The world is plural, multicultural, colourful and beautiful. Not uniform, grey and dull.

If we, hominessapientes, do not multiply as much as our grandparents did, it could become a survival of the fittest among cities and countries in the end. A war for every living soul could be inevitable! But in that case, the most modern and innovative cities and countries, inhabited by the most modern and innovative people and ran by the most modern and innovative officials, are then prepared and know what to do.

COSTA DE LA RUINA: NEGLECTED PLACES AT THE COSTA DEL SOL ALL THE WAY FROM MALAGA TO MANILVE

Sebastian Seyfarth

This chapter deals with the topic of the current situation of hundreds of empty and abandoned construction sites and their relations to their environment. This phenomenon has its roots in the time of mass construction, which was followed by the global financial crises. Nowadays these places are neglected and avoided by local residents and city municipalities. In particular, this paper is going to refer to the example of the Costa del Sol area in the south of Spain as the main case study.

Since the 1950th this area in southern Spain experienced a tremendous urban growth in providing settlements and infrastructure for Mass Tourism. Rapidly it became one of the most travelled holiday destinations for Europeans. Short term vacation tourism, as well as long term and constant residents from Spain and abroad, bought a 2nd or summer resident home at the coast. Hence the major part of the developments comprises residential buildings. Most of these developments especially inland, prioritised time efficiency of construction, not quality of the structures. The developments have almost no reference to the history or identity of that area. This creates the feeling of being in a copy-paste-mass-production-urbanisation, with fences and borders. There are isolated settlements, unrelated to their surrounding and even other neighbouring regions. The levelling of the topography to establish infrastructure for roads and houses caused big scale nature destruction and landscape sealing.

These developments continued until the Spanish property bubble burst in 2008 due to the global economy and financial crisis. Since then plenty of 'in progress' buildings stopped in construction and still remain in that very situation as they came to halt four years ago. Some of the developments could continue but even these structures are empty today. Together with other vacant developments they are generating ghost towns as though nobody ever lived there. What is going to happen with that kind of abandoned and neglected urban obstacles, when there is no money to continue, to transform or to destruct? How can one interact with the residential building typology that appears along the coast and has become part of Costa del Sol's identity?

An area is influenced by its on-going developments. Some of the results are being planned and others not. Does the area itself profits from it, or is it just the individual? Since the speculation business got forced stopping its developmental leadership what are the claims and consequences to residents, nature and the Costa del Sol identity?

THE LINEAR COSTA DEL SOL CITY

The coastline of the Costa del Sol is an elongated urban agglomeration that stretches from Malaga to Manilva throughout 9 different municipalities. While driving along the coast these municipality boarders are barely visible. There are no tangible borders instead they blend into each other. Is it one never-ending suburb or one lengthened city centre?

There are more continuous elements that support this linear perception. Nature surrounds the Costa del Sol from one side with the linear stretch of the Mediterranean coast with the affiliated linear beach plot and on the other side the continuous mountain range. The existing 'National 340' and the 'AP-7' toll highway are the main infrastructural backbones for the Costa del Sol. They connect all the urban developments, conglomerations and inhabitant spaces, allowing a fast and direct linear connection. Whereas it is possible to reach more or less every space at the Costa del Sol along the highway, the places among each other are rarely connected and some neighbouring settlements are only accessible from the highway itself. This makes the car more or less the only transportation medium to move around.

Even though there are all this linear aspects of the coast there is almost no infrastructure to experience the coastline in itself. The highways are facilitating structures, Marc Augé's so called non-place, a transit space mainly to reach a certain destination (Augé 1992). Whereas for experiencing the area by walking, this very highway constitutes a boundary which rather blocks accesses than enable them.

Social situation

What is the residents' perception of their coast and what are their relations between each other, the abandoned constructions, the inhabited buildings and their individual desires for the area? Since the 1950th the Costa del Sol area experienced huge developments concerning all aspects of the Tourism sector. With that also the user-target-group remained the very similar. The coast as an image for relaxation, water, beach and sun. Is there a way to develop something for tourists and local people? Is there a target group who takes the area as it is without becoming artificialized?

There are different actors around the nature-concrete landscape like the investors for whom the Costa del Sol was a residential business machine and the dwellers themselves which we can distinguish in two main sub groups of people, the local residents and the seasonal tourists. Due to the holiday travel concept of predominantly being in an isolated resident complex right next to the beach, these groups differentiate themselves among each other in individual zones. The, on the one hand, overdeveloped real estate market leaded to an, on the other hand, underdevelopment of social activity, common space, cultural offers and traditional everyday habits. Before tourism became the major business at the Costa del Sol, inhabitants used to work in the fields of fishing and agricultural. Due to the 1998 change in the building law in order to access more ground for the real estate market, plenty of traditional farmland had to be sold to residential developers leaving the original land owners with a absents of parts of their identity.

The shrinking phenomenon and de-growth

In the nowadays situation, after the crises, we can find this area with an oversupply in living space. After the banks cancelled the supply of loans, people cannot afford to buy these holiday houses anymore. That is why we can find even new furnished apartments which not get sold, but fall prey to weather and decay over time. Even in terms of a recovery, the new investment would need to consider to demolish the afflicted structures first and then to fully new construct, due to decay and

Progress types:

1. Foundation	Concrete foundation platform with concrete columns
2. Skeleton	Construction of concrete slabs supported by concrete columns
3. Bricks and Walls	Skeleton structures with either adobe brick walls or even plastered walls
4. Finished but vacant	Finished constructions with color, windows and doors, but still empty
5. Abandoned Historical	Buildings which were once inhabit but became abandoned, i.e. old farm houses or mansions

Size types:

1. Single unit	A single solitary ruin
2. Building complex	Two or more ruins belonging to the same construction project
3. Resort	Developments with the size of a whole resort

Table 3-1 Types of construction ruins. Source: Sebastian Seyfarth.

the simple fact that we would never get the same conditions and customers as before the crisis.

What are possible de-growth strategies with this building typology? And would it be a good strategy to just demolish these obstacles to give the Costa del Sol back its initial natural landscape? Does de-growth mean deconstruction? Or what else can happen then with these empty and unfinished houses?

Fascinations and potentials of the abandoned construction ruin

Giovanni Battista Piranesi showed us already in the 18th century with his etchings of the ruins of Rome the very aesthetics in ruin structures. A little later Hubert Robert drew the brand new Louvre in Paris as an imaginary ruin and reveals this hidden mystic layer of architecture. Ruins are different; we immediately bring them in relation with history witnesses the past. We are able to see two worlds at the same time. The one how it originally was and the one how it got transformed and remains today. The Costa del Sol abandoned construction ruins are different form normal ruins because they were never inhabited and some never even finished being constructed. It is a negative ruin, not the classical one when a building falls apart into ruins, but these developments rise up to ruins (Smithson 1967). While working on the Costa del Sol ruins I characterise them into different types. (Table 3-1)

Example of the aesthetics of the stalled concrete Skeletons:

A construction site surrounded by cranes which gives the impression of a still growing urban fabric. However the cranes have been idle for some years and the construction fields abandoned. Even construction debris litters the site, such as ten thousands of bricks still wrapped and unused. The buildings, skeletons, ruins, concrete slaps as floors and columns to support these floors. Simple as it is. The structures are fulfilling the model of basic modern architecture. It is minimalism in its pure form, which means a wide space to move in and a structure to support that space. There is no wall, no separation, no border. It is a minimalistic radical version of the Mies

Figure 3-2 Ghost town in Manilva. Source: Sebastian Seyfarth.

van der Rohe's Farnsworth House. Landscape, nature, sun, air and views are flowing through the unfinished skeleton structure and let people inside experience a much more natural surrounding related interior feeling than in regular types of housing interiors. The design concept provides users with a defined space like a room, but without being in an enclosed space. It is more like a public square, but rather a multi-layered public square building.

Like in Piranesi's etchings of the Carceri series, the staircases are the conspicuous elements of attraction in these skeleton structures and you sometimes cannot be sure where they lead. (Figure 3-1)

Example of finished but never-inhabited ghost-town resort:
Walking along an empty street with many of the same looking buildings all around. All the blinds are shut and there is no single towel on either balconies or gardens. Everything is new and freshly painted. Walking by, one expects to see somebody sitting in the next garden or opening up a window, maybe the neighbourhood kids are skateboarding on the street you are walking on.

The wild grass growing out of the curb stones shows slight evidence that something is not right. In fact, this place is vacant and always has been. Somehow there is no soul. There never were any kids skateboarding on the street. There is no history with these buildings, no relation to anybody. Nobody misses the time growing up there because no one ever enjoyed afternoons with a hot chocolate on the terrace. Because it is in no one's memory, can we easily tear down this place?

With or without the people, on site, we see all the images, stories and history even though there is nobody and the history of the area is a history of construction. We see and imagine stories or possibilities. Such a surrendered and exposed man-made fabric automatically lets us think and create scenarios. The ruins are the means for imagination. (Figure 3-2)

Internet activity

The importance of the digital network in our daily routine is not comparable with the situation even just 10 years ago. Booking, buying, renting and lending became easy and accessible. Going through books, streets and museums all over the world from your laptop is common, as well as being connected with thousands of persons, sharing videos, pictures and impressions from everywhere in the world wireless via your smartphone. The digital world is not just something for the young generation and big global companies to sell products. For example problematical urban areas or local discrepancies could get more participation from neighbourhoods and global contributions to achieve a contemporary solution. Therefore it seems inevitable to involve that digital layer in contemporary urban developments.

THE PROJECT

The project is about creating a new spatial dynamic between all kinds of residents, natural landscape and dense urbanisation. Due to the crisis the construction developments came to a halt. These so far unfinished and neglected constructions are going to become a new place of action. The project is making use of these structures and provides possibilities and gives an answer to the lacks and needs of the Costa del Sol inhabitants. In addition the project will introduce the area to the contemporary generation of travellers and locals. This new target group will bring more variety in the future developments but without considering mass tourism and mass commerce. The project is more about the real-life of the area. Additionally it has the concept of investing no new money by working with the minimal tools of intervention. The aim is to work with the ruins, natural appearance and decay for the need of the area itself. It will bring people together with themselves, with nature and the human creation of concrete structures figuring out the question: How can a participatory design process integrate man, the abandoned and nature and making use of the place as a collective good?

The proposed strategy works with different elements whereas the first and second are more focused on the external representation of the coastal area. The third and fourth element gives answers and scenario based solutions to the various perceived scarcities in the research area.

The first element in particular introduces the area and the phenomenon of abandoned construction ruins and their positive appearance in a new perspective. The second element describes the connection of the sites and therefore a way to individually perceive the already existing linear conglomeration with a new infrastructure. The elements 3 and 4 are dealing with ephemeral vs. permanent interventions in order to create a new spatial dynamic for the site itself. Empower the specific character and spatial quality with a permanent addition, and the architectural supporting module as a replaceable ephemeral object.

Element 1: Rediscovery of the Coast (Information):

The people should become aware of the positive potentials in the neglected spaces. Residential estates appear in such huge presence in the region of Costa del Sol that we cannot deny that these structures became part of the identity already. We have the opportunity to work with these stalled ruins before they get replaced. To just deconstruct what we already destroyed is not an answer. To flatten with bulldozers an area for the second time does not bring us back to

Figure 3-3 Web page draft. Source: Sebastian Seyfarth.

nature. Richard Wagner wrote: 'What is being built is always a tomb, a memorial to failure and disaster...only ruins have permanence' (Huyssen 2003). So the concept is to use that neglected but permanent structures, in order to give them relevance in their uniqueness but also to support the neighbourhood and their individual desires. The places have to remain accessible to everybody in physical and theoretical way. No privatisation, no fences and no boundaries. The place will be for looking, exploring, imagining, reflecting, playing, acting, meeting, doing, creating, exchanging, learning and being.

The abandoned construction ruins, or place of possibilities, will be explored and facilitated on a webpage, which shows all the ruins with specific information about the plots and their surroundings. The internet site introduces different categories of ruin types, pictures of the ruins, texts, notes, imaginations, stories, sketches, and others to discover the new view toward the neglected mass. Basically the webpage introduces and communicates in a contemporary way the topic of the Costa del Sol situation and its special objects. On that platform it is possible to exchange opinions and experience, photos, stories and imaginations. Furthermore the web page is able to grow and therefore provide always new sites and updates which keeps the website and the place worth to go.(Figure 3-3)

Element 2: The path of identity (Infrastructure):
The potential is there, we just need to support the way it can get experienced.

Since these 'dead bodies' are appearing all over the coastline, they form an element of continuity that can be seen as a connected itinerary along the coast. The 'Costa del Monumento' pilgrimage, the enlightenment journey is meant to discover the origins and hybridisation in nature phenomena and artificial human creation.

Hereby the abandoned construction ruins are the eye catching highlights and particular targets to guide you along the path. Possible to create different routes suitable for different extensive day trips. Throughout your trip you discover the exciting ruin typology but you will also experience the coast in its linear outstretch, not just out of a transit non-place. It is important to realise that 'The way is the aim'.

I will introduce the 'IBA - FürstPückler Land' (InternationaleBauausstellung) in Brandenburg Germany where a new infrastructure of bicycle paths around the area were established. They connect cultural activities with the beautiful landscape. Highlights on these paths are the active and the rehabilitated coal mining pits.

The communication of this contemporary traveling tour for alternative tourism is again accessible through the web page. Users are able to interactively design their own personal itinerary and discover this new layer of the Costa del Sol.

Element 3: Activation of the character (Permanent transformation):

The third element confronts the issue of the interactions with the buildings in general and applying a program to the site. Travellers but even more local inhabitants are going to design their neighbourhood and provide a chance to empower the cultural, local and nature activity. The possible implementations at such places are as big as the amount of the sites itself. One example to mention is a skeleton structure which is on former agricultural ground and in between local resident homes. A traditional and contemporary activation of such site would be a common nature-green-house (see Figure 3-4) in which to plant, farm and store. In this sense, the site gets integrated in the Costa del Sol fabric and linear city experience where locals are able to bring back their traditional craftsmanship, meeting and share at these common places the different historic layers of the costal developments with temporary visitors, seasonal tourists and other local residents.

This type of programs would also help the ruin to be one. In terms of perception, which reminded to the words of Robert Smithson in his speech about the Hotel Palenque in Mexico where he talks about the carefulness of how these people tear down a building: 'Slowly with a certain degree of sensitivity and grace so that there is time for the foliage to grow through the broken concrete, and there is time for the various colours on the wall to mellow under the sun.' (Smithson 1972). Robert Smithson is talking about the potentials in decaying and that it shows us the entropy of the presents. The ruins are witnesses of the ephemeral.

The transformed ruin does not ask for anything and the visitors will feel invited. Its charismatics and playfulness let people interact with it and they will ask themselves 'what could be next?' while having ideas and inspirations the person is taking part of the whole interactive process of observing and imagining possibilities which can be transformed into that structure. Therefore the ruin is also the means for imagination itself.

The main element of the already on-going transformation hereby is the nature which is taking back its original space (see Figure 3-5). So, let nature take back its space?

Element 4: The module (Ephemeral supporting object):

The ephemeral addition is a supporting module for the individual activity or the stroll, which can

Figure 3-4 Nature greenhouse scenario. Source: Sebastian Seyfarth.

be installed on each site. One of the biggest challenges in providing a solution to the various desires might be to implement some kind of architecture when it was architecture which failed at these specific places. Therefore the focus lies on the perceived space which is created already by the ruin structure itself. Hence the additional installation will be simple, flexible and just temporary. In fact it is just there as long as a person is using it and its space it creates. The Module adapts the existing incomplete ruin structure and completes it momentary to an individual defined area for a specific person or group.

In order to adjust this flexible structure on all kind of positions, an installation of several hocks around the whole site will be implemented. That is giving the users a variety of different options to define an individual space. By using just a simple and traditional like shade-sail-fabric to implement walls, roofs and benches, one is able to define different size areas by just this minimal and temporary installation (see Figure 3-7 and Figure 3-8). In each site the module will be individual due to its adaption of the ruin, its specific character and the personal user needs and desires. In that way people can establish places for sitting, meeting, selling, sharing, playing, enjoying, sleeping and more, a common space for a collective good.

POSSIBLE APPLICATION IN OTHER CONTEXTS

In terms of an application in other contexts we are going to look at the phenomenon in general. Architectural projects which were resigned for a variety of reasons like design errors, clashing political decisions, inaccurate cost estimates, contractor bankruptcies, evident disregard of building regulations, disappearance of funds and more, have stopped, leaving just a series of ruins, abandoned even before having been used at all.

Figure 3-5 Already on-going nature reconquering process. Source: Sebastian Seyfarth.

Figure 3-6 Uses the existing conditions to create a green roof. Source: Sebastian Seyfarth.

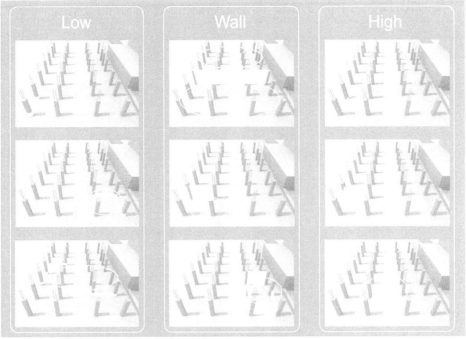

Figure 3-7 Variety of different option to define space. Source: Sebastian Seyfarth.

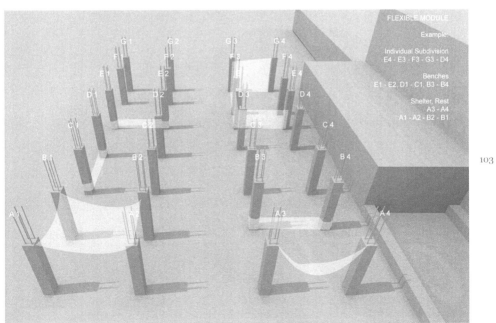

Figure 3-8 One possible constellation of individual space creations. Source: Sebastian Seyfarth.

The phenomenon appears also in other areas of the Mediterranean Sea, just a few examples like in Italy, especially on the island Sicily, where a national survey discovered 156 unfinished abandoned construction ruins. Another conglomeration of unfinished and abandoned constructions is near by the resort town Kusadasi in Turkey, where over 50 abandoned concrete skeleton structures from 4 to 15 floor height are located right next to the Aegean coast.

Due to the contemporary increasing global capitalist economy, buildings no longer just get built due to housing demand, but as a financial investment. This strategy works until the property bubble burst. This did not only happen in the area like the Costa del Sol, but in other places around the Mediterranean and the global world.

The city of Kangbashi in Ordos China was built for around 300.000 people, most of the apartments are sold, but just a few people are really living there. There are plenty of these ghost towns in the bigger urban fabric of Shanghai like Thames Town, Anting German Town, Holland Town and other new towns.

We do not have to go that far away because in Spain we can find a lot more ghost town developments for instance the place El Quiñon. Areas are usually not able to cope with such high population growth. The problem of missing infrastructure like shopping facilities, schools, hospitals and social establishments is eminent. To live in these buildings is rather secondary, so it is usually meant to buy, possess and sell them.

In the end, we can only hope that the crises stops these speculation-based developments, otherwise more ghost cities will grow and we will be left with more ruins and a failing environment.

CONCLUSION

This strategy of transformation creates unique architectural hybrids which generates a forward thinking and contemporary intervention, while strengthening the identity of a region. Architects and planners have to be aware of this character of identity while intervening in the urban and natural fabric. It is important to understand that urban developments are creating large scale environmental changes and could cause nature irregularities. Otherwise, areas will end up as interchangeable non-places with no relation to environment, citizens and traditions.

References

Augé, M. (1992) Non-Lieux. Introduction à uneanthropologie de la surmodernité
Smithson, R. (1967) A Tour of the Monuments of Passaic, N.J.
Huyssen, A. (2003) Present Pasts.Urban Palimpsests and Politics Memory.Stanfort, California.
Smithson, R. (1972) Hotel Palenque.University of Utah.

Figure 3-9 Concrete pillars, today. Fuengirola.Benalmádena. Source: Sebastian Seyfarth.

Figure 3-10 One example of a transformed site.Fuengirola.Benalmádena. Source: Sebastian Seyfarth.

CULTURE HUNGERS: NEW APPETITES FOR CONTEMPORARY CITIES

Serena Maioli

DYSFUNCTIONAL ABUNDANCE

The city is an egg (Price, 1961). The ancient city, hemmed in the physical line of the walls and made up of an historical core, is a boiled egg: we are able to distinguish the borders and its density. During the centuries of industrialization and demographic boom, the city begins to develop itself beyond the walls, taking the form of a fried egg: the periphery is born. The city centre, up to now solid on the core, loses its magnetic force and infects itself with an urban magma which floods everything dissolving hierarchies: the modern city become scrambled.Despite Price's model, our cities entered a new phase, one in which growth and the blending of centres and periphery brings about a new phenomenon of erosion and blurring: it causes the emptying of entire urban parts, towards a porous islands' city model (Ungers, 1977).

We are living in redundant spaces, unfinished or unplanned, revealing a stopped growing process: we are talking about vacant spaces or, more often, completed spaces with function but without sense. We can define those spaces 'urban lacunas'; they are protagonists in the loss of meaning of the whole work which is the city. Is abandonment a symptom of crisis or the result of a natural selection? We cannot continue categorizing shrinkage as a contemporary wound or a sign of decline; rather, we have to admit it is the expression of latent social behaviours and economic trends which bring us to reconsider quantity and quality of the space.

The emptying scenario is a topic in the debate among local community and hyper-community (political and economic), two opposite fronts both for aims and kind of space use.To understand the reasons of shrinkage we have to observe how people meet, how they eat, what they buy, how long they live in public space or in private: substantially, it's time to study the culture space capable of synthesizing the identity of a bigger de-territorialized community.

NOTHING IS REALLY ADAPTIVE BUT CULTURE

[...]The city must actually create new appetites, new hungers - not solve problems. The architecture is too slow to solve problems.

Culture is a cluster of ideas almost impossible to merge: it's the set of mental qualities (knowledge and beliefs) and behaviours features (customs and traditions) which are expressed by human displays such as art or ethic. Moreover, culture is a social legacy achieved by populations during the centuries by the strengthened relationships among individuals, groups, countries; culture is the product of ethnicities. Talking about culture in urban planning means listening to changes in society: culture is the way people react to poverty; the way they define hierarchies and limits among public and private sector. It is made by the myths we invent and by the trends we follow.

Why, then, do we need to investigate the regenerating potentialities of culture in the shrinking city? The reasons why towns are reshaping their spaces results from a friction between the ambitions of the growth-oriented economic model and its social externalities on using urban and rural areas.

Studying this context we are able to understand how to steer the urban agenda: culture becomes a survey-tool, much like a magnifying glass, but also a development strategy which enables the translation of phenomenological codes into technical learning and vice versa.

Culture presents the chance to transform social experiences into urban experiences and to tie up again the lost relationship between people and places.

The arrhythmia between city and urban life is one of the first causes of urban decay and derived by its inability to engender sense of belonging and identification: the breaking-off between community life and space produces unconcern in the best case scenario and social exclusion in the worst one.

The life cycle of a building, a district or a park, starting from planning until its demise is much slower than the social time which is capable of creating innovations, of broadcasting impulses and trends, activating exchanges among people every minute. The time-planning of urban scale has to follow the culture road trying to outguess cultural transformations.

To understand how the city creates culture and how culture becomes praxis and symbolic representation of society, we need to study the so-called soft infrastructures as the relational and information resources of the city (Branzi, 2006). New fields of study may help urban planning in ordering complexity and in showing how we perceive space (environmental psychology), how we interact with it (interactive design) and how we communicate thanks to the urban space (communication).

Cultural tools: environmental psychology

There is a deep gap between the city we plan and the city we live in. Which spaces do we live in and which ones make us feel good or express safety, energy, excitement, calmness or daze? The environmental psychology measures the effect of the physical environment on the individuals and the community well-being.

Wellbeing has come into the technical vocabulary of architects, planners and governors: it is a complex condition which involves senses, expectations, attitudes and it depends on the particular context and reference culture. The sense of well-being is influenced by measurable facts as lighting and noise, smell and proximity to obstacles, but its perception is eminently subjective and derives from the interweaving of mental attitudes and social interaction.

The acceptance of a refurbishment project by the local community is strictly dependent on the quality of the urban condition or situation generated, on the skilful mix of surprise and reassurance: the synergy between new intervention and place identity and history, that is actually its widespread culture, gives to the project one more chance to succeed.

Querying on the dynamics of flows and places to stop, we can understand why some spaces have been preferred to others and, afterwards, what is the method to activate the shrunk spaces of the city.

Cultural tools: interactive design

The interaction design, as a quite distant subject from urban planning, both for applications and work tools, may be considered extemporaneous: however, it has been born with similar aims than those of urban design and it uses work's methods that follow the same direction of the culture-based approach to planning so far enunciate.

This design branch deals, in fact, with the analysis of interactions between man and computer devices with the purpose of generating market products fulfilling as much as possible human necessities, always considering a specific context. Interface, usability, interaction define the relationship between users and machines (Steenson and Scharmen, 2012).

During the design process, from idea to product, we can observe an interesting method used to evaluate the responses of the interactive object to the user's needs: the first phase involves a market and target research, which is followed by the idea's conceptualization into some specific solutions. The most important part of the process, however, is the realization of a prototype that gives a quick and low-cost feedback on the acceptability of the product.

If we define the urban spaces as one interface within, and of, communities, is it possible to plan their interaction with the citizen's needs? The cities' architecture is not only physical planning of space, but the definition of its dynamic relationships with people: to combine the world web potentialities with the ones of the real geography not only do we have to create interactive maps of the city but also to promote interactive and narrative cities. Our cities need to be narrated: a space storytelling, capable to highlight the functionality and the responses of the land to the change in time and uses, giving the citizens a constant feedback on the political urban decisions.

Cultural tools: communication

The future cities have to take charge of an important task: to increase the imagination of local communities, enabling them to learn patternthinking. Today the cities talk through road signs, commercials, lighting and neon signs; they talk about happiness, desire and possession addressing themselves to the individuals rather than to the whole community.

The urban communication turns out to be as much important as urban planning in the new-born media age: cities have to seize the opportunity of branding themselves, developing communication strategies to present themselves as attractive.

First of all, we need to focus people's attention on the abandoned places of the city, on the fragile and marginal dots keen to be brought back to the urban storytelling. A new crisis-communication has to evolve, responsive to the critical events, capable of involving local and external stakeholders in regeneration projects: crisis may be interpreted as signs of change and, because of it, there become the ideal settings in which to create new scenarios.

The public space is the stage of urban communication and the governors have to spend time and resources on reshaping it, in order to improve the relationship between local government and civil society actors.

AVANT-GARDE

Back to visibility

During the Five Days of Milan in 1848, the street fighting against the Austrian monopoly has put side-by-side a multitude of Milanese revolutionaries, coming from different social and cultural ranks, to claim for a common identity and land that once had been usurped from them.

In May 2012 something happened in Milan which, not being comparable to the independence fight, took its origin from same desire reclaim back a lost piece of land and identity: the ten days occupation of the Galfa Tower by artists and intellectuals reveals the demands of a large and creative social group, focusing their attention on wealth, spaces and visibility redistribution; confinement and exclusion from the labour market and urban life were the reasons which brought the Art's workers association to outline the perspective of a cultural resurgence.

If we think that social inclusion starts from the sense of belonging to our places, we can easily explain the Art's workers choice to occupy a vacant skyscraper located in the city centre, in order to give strength and visibility to their cultural protest.

The Galfa Tower bears the name of the two streets which it overlooks, Galvani and Fara streets: after serving as a base for an oil company and, from the fifties on, the base of the BancaPopolare di Milano, since 2006 the tower belongs to SAI, an insurance company; ever since, the skyscraper with its thirty-one abandoned floors is still looking for a renovation.

Why have they occupied the Galfa Tower instead of a place already programmed to accommodate cultural activities? According to some young participants, culture cannot stay enclosed in the usual institutional borders but must overrun other spaces. The Art's workers criticized the way Milan produces cultural events like the EXPO 2015, which is capable of attracting huge masses of consumers but, simultaneously, requiring large investments in new built up areas and reinforcing socio-spatial fragmentations and inequalities: the slick showcase of the most recent regenerative plans and models of Milan actually seems to use the same vocabulary of previous concepts and visions, for instance the theme of green and greenery as the city panacea and the inevitable concrete employ in order to claim the design victory.

In this context, the occupation of the Galfa Tower reveals a desire to come out of the dark, social magma of the city; beyond this gesture there is the hope to give visibility to social and urban issues: social atomization and urban shrinkage.

The skyscraper isn't just an icon of capitalism, building speculation and the culture of the urban standard: as GiòPonti said, the Galfa Tower is the symbol of Milanese industriousness and widespread energy of the city (Ponti, 1961).

Macao is the name chosen to reinforce the project branding: the association's network allowed a cross-communication through the web and informed the Internet users about the experiences collected, debates, propositions and news. The occupation led to the discovery of an abandoned world, in order to reshape it and to get back producing culture. Different working groups organized video installations and architecture workshops in order to fit out the interiors; events planning to attract people and artistic announcements to involve citizens all over the world in building a new community of professionals. Macao seemed to be a collective and inclusive demonstration in which different fields of culture (literary, design, art, music and many other) and different social ranks collaborated.

The failure of Macao came on the tenth day with the order to evacuate the Galfa Tower rooms: the institutional legality continues prevailing against illegal and explosive creativity. Macao doesn't stop, however, and moves to the public space, from the new-born Macao Plaza to Piazza Duomo trying to reorganize a new committee. What will its future be? Is Macao searching for a space in which it could come true or are the abandoned places in the city desiring for the arrival of a project like Macao?

The main critical point of this kind of demonstration against a complex system of institutionalized values is the impossibility to embed them into society: they haven't been interiorized as being part of the collective culture yet. The reason they blossom is the same of their failure: the detachment between urban planning and urban sub-culture. All that we can get from this Italian experience cannot be seen as an accomplished fact because it is still not accepted as taking part of our conscious imaginary, but the beginning of a trend: the trial of a bottom-up undertaking without any planned intervention by politicians and technicians. The ground-breaking boost for an urban change and for the transformation of inner structures (market, production, social relationships) comes again from the creative part of the society.

In the interview given in the 2011 during the 'Festival dellamente' in Sarzana, Zygmunt Baumann said:

'Every majority, historically, is born from a minority. [...] We call them minorities but they are not inactive. They don't appear in the statistical boards, for this reason we don't notice them. However, I'm quite persuaded that, somewhere in the world, some alternative programs of action are coming out.'

A city caused by learning

The Potteries Thinkbelt is born as a taunt, during an half architectural half institutional conversation between Cedric Price and the British Ministry of Education, Lord Kennet. The meaning of education in the contemporary age and its physical display in the city was the crucial theme of the discussion: according to Price's statements, education infrastructure represents better than others the paradox of an architecture out of phase despite the social evolution. Is it still possible to learn the world's properties and at the same time to invent new worlds when knowledge is kept within brick fortresses?

Cedric Price doesn't think so and defies Lord Kennet to look back at its role as governor and key decision-maker on British education policies.

Price: 'Why don't you really think about what education is about, what learning is about? How people access it?'

Lord Kennet: 'If you are so clever, why don't you do it?'

Price: 'I bloody well will, then.'

Access is the key-word we should focus on to understand the creative sparkle that brought Price to the conceptualization of the Thinkbelt. The access to learning includes many meanings: first of all, it refers to physical access, through infrastructure, of students to learning facilities; secondly, access refers to how young people embrace, on a daily basis, an educational career, their dynamic interactions, the way they experience knowledge and produce it. Today, the access is overall connected to the virtual linkage or the possibility to network people and information all together. Price considers the students as one of the most dynamic social groups due to their adaptability and reactivity. But the place in which they have to perform their creativity appears paradoxically static, introspective and stiff: they live in a space which is unsuitable to host any change.

The Thinkbelt project uses an abandoned railway as a networking catalyst for an urban settlement in which industrial activities have been replaced by production of knowledge. Rem Koolhaas notices that Price's project deals with the theme of 'the derelict' or 'the ruin' that preserves a vital sparkle inside itself: Price finds in ruins the essence he needs to start a transformation process (Koolhaas, 2004). The ruin has lost the epochs' images and remains as a sign of the landscape in its deep sense, deprived of the ornaments time has put on it. It's a track, a stop or an interchange point: it loses the exterior skin but not the capacity to generate situations. The rails and the rail-tools are used for moving and transferring prefab classrooms, laboratories, storages and services: as in a giant dockyard, three hub-stations allow the moving of containers with different functions through the use of a crane, depending on the needs.

Those transfer areas, Pitts Hill, Madeley and Meir set up a triangle of local infrastructure connected to the regional ones in which the housing areas are located. The housing blocks are also made of prefab units which can be assembled in four different ways according to specific site conditions.

Price thinks that the mobile learning, as well as the dynamic management of learning facilities, could spark off positive reactions: the project would encourage flexibility and enable experimentation; in order to boost them, he decides to build from the beginning only ephemeral and adaptable architectures.

At the base of the settlement strategy of the Thinkbelt, Price grants free access to learning in a way that would become the starting point for creating a new industrial class as a driving force of the country.

Price believes in the virtuous synergy of tangible and intangible production enhanced by the physical connection of the railway networks.

From the knowledge cathedral to the Potteries' containers there is a huge conceptual leap of monumentality: the building loses its symbolic centrality and becomes one of the knots of a complex web in which the link itself rises to the rank of monument. The project deals with the first signs of industrial decline which led, in the following years, to the progressive abandonment of industrial and tertiary areas: Cedric Price, sooner than other artists and technicians, understood the potential of dispersal as an opportunity to build a new landscape, an information landscape. The Thinkbeltrail-scape merges and crosses the architectural and the geographical disciplinary corpus, using terms related to geography such as limit, dimension, coordinates.

To the question 'is it necessary to build?' Price answers with a certainty: enabling is better than building. Thus, if we would like to see a contemporary appropriation of Price's statements, we should shift our attention from city planning to interactive design: Thinkbelt is one the very first cases of interaction design because it sets up synergies between man, computer devices and architecture. The output of an interactive design process could be defined as a plan of interfaces rather than a physical building project: it turns away from the idea of formal representative architecture. The evolutionary nature of architecture and city's forms brings us to two different considerations: first of all, architecture could keep on living if they it results capable of adapting in time; secondly, if architecture cannot adapt itself, landscape will transform it into its original (in the sense of non-historical) configuration. All we can learn from Price's lesson is the capacity to fit in the change under way and encourage it. The peculiar open-endedness of his model, even if strongly critical, does not fight against capitalism effects, rather it elicits from the fail of capitalism the strengths to build a new idea of learning-society. He doesn't criticize mass culture: on the contrary, he desires that such trend causes the spread of creative sparkles, qualifying and connecting them exponentially through networks.

Rules and roles

Macao and the Potteries Thinkbelt haven't been brought to completion because of the political situation and the urban rules they had to interact with: the final aim of this culture planning essay is to understand how these kind of projects could be set up in our towns and which values, methods and tools we can get from them in order to define new political lines for the regeneration of shrunk parts of our cities.

First of all we see what new behaviour patterns rise from the urban projects so far analysed: the collective accountability, the free access to information and cultural production, the extending of the participation in planning despite the hierarchical and top-down urban planning, the design of change against that one for an immobile present. These new behaviour rules involve taking a positive account of change and the concept of adaptability: first of all adaptability of functions to needs (i.e. human-oriented design), then adaptability of architecture to functions (i.e. flexibility); a growing fluency of expertise among disciplines; finally the city needs urban policies to be changeable in time, instead to be rigid and self-referring.

The two above mentioned projects enunciate several methods:

Professional diversity and/or multi-disciplinarity requires and enables a new mind-set (artistic, creative, user-oriented, narrative) on how to solve urban problems: seeing the same issues from different perspectives helps in making projects suitable for future needs and users.

The strategic use of infrastructures as the only fixed systems for the connection of mobile structures permits not to plan the urban settlement a priori, but to make it pliant.

Using the computer to monitor and update projects and plans supervising its functionality and its social responsiveness.

An open-design method which enhances the unfinished as a condition for incremental improvement: from a prototype (or micro-interventions) to more complex settlements which have both time and ability to settle in the city being appropriated by people.

In order to reach adaptability in planning, some new practical tools have to involve the field of urban education [1], social research and a penetrating review of the regulatory frameworks urban growth management strategies.

Training and inclusion of new professionals in planning is outstanding: in a competitive city the scientific and the technical expertise has to be assisted by social sciences and by artistic disciplines. Artists, sociologists, psychologists, technicians and building surveyors, engineers and designers have to confront each other in order to have a global vision of their cities and to steer its constant changing. In addition to this, we have to improve creative communities as indicators of the breaking point in our societies: they are a visible social thermometer which directs the trends and defines future scenarios.

Ultimately, our cities have to train crisis managers, that is, coordinators able to manage cyclical crises not as dramatic and isolated events but as a structuring feature of modernity.

The transition from our growth-oriented urbanism to a planned de-growth control requires strategic, slim and fast plans, able to offer long-term city visions: these plans design diagrammatic solutions, economical direction, but first of all a set of cultural ideas for the city.

Which behaviours have to be encouraged in order to fill the gap between shrinkage and hyper-urbanization?

Which kinds of places allow them to establish?

We have to devise a building evaluation system which isn't based on square meters only,

but instead on the energy amount and natural resources consumed by buildings, on the quality and flexibility of their spaces, on the efficiency of the infrastructures which serve them.

---

1   See, as example, the experiences driven by CUP (the Center for Urban Pedagogy, based in New York). http:// welcometocup.org/

The methods so far analysed can be applied to other contexts keeping in mind that culture can't be outsourced and set randomly; otherwise we could lose its authenticity and reciprocity between society and its urban project.

However, it's possible to underline common features between different territorial systems.

The interactive settlement of the Potteries Thinkbelt could be applied easily into the European urban agglomeration or metropolitan regions: the Dutch Randstad, the Baltic region, the hyper Milanese region or even some less known and smaller territories such as the Emilia-Romagna region in Italy, which is formed by a series of small strongly connected industrial knots.

To develop such network plans, based on technological innovation and on advanced idea of knowledge economy, means to aim at urban density on one side, and to material and immaterial infrastructure on the other: the localization doesn't influence anymore the investors choices, and for this reason these territories have to focus on the cultural vision, first, and then on the technical project. In this sense, infrastructures have to be the channels through which people can flow across the territories, boosting local identities without forgetting to connect them.

Finally, experiences such as Macao can be defined as micro-interventions which often do not involve the whole city but just one abandoned building. The effort of mapping abandonment in our cities enables not to isolate Macao as a single event, but to reinforce it through a widespread know-how: isolated territories cannot face the 'big effects' of our economic stagnation, rather linking experiences, expertise and citizens each other would empower communities self-determining.

CONCLUSIONS

The possible must become more important than the probable. (Price, 1968)

The city is an open-work in which the main actors are the communities: for this, it cannot be bounded as built-up space but should express itself through it when the shrunk, fragmented, arid space gets back its cultural value. The urban is intrinsically connected to social conditions, to political themes of legality and public works, to economical issue of employment: the city is actually society, policy and economy itself. As long as urban planning remains sectorial and driven by standards or forcedly visionary but with no relation to local cultures, a widespread displeasure will cause the place's abandonment, social distress and conflict.

Cultural planning immerses the city in a virtuous circle, or better a spiral of ascending development: the never ending spiral continuously re-sets its own direction without coming back to the origin. In the same way planning processes culturally oriented consider the spatial needs as the results of relationship developing in time, nor in a linear neither in a cyclical sequence of events, but in a spiral idea of progress. 113

References

Branzi, A. (2006) Modernitàdebole e diffusa. Ilmondo del progettoall'inizio del XXI secolo, Milan: SkiraEditore.

De Solà-Morales M. (2009) Public spaces, collective spaces, in Avermaete T., Havik K., Teerds H. (2009) Architectural positions. On architecture, modernity and the public sphere, Amsterdam: Sun Publisher.

Ferguson F. (2006) Talking cities: the micropolitics of urban space, Berlin: Birkhauser.

Meroni A. edited by (2007) Creative communities | People inventing sustainable ways of living,

Milan: EdizioniPOLI.design.

Price, C., Obrist, H.U., Isozaki, A., Keiler, P., Koolhaas, R. (2000) Re: CP, Bael-Boston-Berlin: Birkhäuser.

Ungers, O. M., Koolhaas, R. (2012) The City in the City – Berlin: A Green Archipelago, Berlin: Lars Müller Publishers.

Wright Steenson, M., Scharmen, F. (2012) L'architetturadeveinteragire, Domusweb June 2011.

Macao project: http://www.macao.mi.it

Exhibition 'Cedric Price: Think the Unthinkable exhibition', created by Architecture+Design Scotland and shown at The Lighthouse in 2011: http://ads.org.uk/ms/access/cedric/index.html

SPATIAL ASSEMBLAGES:THE PRODUCTION OF SPACE(S) BEYOND THE IMPERATIVE OF GROWTH
Rui Santos

What sort of spatial practices may respond, in a systematic way, to the challenges of post-growth economies? Though stressing social and environmental concerns, politically committed spatial practices and their theoretical counterparts emerging since the 1960's have not aimed at responding directly to such challenges. 1 In the light of the present, and of successive, financial and economic crisis, this may be, however, a relevant question for spatial disciplines, particularly for architecture and planning practices which have been lately involved in the production of 'global commodities'. As debates on 'shrinking cities', growth imperatives and socio-environmental externalities of economic development gain public recognition, a radical revision of processes concerning the production of space(s) is being called upon to accommodate claims from ecological economics and political ecology. It could be argued, therefore, that spatial disciplines are ill-prepared for future challenges and that a new set of spatial practices must be convened and debated. But, in order to do so, one must previously clarify 1) what is meant by post-growth economies, 2) what are their founding assumptions and 3) how can they be translated into a set of urban policies consistent enough to inform spatial practices. Only then can we try to understand what sort of practices may be convened, what concepts can act as mediators between them and possible framing discourses, and finally argue on their expectable impacts.

WHAT DOES 'POST-GROWTH ECONOMIES' MEAN?
Post-growth economic models comprise a series of different discourses and scenarios. A clear-cut separation must be made, firstly, between unintended shrinkage and planned degrowth. In the words of Herman Daly:

> A condition of nongrowth can come about in two ways: as a failure of a growth economy, or as the success of a steady-state economy. These two cases are as different as night and day. No one denies that a failure of a growth economy to grow brings unemployment and suffering. It is precisely to avoid the suffering of a failed growth economy (we know growth cannot continue) that we advocate Steady State Economy (Daly 1992, 186).

Claims such as this have a long history in the discipline of economics. Adam Smith, John Stuart-Mill and Keynes have all predicted a time when economic growth would become unsustainable and even unprofitable, thus giving way to deeper concerns with overall prosperity and well-being in a zero-growth economic environment (Martínez-Alier, et al. 2010. However, it was in 1972 that this concept earned scientific and political legitimacy with the publication of 'Limits of Growth' report (Meadows et al. 1972) which presented to the United Nations assembly the irreversible effects of human activity on finite natural resources, asking whether or not we could continue expanding our economies within a limited world. Approximately at the same time, Nicholas Georgescu-Roegen, a former student of Schumpeter, came to question the idea of economic development by applying the second law of thermodynamics - the Law of Entropy -, to economic theory. Considering the irreversible losses of energy implied in every act of ordering, Georgescu-Roegen predicted that in the nearby future economic growth would surpass the earth system's carrying capacity: the continuous depletion of finite water, land and mineral resources would cause an inescapable economic recession despite all attempts to dematerialise economics by means of continuous technological advances. Confronted with his own findings, Georgescu-Roegen concluded that a planned downsizing of economy would be as inevitable as advisable, a process he coined as 'degrowth' (Georgescu-Roegen 1971).

Since then, the concept of degrowth has followed different and diversified paths. In the words of Martinez-Alier, 'it is not simple to capture the meaning of sustainable de-growth in a nutshell. Such explicit opposition to the motto of sustained growth does not imply an exact opposition to economic growth. It advocates instead a fundamental change of key references such as: the collective imagination (changementd'imaginaire) and the array of analysis, propositions and principles guiding the economy' (Martínez-Alier, et al. 2010, 1742). Serge Latouche, the main Francophone intellectual of degrowth, claims that 'the motto of de-growth aims primarily at pointing the insane objective of growth for growth' sake (Latouche, Le Pari de la Décroissance 2006, 6). Thus, in his own words, degrowth is a 'political slogan with theoretical implications' (Idem).

More recently, degrowth and steady-state economic models seem to have been enjoying wider public recognition in developed countries: Tim Jackson's 'Prosperity without Growth' (Jackson, 2007) has been widely read and accepted, the First International Degrowth Conference was held in Paris, in 2008, and the Club of Rome presented a new report on economic degrowth to the European Commission in 2009. This legitimation of steady-state or degrowth economics may, however, be apparent and reflect a concern, above all others, with the on-going financial crisis and the consequences of globalization, urbanisation and (de)industrialisation in the developed world. It is well known, many cities and regions in the 'Global North' are facing processes of demographic shrinkage and economic recession due to these combined factors and despite major public efforts to encourage private investment. Given, then, the visibility and proximity of this problem in developed countries, it is more likely that 'shrinkage' caught the attention of northern governing institutions and audiences instead and ahead of degrowth with its far removed concerns with, to use an example, the uneven distribution of development benefits throughout the globe. Also, one should probably argue, it would be very surprising (and, perhaps, contradictory) if dominant discourses and institutions would fully accept - obsessed as they are with sovereign debt sustainability and economic recovery – such an explicit antagonism and radical critique to existing power structures and modes of production as the one advanced by studies on degrowth.

'POST-GROWTH' POLITICS?

As the Italian sociologist Onofrio Romano argues, degrowth ultimately stands as a pretext and figurehead argument for radical democracy proposals. What is being discussed in degrowth, says

Romano, are some founding political values by means of an scientifically legitimised argument that, conveniently, speaks the same language of modernity's hegemonic discourse: the (suspicious) language of economy. In a tone of admonition, he remarks that:

> If the project is about radical democracy, degrowth cannot be a foundation for the same reason as degrowth advocates do not believe that 'growth' should be a foundation. Both 'proposals' are bound to merge in the melting pot of the thousand options that cross the democratic regime. Growth and degrowth, in this scene, rest in the same paradigm of the autonomous subject: their validity is the function of historical constringents and neither of them can aspire to the throne of constitutional dogma (Romano 2008, 245).

Confirming Romano's remarks, the website of Le Parti pour la Décroissance declares the objectives of degrowth to be 'emancipation, wellbeing and fulfilment through voluntary simplicity' (Quellestratégiepolitique pour la Décroissance?n.d.) and 'the building of other worlds, environmentally and socially responsible, humanly decent and democratic' (Idem). These overall objectives comprise a whole strategy of '(re)localism' for housing, transportation, production and distribution to be implemented by measures such as: 1) the adoption of LETS, 2) the emancipation from forced (paid) labour, 3) the establishment of minimum and maximum incomes, 4) free public services, 5) a sustainable usage of natural resources, 6) the implementation of an 'energy descent' plan, 7) renouncing the cult of technology, 8) the emancipation of educational and cultural institutions from competitive towards cooperative behaviour, and finally, 9) the deepening of democracy to prevent people from being caught by power. Similarly, the programme defended by The Green Party of the United States - which stands for 1) grassroots democracy, 2) social justice and equal opportunity, 3) ecological wisdom, 4) nonviolence, 5) decentralization, 6) community-based economics, 7) feminism and gender equality, 8) diversity, 9) personal and global responsibility and, last but not least, 10) future focus and sustainability (The Ten Key Values of The Green Partys.d.) – points out to this intertwining of radical democracy and political degrowth agendas.

WHAT SORT OF 'POST-GROWTH' CITIES?

Not surprisingly, the same correlation between political degrowth and a '(re)localised radical democracy can be observed in terms of urban policies. In the II Conference on Economic Degrowth for Ecological Sustainability and Social Equity that took place in 2010, in Barcelona, a set of working groups has been assigned to discuss the relation between degrowth and the various dimensions of urban lifestyles and public policies, addressing topics of infrastructure, housing, cities, consumption, education, etc. The group working on cities presented a 'work-in-progress' vision for a 'degrowth city', a vision resembling a 'transition town' with, maybe, deeper undertones of 'criticality' (given its on-going debating of 'squatting', 'cohousing', liberation from paid work, etc.). Regrettably, and despite the much emphasised provisionality of this vision, this 'degrowth city' has reflected no more than a meagre and instant assemblage of the 'compact city' model, 'cradle to cradle' production processes and a set of explicitly translated 'right to the city' claims.

'Degrowth city', for instance, concerns 1) urban renewal instead of urban sprawl and the building of 'edge cities', 2) the deepening of democracy through participatory planning and co-design strategies, 3) the disinvestment in mega-projects and infrastructures, including those of transportation, 4) food sovereignty, 5) the extension, collective management and governance of common resources, etc. Disregarding the multiple and persistent critiques to 'localist' and 'progressive/leftist ideal(s)' (Fainstein 2006, 3) of cities that underline the 'practical difficulties of implementation, and [its] inequitable outcomes' (Idem),2 growth objectors attribute these shortcomings to the capitalist system in which space is being forcefully produced. In their viewing, it is capitalism that prevents the translation of urban ecology and human rights into a coherent set of urban policies: sustainable urban development, as it is being promoted worldwide by all kinds of governing institutions, remains indifferent to the accounting of most socio-environmental externalities despite on-going studies on ecosystem services. Yet, not only capitalism, but also disciplinary boundaries of sciences so dear to degrowth partisans as urban ecology, make it difficult to translate further ecological concerns into a set of consistent post-growth urban policies. Focusing solely on the environmental consequences of urban nature's metabolism, urban ecology perpetuates (maybe unintendedly) the artificial nature-society divide by ignoring the fact that 'the social appropriation and transformation of nature produces historically specific social and physical natures that are infused by social power relationships', (Heynen, Kaika and Swyngedouw 2006, 7); and in doing so, urban ecology excludes the concerns for socio-environmental justice that, though uncomfortable for 'green capitalism', cannot be disregarded in the light of an increasingly uneven process of global urbanisation.

Contrarily to the previous, research on 'shrinking cities' (Oswalt 2006) has extended the debate on post-growth beyond the separate discussions on 'civil rights' and 'ecology' by looking closely at the intertwining of political, economic, cultural, social and environmental implications of actual city-wide (unintended) shrinkage. It has taken shrinkages not as a taboo or a problem to be reversed by 'green development' or 'instant utopias' but, inevitably, as a starting point for a profound and transformative cultural change that cannot be thought without a correlative transformation of epistemological and ontological frames steering the construction of knowledge.3 Consequently, it departs from the studying of actual cities' survival strategies - in their succeeding or failing capacity to transform institutions and institutionalised behaviours (Idem) – to, only then, launch itself into inconclusive debates on property regimes, economic models, work policies and cultural actions that, altogether, accommodate interdisciplinary critiques to current modes of production of the built environment. Indeed, if there's one conclusion to be taken from these studies, is that shrinkage remains a widely unknown territory for 'planners of growth', thus revealing the inadequacy of standard spatial planning approaches and tools to embrace it as a potential instrument for transformation. In this light, it can be argued, research on 'shrinking cities' offers a cautionary argument, based on existing examples, to premature 'assemblages' on what post-growth cities should be composed of and how, by taking 'the production of space' as a primary matter-of-concern (Latour 2005).

Concerns with 'the production of space' are far from being novel; they have long entered the social sciences debate with the contributions of Burgess, Park and McKenzie on the 'mosaic city' - 'The City: suggestions for the study of human behaviour', published in 1925; Lefebvre's reflections on 'the (social) production of space' - 'The Production of Space', published in 1974; Foucault's rendering of the spatialisation of discipline and punishment – 'Discipline and Punish', published in 1975; and, De Certeau's argument for deviational tactics in the making of everyday life against institutionalized and technocratic strategies - 'The Practice of Everyday Life', published in 1980. Later becoming a central theme for Urban Anthropology (Low, 1999; 2003), the production of space also influenced theories of collaborative planning (Healey, 1997), strategic design (Manzini&Jégou, 2003) and collaborative (urban) governance (Kooiman, 2000).

In regards to the architecture discipline, the production of space also influenced numerous collaborative practices throughout the world and has been debated in texts such as Giancarlo Di Carlo's 'Architecture's Public', published in 1969; Colin Ward's 'Housing: an anarchist approach', in 1976; John Habraken's 'Supports: An Alternative to Mass Housing', in 1972 and John Turner's 'Freedom to Build: Dweller Control of the Housing Process', published in 1972. With the economy and financial market's globalization in the 80's and 90's, however, pushing architecture to produce 'global commodities' within a 'starchitecture' system (Benítez, 2010), the production of space as a process by which the collective is composed (Latour, 2005) lost its primacy as a crucial matter-of-concern for architecture. Nevertheless, and considering the current economic crisis and the questioning of 'business-as-usual'- or status quo - modes of production of the built environment, it may well claim back its centrality, particularly if backed up by politically and socially relevant spatial practices.

'POST-GROWTH' SPATIAL PRACTICES: SPATIAL ASSEMBLAGES?

Having reached this point, time to ask again: what sort of spatial practices may respond to challenges of shrinkage or degrowth? In order to try an answer, we may now have to look for 'spatial assemblages', or, local and creative processes of collective and interdisciplinary composition of space(s) aiming at transformative social change (Schmidt and Hersh 2000). The term 'spatial assemblages' is here advanced to cluster both Lefebvrian notions of 'differential space(s)' and urban studies' readings of assemblage theory. Ignacio Farías, in its introductory chapter to the book 'Urban Assemblages' (2010), describes how the concept of assemblage allowed urban studies to look at cities, for the first time, as hugely complex sociomaterial and sociotechnical landscapes; an assemblage of assemblages being composed of relational – and diagrammatic - sets of human and non-human actants ever actualising as precarious (and heterogeneous) agencements. Embracing, on the one hand, Deleuze and De Landa's stances on 'assemblage' and, on the other, Science and Technology Studies research on Actor-Network Theory (Latour 2005), Farías follows to suggest that 'urban assemblages' bear the emergent capacity of enabling agency (Farías, 2010, p. 15) in their continuous movement between (re)territorialisation (formation of habits) and deterritorialisation (breaking of habits) (Dovey, 2012) processes. Thus, the borrowing of the term 'assemblage' here presented is intended to highlight spatial practices that potentiate the creation of difference (and social transformation) in their mobilisation of agency4.

'Spatial assemblages' include CBO-driven planning processes, initiatives of artistic activism, actual buildings or even critical readings on cities and the production of space. Some of these transformative spatial practices have already been categorized and described by various authors over the last decades, resulting in publications such as 'Action Planning for Cities' (Goethert and Hamdi 1997), 'Architecture and Participation' (Blundell Jones, Petrescu and Till 2005), 'Architecture of Consequence' (Bouman 2009) and, more recently, 'Microplanning' (Rosa 2011), 'Collective Architectures' (Benítez 2010), 'The Nightmare of Participation' (Miessen 2010) and 'Spatial Agency' (Awan, Schneider and Till 2011). In 'The nightmare of participation' – part three of a 'participation' trilogy -, Markus Miessen (2010) argues for unsolicited interdisciplinary 'Spatial Practices' that, within Chantal Mouffe's agonistic approach to democracy, use conflicting interests and topics to prepare the ground for potential (social) change. Awan et al (2011) present 'Spatial Agency' as motivating spatial (transformative) praxis – buildings, installations, exhibitions, maps, networks, sets of instructions - that, being able to engage transformatively with organizational and social structure(s) present a new paradigm on how to operate in architecture.

Benítez (2010) presents Santiago Cirugeda's 'Urban Prescriptions' as collectively produced and politically committed projects that, working in contexts of 'social emergency', aim at the creation of a 'Manual for Open Code Architectures' that fuse technical and legal questions such as assembly instructions, legal supports, safety conditions. Finally, Rosa (2011) documents 'Microplanning' initiatives in São Paulo, Brazil, as bottom-up 'urban creative practices' capable of creating common spaces for people living in destitute neighbourhoods by consolidating intra- and inter-neighbourhoods' social connections.

Given the divergent theoretical renderings of all these practices, their grouping as 'spatial assemblages' might seem problematic and, indeed, raises crucial and still pending questions: do all these practices aim at being 'situated micro-utopias' (Benítez 2010) or participate in the construction of an 'emancipatory common-sense' (Santos 1991)? Do they all relate in the same way to democracy, 'spatial justice' (Soja 2010) or political ecology? Are (all) these practices interchangeable? These questions wait for a thorough and proper answer. However, and regardless all their possibly describable differences, one can still assert that 'spatial assemblages' share two major matters-of-concern. Firstly, they push for transformative social change and, secondly, they all consider the 'production of space', even if unwittingly, as a shared/collective, impermanent/dynamic and political enterprise. Whatever their specific objectives and outcomes, therefore, all 'spatial assemblages' aim at transforming a current 'state of affairs' in trying to irreversibly change its most obstructive components: the behaviour of intervening actors, constraining regulations, bureaucratic planning procedures, etc. Secondly, 'spatial assemblages' address the production of space(s) beyond its physical or abstract dimension in order to compose (a) 'differential space(s)' of, and for the intrusion of 'otherness'; in other words, 'spatial assemblages' take space as a matter-of-concern and not as a matter-of-fact (Latour 2005).

WHAT, THEN, MIGHT 'SPATIAL ASSEMBLAGES' EXPECTABLE IMPACTS BE?

It may be argued that 'spatial assemblages', as concerned with the production of differential spaces contribute to the spatial sustainability debate beyond 'eco-friendly' or 'green' concerns (Daly and Farley 2004, Jackson 2007, Latouche 2007). 'Spatial assemblages' provide a counterpoint to the current economic crisis debate and, in their concern with transformative change, create interstices of other possibilities beyond those attached to the so-called 'irreducible' need for economic growth. Indeed, and as the mentioned debates on 'Shrinking Cities' and post-growth economic models - and its political translations - gain public recognition, these heterodox practices may be important field experiments for urban sustainable living in the light of recent redefinitions of 'prosperity without growth' (Jackson, 2007).

Additionally, 'spatial assemblages' may also contribute to the questioning of architecture's production processes, boundaries and political responsibility. Firstly, they dangerously invite architecture to draw its attention from 'objects' to 'processes', that is, to analyse its recent production processes and products; now, as most contemporary architectures became 'global commodities', to accept this suggestion eventually means to scrutinize these commodities as 'black boxes' (Latour 2005), enquiring their eventual externalities or (lacking) transformative potential (Benítez 2010). Secondly, 'spatial assemblages' press architecture to work on an expanded and interdisciplinary field, intersecting the boundaries of planning, art and political activism. As once the acknowledging of objects as being socially constructed allowed sculpture to expand its field towards architecture and landscape (Krauss 1979), a similar process might now occur to architecture by hand of 'spatial assemblages'.

Finally, 'spatial assemblages' may imply a critical assessment to the 'immutable mobiles' (Latour 2005) or, the institutional and regulatory 'frames' in which spatial (organization) disciplines operate. Though the topics of 'informality' and 'governance' have long invaded the urban discourses and policies (Healey, 1997; Kooiman, 2000; Roy, 2005), most countries are still recalcitrant when it comes down to implement de facto non-statutory instruments based on negotiation and shared decision-making. It is expected that 'spatial assemblages', if well-equipped and constructed, significantly reverse this tendency and push forward framing institutions and regulations.

WHAT ACTORS, THEN, MUST BE IN PLACE FOR 'SPATIAL ASSEMBLAGES' TO SUCCEED?

Beyond contributions for the widening of sustainability debates and architecture's disciplinary corpus, it has been mentioned that these practices aim at pushing political and regulatory institutions towards a new paradigm that acknowledges space as a collective and political enterprise. For 'spatial assemblages' to fulfil their potential, then, many more actors - and their networks - must be allowed to participate in the production and governing of space. This is not a new claim, but one needs to stress it continuously due to the tendency of experts and governing institutions to avoid devolving their power beyond tokenism.

Unfortunately, the mental frame of most planners, architects, engineers, politicians, development practitioners, is still that of 'après moi, le déluge!' a frame consistent with linear modernity. This modernity, however, has been long and thoroughly criticized and does not fit our currently globalised - and liquid - world. Change is becoming a growing necessity more than a choice; this change however, in Marina Silva's opinion - a Brazilian politician and activist - does not aim at adaptation but rather at a slow and creative inadaptation process. The predicted 'revenge' of a silent Gaia may urge us to collectively engage into a new ecology of practices.

'Spatial assemblages', though operating in a 'local' scale, provide the right strategies and tools to embrace this collective endeavour. In their urge to invent 'differential space(s)', these practices are privileged actors in the (re)activation of political subjects and communities. This, however, is not enough to affect structural change: the empowerment of political assemblies requests consistent and continuous efforts and attachments to solid networks, whether rhizomatic or hierarchically organised. But if collective inadaptation is as inescapable as shrinkage or degrowth, one should not be concerned: all institutions may be eventually summoned to participate in the making of unsolicited 'spatial assemblages'.

Acknowledgements

This paper has been partially developed with the kind contributions of Dr Tatjana Schneider, Senior Lecturer at the Sheffield School of Architecture.

References

Agier, M. (2009).Antropologia da Cidade: lugares, situações, movimentos. São Paulo: Terceiro Nome.

Awan, N., Schneider, T., & Till, J. (2011).Spatial Agency: other ways of doing architecture. New York: Routledge.

Benítez, P. V. (Ed.). (2010). Collective Architectures: Camiones, Contenedores, Colectivos. Seville:

EdicionesVibok.

Blundell Jones, P., Petrescu, D., & Till, J. (Eds.).(2005). Architecture and Participation. Oxon, England: Spon Press.

Bouman, O. (2009). Architecture of Consequence. Rotterdam: NAi Publishers.

Daly, H. (1992). Allocation, Distribution and Scale: towards an economics that is efficient, just and sustainable. Ecological Economics, 6, pp. 185-193.

Daly, H.,& Farley, J. (2004). Ecological Economics: principles and applications. Washington: Island Press.

De Certeau, M. (1980).L'Invention du Quotidien. Paris: Gallimard.

Dovey, K. (2012).Informal urbanism and complex adaptive assemblage.International Development Planning Review, 34 (4).

Fainstein, S. (2006). Planning and The Just City. Searching for the Just City. Columbia University, New York.

Farías, I., & Bender, T. (Edits.). (2010). Urban Assemblages: how actor-network theory changes urban studies. Abingdon, England: Routledge.

Foucault, M. (1975).SurveilleretPunir. Paris: Gallimard.

Georgescu-Roegen, N. (1971). The Entropy Law and the Economic Process. Cambridge, Massachussets: Harvard University Press.

Goethert, R.,&Hamdi, N. (1997). Action Planning for Cities: a guide to community practice. Chichester, England: John Wiley & Sons.

Healey, P. (1997). Collaborative Planning: shaping places in fragmented societies. Vancouver: University of British Columbia Press.

Heynen, N., Kaika, M., &Swyngedouw, E. (2006).Urban Political Ecology: politicising the production of urban natures. In N. Heynen, M. Kaika, & E. Swyngedouw (Eds.), In the Nature of Cities: urban political ecology and the politics of urban metabolism (pp. 1-19). Oxon, England: Routledge.

Jackson, T. (2007).Prosperity without Growth?The transition to a sustainable economy. Retrieved 11 15, 2010, from Sustainable Development Commission: http://www.sd-commission.org. uk/publications.php?id=914

Keynes, J. M. (1936). The general theory of employment, interest and money. London: Palgrave Macmillan.

Kooiman, J. (2000). Societal Governance: levels, models, and orders of social-political interaction. In J. Pierre (Ed.), Debating Governance (pp. 138-166). New York: Oxford University Press.

Krauss, R. (1979). Sculpture In The Expanded Field. October, 30-44.

Latouche, S. (2006).Le Pari de la Décroissance. Paris: Fayard.

Latouche, S. (2007).Petit Traité de la DécroissanceSereine. Paris: Éditions Mille etunenuits.

Latour, B. (2010). An Attempt at a 'Compositionist Manifesto'.Obtidoem 04 de 2012, de Bruno Latour: http://www.bruno-latour.fr/sites/default/files/120-NLH-GB.pdf

Latour, B. (2005). From Realpolitik to Dingpolitik: an introduction to Making Things Public. In B. Latour, & P. Weibel (Edits.), Making Things Public: atmospheres of democracy (pp. 14-41). Cambridge, Massachusetts: MIT Press.

Latour, B. (2005). Reassembling the Social. Oxford: Oxford University Press.

Lefebvre, H. (1974). La Production de l'Espace. Paris: ÉditionsAnthropos.

Lefebvre, H. (1968). Le Droit à la Ville. Paris: ÉditionsAnthropos.

Low, S. M. (Ed.). (1999). Theorizing the City: the new urban anthropology reader. New Brunswick:

Rutgers University Press.

Low, S. M.,& Lawrence-Zúñiga, D. (Eds.). (2003). The Anthropology of Space and Place: locating culture. Oxford: Blackwell Publishing.

Manzini, E., &Jégou, F. (2003).Sustainable Everyday: scenarios of urban life. Milan: EdizioniAmbiente.

Martínez-Alier, J., Pascual, U., Franck-Dominique, V., &Zaccai, E. (2010). Sustainable De-growth: mapping the context, criticisms and future prospects of an emergent paradigm. Ecological Economics, 69, pp. 1741-1747.

Meadows, D. H., Meadows, D. L., Randers, J.,& Behrens III, W. W. (1972). Limits to growth. New York: Universe Publishing.

Miessen, M. (2010). The Nightmare of Participation: crossbench praxis as a mode of criticality. Berlin: Sternberg Press.

Oswalt, P. (Ed.). (2006). Shrinking Cities (Vol. 1: International Research). Ostfildern-Ruit: HatjeCantz.

Quellestratégiepolitique pour la Décroissance? (n.d.). Retrieved July 2012, from Parti pour la Décroissance: http://www.partipourladecroissance.net/?p=6848

Romano, O. (2008). The Anthropological Stakes of Degrowth. First international conference on Economic De-growth for Ecological Sustainability and Social Equity, (pp. 243-247). Paris.

Rosa, M. L. (2011). Microplanning: urban creative practices. São Paulo: Editora de Cultura/Asahi.

Roy, A. (2005, Spring). Urban Informality: towards and epistemology of planning. Journal of the American Planning Association, 71 (2), pp. 147-158.

Santos, B. S. (1991). Ciência. In M. M. Carrilho (Ed.), Dicionário do PensamentoContemporâneo (Vol. Dicionário do PensamentoContemporâneo, pp. 23-43). Lisboa: Publicações Dom Quixote.

Schmidt, J. D.,&Hersh, J. (Eds.). (2000). Globalization and Social Change. London: Routledge.

Smith, A. (1776). An inquiry into the nature and causes of the wealth of nations. London: W. Strahan and T. Cadell.

Soja, E. W. (2010). Seeking Spatial Justice. Minneapolis: University of Minnesota Press.

Soja, E. W. (1996). Thirdspace: journeys to Los Angeles and other real-and-imagined places. Malden, Massachussets: Blackwell Publishers.

Stengers, I. (2005). An Ecology of Practices, Introductory notes on. Cultural Studies Review, 11, 183-196.

Stuart Mill, J. (1848). Principles of Political Economy. London: John W. Parker.

Swyngedouw, E. (2003, November). Urban Political Ecology: justice and the politics of scale. Antipode, 35 (5), pp. 898-918.

The Ten Key Values of The Green Party. (s.d.).Obtidoem 07 de 2012, de The Green Party of the United States: http://www.gp.org/tenkey.php

RE-USING OUTDATED INFRASTRUCTURE: THE CASE OF GUADALMEDINA RIVERBED

Ramon Marrades Sempere, Chema Segovia

In this paper we present an urban process that will foster the benefits of an outdated infrastructure through public use, which works as a catalyst for economic revitalization. Guadalmedina River, in Málaga (Spain) is a dried river that splits the city in two parts. Architects drew up plans to recover this area as a public space. Politicians convened hearings. Editorialists wrote impassioned commentaries. But everything they planned was too costly and nothing happened for decades.

The open model of Guadalmedina public use as presented in this proposal is an example of new forms of urban intervention in a context characterized by difficulties in making major interventions involving heavy investment efforts. It belongs to the orbit of the new trends in planning intervention based on the creation of new spaces of social opportunity, high impact, high effectiveness and low budgets. It involves the mobilization of underutilized resources of the city, in this case the Guadalmedina and all its area of influence, urban intelligence and opportunities to generate new resources for economic development and social enjoyment.

The activation of these resources as multiplier effects doesn't only imply a physical renewal, but also, the generation of new activities to invigorate the local economy and civil society.

The integration of urban projects in the local economy is positive in every possible way: it generates opportunities for launching new activities to encourage local trade, new tourist attraction activities and the reuse of existing capabilities in the city.

The Guadalmedina strategy I propose is based on the following propositions. (i) Do not wait any longer to enjoy the city. (ii) Maintain, facilitate and enhance existing uses. (iii) Without building in the riverbed. (iv) Bring the city close to the river. (v) Neighbourhood implication. (vi) Join sea, mountain and city. (vii) Retrieve the Alameda (Main Street crossing the Guadalmedina) as the urban lounge. (viii) Foster citizens' identity with the Guadalmedina. (ix) Work downstream.

FRAMEWORK

The modern methods for urban planning have got us used to formulating urban issues in the future tense. The contemporary approach, of a rationalist nature, still dreams of the ideal finished city. This entelechy puts the need for control before order, as it has met in the accuracy of design a fictitious solution to problems. Thus, in most cases, our cities' definitions are based on free-handedly scribbled future statements.

In the current urban scenario, this model is opposed to that of the focus on the urban built environment. The economic crisis – which ought not to be considered as a temporary accident –

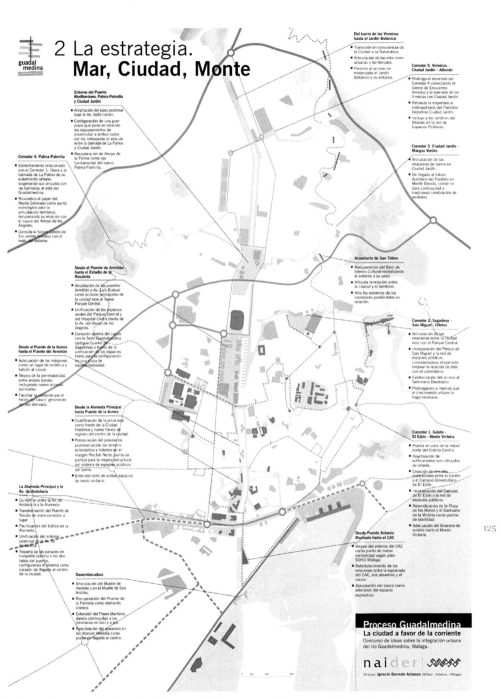

Figure 3-11 ProcesoGualamedina. Entry to the ideas competition. Source: Ramon Marrades/NAIDER.

has confirmed the fact that we need to promptly deal with a series of debates that were once open. They point to the need to give preference to the present moment over the promise of the future by stimulating the exploitation of existing resources, the promptness of response and the value of citizens. There is a need to bring our viewpoint on urban building back to basics: to tend to daily needs, to give space to the new agents that play a part in the urban process and to coordinate every participant's efforts. This philosophy represents a revision of the previous model leaning on three legs: use of the city, urban design and governance.

For starters, we should claim the use of the city as the most powerful tool for citizen participation. The trend of basing urban spaces on design has forced potential uses out of our city plans and projects, and has therefore affected our urban attitude, inhibiting our individual capacity to conquer, make happen, build and enhance our habitats. In the Urban Built Environment the use of the city represents the main tool when it comes to conquering spaces providing them with meaning and value.

In the second place, the focus on the Urban Built Environment considers design as a service and not an imposition. The condition for design is that it embraces individuality within the socializing framework. In this way of thinking, it is a good idea to pick up again the idea formulated consisting of making design contingent on use, and suggesting the possibility of opening up spaces with little treatment, subjecting them to the citizens use and solidifying the resulting situation. It is not about denying the role of design, but about transferring its hegemonic prominence to the importance of humanizing our cities.

Finally, governance will safeguard the sustainability of any urban project. To that end, it should be approached from the exploitation of resources, the relations of synergy and the coordination of tasks. The final challenge will consist on reviewing the traditional instruments for urban planning, regarding the value of the process –complementary to that of the results– and recognizing, supporting and stimulating those practices of urban innovation born outside the mind-set of planning and committed to the citizens.

In this paper we describe a proposal presented to a public contest concerning the recovery of the Guadalmedina riverbed in Málaga. We were part of a multidisciplinary team (economists, lawyers, architects and designers) leadby Iñaki Barredo (from NAIDER, a consultancy company based in Bilbao, Spain).

The case of Guadalmedina riverbed in Málaga (Spain) represents a paradigmatic example of the most common mistake in urban planning which concerns the gap between drawing plans and accomplishing them. In essence Guadalmedina is a dried riverbed that splits up the city in two parts. Among the several plans presented along the last decades, the local government opted to cover the riverbed and build a great avenue there; but it was too costly and nothing was constructed.

Nowadays, when local governments are facing a deep economic crisis, those projects are merely unrealizable, and innovative ideas are needed to provide temporary (and maybe permanent) solutions that allow people to enjoy their cities.

When preparing a proposal as the Guadalmedina process, the first step was exploring the most innovative urban experiences that faced similar conditions. The recovering of outdated infrastructure through public use acting as a catalyst for economic revitalization is not a very common situation, if we scale examples similar to the Guadalmedina.

The Promenade Plantée (Paris, 1993) was an old longitudinal railroad recovered as a city park. This model was followed in the High Line Park (New York, 2009) and the proposed

Bloomingdale Line (Chicago, 2012). These projects take as example the recovery of the Turia Riverbed in Valencia (Spain). The distinguishing feature of the High Line Park in New York is the public-private partnership in its management and financing, since it is an area publicly owned but privately run where the recovery was largely financed with private capital.

The most similar experience to Guadalmedina is, as I mentioned, the river park of the Turia in Valencia, so we ask the opinion of Ricard Pérez Casado, who was the political head of two towns closely related to their rivers. He was mayor of Valencia between 1979 and 1988 and the EU administrator in Mostar (Bosnia and Herzegovina) in 1996. His task in Mostar was focused on facilitating direct democratic elections and the reconstruction of the city. In Valencia he laid the foundations that have transformed it in a more liveable and recognizable city. During his tenure in Valencia, the old Turia riverbed -dried after being deviated in order to prevent flooding- was recovered as a public space (now it is a city park of 110HA, the largest urban park in Spain and also the most visited).

In his opinion 'the Guadalmedina has to be understood as a virtue rather than a threat, taking advantage of its role as the backbone of the city.' It is important to value the items on its margins as 'starting points for the recovery process', in order for it to become irreversible, although 'the first thing is cleaning, and then performing micro-interventions'. The urban action should also serve to 'improve the mobility system' prioritizing non-motorized modes and to let 'the public appropriate the project; only if they're able to, the project will be successful'. Finally, he found it was necessary to create a management tool, a discussion forum to voice the aspirations of the people, which should be participatory, but professionally directed. That was our starting point.

THE PROJECT

We were inspired as well by temporary solutions that allow the immediate enjoyment of the 'hidden' parts of the city. One of the main examples in Europe is the case of Tempelhof Airport, which was recovered as a public park by only opening its doors and planning the transformation in a gradual way, which means that construction processes do not interrupt enjoyment and public use.

We understand that the Guadalmedina does not represent an urban problem for the city of Malaga, neither a hydraulic problem. The Guadalmedina can be understood as a scar, primarily social in nature, which could and should be closed, bringing the city closer to the river, and focusing on joining both margins. Our recommendation of public appropriation of the riverbed addresses the immediate use of an obsolete infrastructure. The bed, dried most of the year, must be given back to the citizens, without altering the hydraulic conditions thereof, allowing safe water floods when they occur.

Why should we recover the Guadalmedina?

It is a unique chance because of the opportunities offered in terms of mobility and open spaces (housing and land markets cannot provide anything similar), because Guadalmedina is an infrastructure per se, since it is a territorial connector that can work without major reforms and will also work in favour of public benefit. The recovering project, paid with public money and regulated by a public entity, offers enormous potential benefit. Enjoying Malaga from the riverbed means a unique linear experience, and it entails a strengthening of community relations through the use of public space.

In addition, an enhancement of Guadalmedina's environment must result in the alignment of interests of different stakeholders (public sector, citizens and enterprises) and act as a catalyst in an economic development process serving to attract new residents, entrepreneurs and tourists.

Recommendations on the use

The process should allow continued, strong, attractive, economically productive and socially constructive community use, and therefore become a driver for improvement of the socio-economic environment.

First, citizens should enjoy a maximization of open space. Open space, which is safe and healthy, which respects nature and specificities at neighbourhood level. It would mean the empowerment of the right to fresh air, and the support of commercial, industrial and artistic existing uses. For entrepreneurs the initiative should mean new opportunities for development.

On the other hand, including a strategy that fosters mobility shifts to non-motorized transport will have positive effects on local businesses, beneficiaries of increased interactions between citizens. It should also serve to mitigate the associated costs of private transportation (congestion, accidents and pollution).

For the city and public administration, our proposal is characterized by flexibility and scalability of urban renewal. All planning must be designed for implementation in phases, so as to allow an immediate use. It also seeks an increase in income in terms of taxes and fees related to new offices, commercial and residential spaces. But mostly seeks at the enhancement of existing uses. Management models, participation and new governance should be effective tools for reaching consensus and private sector involvement.

We propose a continuous schedule of activities with a realistic economic program to encourage private advocacy and programming for public uses, including local crafts, food markets and artistic and commercial opportunities.

Design recommendations

Our main indication is to be consistent with the urban reality of Malaga, carrying out a renewal process that remains sensitive to local conditions. The Guadalmedina is a single body through the built environment. Therefore, the public space must be understood so that the enjoyment can be experienced as a continuum. At the same time, without assuming a contradiction with the uniqueness of Guadalmedina, citizens must be able to enjoy a variety of environments in the length of a singular linear space. The view, the density of the built environment and the landscape design will vary in line with current conditions (use, type of construction, etc.). Access points, which represent natural start and end points; the entrances and bridges are the fundamental elements of the interaction with the Guadalmedina and therefore must be suitable for all citizens, eliminating, wherever possible, barriers in terms of accessibility. The interior of the riverbed should be a pedestrian corridor. The native spontaneous vegetation must be enhanced as well, the 'weed' may be more relevant than artificial decontextualized vegetation.

In conclusion, the primary identity of Guadalmedina must be that of a public open space that serves the mobility and interconnectivity, recreation and contemplation, further enhancing the commercial use in its immediate environment. It should encourage the use of space and should help create a safe environment, in addition to serving as a catalyst for economic development.

Recommendations regarding the intervention strategy

The Guadalmedina has become the major current urban concern of Malaga. For different reasons, the project has stalled in every option that has been referred throughout time. The opening of a competition of ideas that does not set conditions or a given solution would be a good option to turn off the controversy and inaction.

From this need to create conditions to facilitate consensus on Guadalmedina, the intervention strategy embodied in this proposal seeks to provide a framework for a stable and open intervention, through successive stages and generating adapted responses and an active management.

Propositions

Guadalmedina Process is an urban strategy based on the following propositions:

1 *Do not wait any longer to enjoy the city.* The basis of the project is the immediacy of actual use, which is compatible with an urban and territorial planning. We do not wish to provide just a solution for the future, because the urban environment is what we enjoy while making a plan. Guadalmedina is an opportunity of present, proximity and urgency.

2 *Maintain, facilitate and enhance existing uses.* We understand the channel as a space of freedom where the first step is evaluating and revealing the public situations that take place in it. So it is as simple as it is necessary to visualize the cleaning and maintenance of the riverbed to put up with almost no resources, but with creative actions and uses already embraced by citizens in an informal manner.

3 *Without building in the riverbed.* The hydraulic solution we adopted is to not modify the boundaries of the existing runway to avoid a mortgage in terms of investment on the future of the city. The current situation of the river can be improved without major engineering justification, which although necessary, should not be an excuse for not starting the recovery of this public place.

4 *Attracting the city to the river.* If the riverbed is not the problem, Malaga is the solution. Thus, we should favour urban uses in the margins and, acting as a zipper, unifying east and west of the city. It aims to harness the rereading of the river as an instrument capable of posing a cohesive and balanced city model.

5 *Neighbourhood implication.* This is not a linear project, but a transversal one, where the space adjacent to the river is the priority, the first in which we must act by micro-interventions that prove relevant to the needs of each neighbourhood instead of sectionalizing on a purely functional way. It means to discover the possibilities and problems from the river's margin to the neighbourhood.

6 *Joining sea, mountain and city.* The transition from urban to rural environment can be retraced on foot using the different proposed corridors from Guadalmedina to the small mountains that surround Málaga, considering at the same time the possibility of a longitudinal path (walking or cycling) from the port to the botanic garden through the riverbed.

7 *Retrieving the Alameda (Main Street crossing the Guadalmedina) as the urban lounge.* La Alameda is the urban lounge of Málaga and the balcony to the Guadalmedina and, unfortunately, it is nowadays full of cars. La Alameda has to be recovered, humanized and dignified. In addition, it should extend its virtue to the west (Avenida de Andalucía), undertaking a project of sustainable mobility.

8 *From the river mouth to the centre.* The entry of salty water from the sea aims to promote attractive uses for tourists and reuse obsolete port facilities in order to reconcile the city centre with the end of the river, along the promenades. This can act as a business card, precursor of further phases.

Figure 3-12 La Alemada as an urban lounge. Source: Ramon Marrades/NAIDER.

9 *Fostering citizens' identity with the Guadalmedina.* From branch managing of Guadalmedina to the active involvement of citizens, or from training to research, we can reconcile city marketing with the satisfaction of citizens' usual needs. With the attractive public space that the Guadalmedina generates, we can revoke the negative connotation of the riverbed and relate it to Málaga's identity.

10 *Working downstream.* The crisis of urban planning invites us to take a position suitable for our time, which gives room for taking care of the urban and social fabric through simple urban practices, no less effective, even as a whole, and with long term economic benefits.

ECONOMIC AND MANAGEMENT MODEL

Recovery through public use needed a specific management tool to direct the process, taking into account the adequacy of a public-private partnership in management and financing methods. We specify a management model to allow a flexible management of the four main branches of tasks: (a) cleaning and maintenance of the riverbed, (b) actions to improve accesses and urbanization, (c) actions to improve surrounding areas, and (d) actions related to revitalization activities.

Activation of the Guadalmedina as the main resource of the city in the coming years requires a management model with capability to put work together and stimulate commitment and participation. Our intervention is rather an open and unfinished process and therefore need its own spaces for conveyance.

Three main areas will form this institutional motor for Guadalmedina:

1 *Inter-institutional agreement area.* In order to bring together all levels of government with executive and legislation powers on the scope of intervention, capable of ensuring administrative processing and fast approval of the interventions. It will be an institutional space for dialogue and consultation between all government levels to be formed under the legal concept that is most suitable among its members.

2 *Municipal coordination area.* Attached to the Planning Department or directly to the City Hall, bringing together all local authorities involved in the development of initiatives likely to take place in the Guadalmedina.

3 *Social mobilization area.* It will be a social participation entity that will involve civil society entities to become interested in using the Guadalmedina as a public space and as a resource for strengthening their activities.

These three levels will be complemented by capacity management techniques as Guadalmedina Office, with sufficient human capital, materials and budget. Thinking of Guadalmedina renewal as an open process, one of the keys to its success will be its capacity to attract ideas from the public, to mobilize them, to find public and private resources to make them possible, etc.

CONCLUSION

Adaptive planning means going beyond old disciplines' boundaries and sharing knowledge within different fields of expertise. Moreover (as Einstein once wrote) we should be on our guard not to overestimate science and scientific methods when it is a question of human problems; and we should not assume that experts are the only ones who have a right to express themselves on issues affecting the organization of society.

A multidisciplinary team (in which we were involved) has executed this proposal understanding that the way we act in the city, how people use public space, is the first and most important first participation tool. Not only, but especially in times of great scarcity, planning should not impede

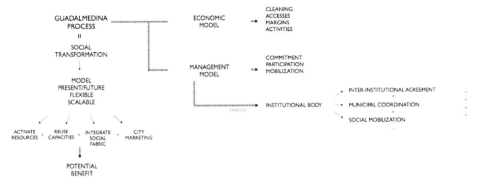

Figure 3-13 Diagramming the Guadalmedina Process. Source: Ramon Marrades/NAIDER.

transitional uses of public space. We summarized a specific proposal but its essentials can be replicated anywhere: scalability, flexibility, low budget, enhancement of exiting uses, facilitation of activities with an ad hoc management tool and making the best out of spontaneous dynamics in the city.

Figure 3-14 Influence of globalization on cities: shopping malls, residential zones, skyscrapers, infrastructure, office complexes, transformation of historical centres, Source: Anna Háblová.

INFLUENCE OF GLOBALIZATION ON CITIES:
SHOPPING MALLS IN CZECH REPUBLIC 1992-2012
Anna Háblová

The information revolution and globalization has caused an overall awareness of the limited resources of the Earth. The basic social values are no longer only economic indicators such as efficiency, speed and mass production. There has been a transformation of social values and social paradigm and awareness of Scarcity as the fundamental economic problem of having seemingly unlimited human wants and needs in a world of limited resources. From the perspective of the new paradigm are shopping malls unsustainable and unacceptable. What helped to recognize Scarcity was interconnection of information technology around the world, which was followed by economic globalization. Globalization is still unfinished, spontaneous and uncontrolled process of increasingly intensive integration of the countries of the world in a single economic system, which occurs since the seventies of the twentieth century (Sýkora, 2000). Globalization affects all disciplines, including architecture and urbanism. For work with large areas occurs change in solving urban problems. It is not possible to take into account only the site itself. When working with a specific area we already begin to look elsewhere than just in the immediate neighbourhood of solved area.

 Power that is moving from public to private sector is the key to naming influence of globalization on cities. Everything connected with multinational companies relate to globalization: the need for companies to be seen (tall buildings, skyscrapers), the expansion of branches (office complexes), the expansion of products (shopping centres), the need for rapid movement of human capacities (transport infrastructure), spatial separation of representatives of companies from the poorer part of town (residential zones - gated communities), relocation of production to other parts of the world (brownfields).

Shopping centres are one of the themes of globalization. Multinational companies and large

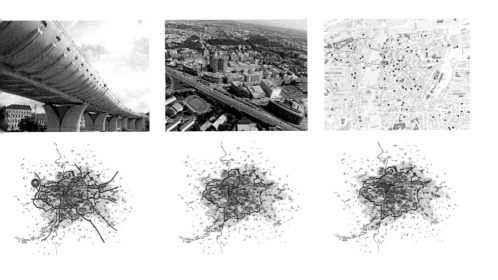

investors are entering into territories with the requirement to capitalize on their projects, and for public administration it would be a challenge to be equal partners. But in most cases public sphere does not have sufficient basis for responsible decision-making. And therefore the formation of the 'no-place' and the residual space in the vicinity of shopping centres. There is a waste of very fertile soils, poor pedestrian permeability area, increase of crime in these areas, the mono-function and poor quality of public spaces.

The aim of this paper is to understand background of shopping centres, describe the situation in Czech Republic and outline the future of shopping centres and ability to reuse from perspective of Scarcity.

INTERNATIONAL PERSPECTIVE

The trading of goods and knowledge has been always the primary activity shaping settlements. Trading has been in constant change throughout history due to diverse factors and this has been reflected in the morphology of cities and building types. The forum in the roman cities, market towns and bazaars in Arabic cities are some examples where trading influenced the settlements.

The shift from a market economy to a culture of consumerism, based on intensive circulation of goods, have occurred in the first environment of mass consumption, the prototype of which was Paris store, opened in 1852. A huge number of products presented in one place, and fixed price products, changed social and psychological relationships of marketplace. From there it was only a small step to shopping centres, for whose first father is considered the J.C.Nichols for his role in development of Country Club Plaza in Kansas City in 1922. He established there many financial, administrative and business concepts that are essential for the post-war city. In 1945 he published 'Mistakes we have made in development of shopping centres', where he described his experience with 150 points, which covered everything from strategy through ensuring political support to adequate ceiling height. But the most important knowledge was that the key to the success of the shopping centres is unlimited parking space.

The first roofed shopping centre with a controlled indoor environment, built in 1956 by the architect and theoretician of shopping centres Victor Gruen, became the Southdale Mall in Edina, Minnesota. He created a completely introverted building type, which interrupted all communication with the surroundings. 'This fantastic urbanism was cleared of all negative elements of the city. Bad weather, cars and beggars' (Paquet, 2003:25).

The principle of the shopping centre, as was in America created in the fortieth and fiftieth years of the twentieth century, has not much changed to the present day. Between 1960 and 1980 was the principle by systematic repetition perfected to the sum of iron rules applied throughout the world. The rules are simple: information about population density, their incomes and purchasing power.

CZECH REPUBLIC FOCUS

The post-communist period after 1989 marked the transformation of the Czech economy, which is essentially the transition from CPE (centrally planned economy) to the operation principle of a market economy. A key step in this transformation was a change of ownership. Possibility of private business boomed through the entry of new businesses and small or large privatization assets concentrated in existing state enterprises (Spilková, 2010). Among the first who managed to replace existing counter stores in modern retail were Dutch group Royal Ahold (Mana) and the Belgian Delhaize le Lion (Delvita).

Even during the second half of the ninetieth years could be seen between the major trading firms also some home. Gradually, however, the local firms faced economic difficulties and were bought by foreign companies (Weidhofer, 2010). After the entry of foreign firms in the Czech market, having introduced modern retail formats (discount supermarket and hypermarket), began Czech Republic in the late nineties to attract developers and large shopping centres, which were already in Western Europe long-established. Full development of shopping centres in Czech Republic came after almost 10 years after the fall of communism.

Development of food chains began by supermarkets. The innovative role played hypermarkets, which helped launch the first truly shopping centre. The first shopping centre in the Czech Republic was the centre Černý Most in Prague built in 1997. At the beginning of 2003 were in Czech Republic 127 shopping centres and at the beginning of 2010 were in Czech Republic 230 shopping centres larger than 5,000 m2 (Spilková, 2012:31). Most shopping centres are in Prague, followed by South Moravian Region (Brno city) and Silesian Region (Ostrava city). Only one shopping centre is located in Jihlava city Region (see Figure 3-15).

The number of shopping centres in each region does not match the purchasing power of the population. For example, the Silesian Region has one of the lowest purchasing power, but on its territory are seven shopping centres. A similar disproportion is in the Ústi Region, which has 5 shopping centres, what is still more than in the Plzeň Region, which is comparable to the purchasing power of the Prague Region with 24 shopping centres.

This fact is one of the indicators of unorganized development of shopping centres in the country. Figure 3-16 shows the localization of shopping centres in Prague. Shopping centre Eden was built close to the shopping centre GalerieFlóra; GalerieButovice was built close to the shopping centre Stodůlky and Zličín zone. It affects the balance of the retail network in the area and it can lead to closing of some shopping centres. The first shopping centre that closed in CZ in 2009 was StodůlkyCenter, later converted into a hypermarket with furniture.

It would seem that Prague is filled enough with retail areas, and even reaches the level of West

Company name	State	Year of the entry
Ahold Czech Republic, a. s. (Royal Ahold, púv. Euronova)	Netherlands	1991
Discount, a. s. (Delhaize Le Lion)	Belgium	1991
Billa (Rewe)	Germany	1991
Asko Nabytek	Germany	1991
bauMax, s.r.o. (bauMax)	Austria	1992
Spar ČR (ASPIAG, SPAR Ostbayern)	Austria	1992
Plus Discount (Tengelmann)	Germany	1992
Bauhaus	Germany	1993
Julius Meinl	Austria	1994
OBI	Germany	1995
Sconto Nábytek (Hoffner)	Germany	1995
IKEA	Sweden	1996
Tesco Stores CZ, a.s. (Tesco plc.)	Great Britain	1996
Globus ČR, k.s. (Globus)	Germany	1996
Carrefour ČR, s.r.o. (Carrefour)	France	1997
Makro Cash and Carry ČR, s.r.o. (Metro AG)	Germany	1997
Kaufland (Lidl and Schwarz)	Germany	1997
Penny Market (Rewe)	Germany	1997
Hornbach	Germany	1998
Lidl	Germany	2003

Table 3-2 Overview of the entry of foreign companies on the Czech market. Source: Starzyczná, 2010.

European cities. Although it is planned developing of new shopping centres (StromovkaRustonka, Bořislavka, Dejvice Centre or a new outlet at the airport Prague - Ruzyne). It is clear that the role of local government is small and there has been promoting development goals without a deeper analysis of catchment areas (Spilková, 2012).

Development of shopping centres in Prague, as in other cities of Czech Republic, took place from the peripheral zones to urban centres. The reason for development of shopping malls on the edges of city was lower prices of land, clear ownerships, integrity of land and absence of land use plan. After use of peripheral parts of the city, new shopping centres moved to the inner city, as in the case of New Smichov (2001), Flora Palace (2003) and Palladium (2008).

As mentioned above, shopping centres in the Czech Republic were built unorganized and uncoordinated. Analysis of developers and free market is not working for hundred per cent, as it might seem at first glance. If we consider asking whether it is necessary to regulate the emergence of new or expanding existing shopping centres in Czech Republic, we should answer by foreign experience, which is very diverse. But regulations which prevent the development of shopping centres that follow the existing city structure and do not disrupt existing retail networks prevail. One tool for planning retail is the RIA study. RIA (Retail Impact Assessment) originated in Great Britain in the 60th of the last century as a result of ideas procedural planning and social engineering. Over the next decade, evolved from theoretical models and system approaches in the seventieth, despite the neo-Marxist models and free-market ideology to a more pragmatic form of the nineties. Retail impact assessment and RIA study as its output can help to understand the potential impact of changes, to control public spending, to preserve the effectiveness of the system and to ensure the same level of service for all consumers. The advantage of such independent study is to get enough objective information on the impacts of the project. This study is not used in Czech planning legislation. Its introduction, however, could help to unify the procedures for planning in the retail area and avoid future negative consequences of uncoordinated construction of large shopping malls (Spilková, 2012:76).

If we compare countries with a long time liberal planning practice (France, Germany, Great Britain, Spain, Italy) with countries that have a long history of restrictive planning policies (Belgium, Denmark, Finland, Switzerland, Norway, Netherlands) it is clear that the regulation reflects the overall quality of individual settlements.

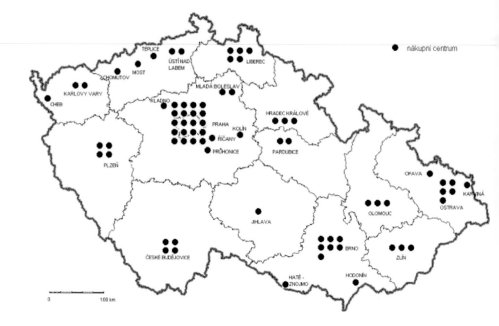

Figure 3-15 Number of shopping centres (black points) in Regions of Czech Republic. Source: websites of the shopping centres, processed by Anna Háblová.

SOLUTIONS IN TIMES OF SCARCITY

The uncontrolled expansion of large-scale shopping centres can cause wrecking and desolating of shopping malls. To that cause can be added increasing price of oil, online shopping and unsustainable buildings. Moving this idea on, the situation can be similar as the issue of abandoned brownfields. The period of production was replaced by the period of consumption, and that can be replaced by another one. And we will deal with abandoned shopping fields and their reuse, demolition or heritage protection.

In the few past years, in America was closed many 'big boxes', and even the reason is different from the mentioned above [1], abandoned shopping centres, so called ghost malls, are real threat for the American suburban landscape.

At the beginning of the sixties of the last century were spread in the USA so-called 'big boxes' (among other large-scale retail buildings), owned by two main chains: Kmart and Wal-Mart. The name 'big boxes' has become known thanks to the simple, pragmatic visual style of these shopping centres. In recent times are hundreds of these big boxes across the United States becoming deserted places, called 'ghost malls'. At the moment, Wal-Mart offers on its website (www. walmartrealty.com) a total of 656 of its empty buildings for rent. However, when counting with other chains such as Kmart, The Home Depot, Kroger's, etc., we would get up to several thousands of abandoned buildings (Christensen, 2008).

---

1   The reason is expanding of chains to bigger and newer boxes not far from old ones. They left the old buildings empty, not leaving them to competition chains.

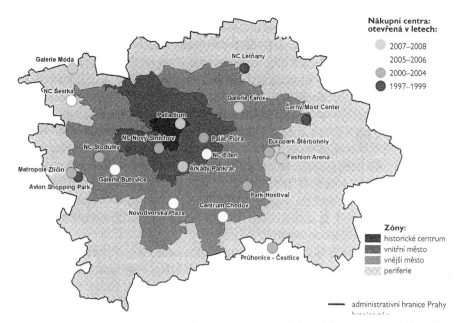

Figure 3-16 Localization of shopping centres in Prague. Source: websites of the centres, student work U6, Anna Háblová's investigation.

The question is, whether it doesn't expect European shopping centres, where failing of shopping centres is not happening. In Czech Republic failed only one shopping mall in 2009 in Prague, Stodůlky. Problems with lack of customers already recognize shopping malls NovéButovice, Futurum or Tesco.

Adaptive reuse is happening all around us, as it has been since people began constructing this built environmental upon the Earth. Each building has its own personal timeline. The definition of 'reuse' according to the dictionary is 'the act of using again in different way after reclaiming or reprocessing'. The first part infers an action, but the words 'reclaiming' and 'reprocessing' refer to a conceptual act – a decision, an imaginative and creative moment. Reclaiming a structure is a process that also must occur in the minds of the people who are enacting the reuse.

That is current topic in many American cities which are surrounded by many empty big boxes. And it is not excluded that this problem will face one day also some European cities.

Figure 3-18 shows proposals of student from Faculty of architecture in Prague, who, under the author´s leadership, processed information about shopping centres in Prague and tried to propose another possible use of shopping centres in case of no longer serving its original purpose. These are mainly large shopping centres on the outskirts of Prague, which are characterized by the largest number of similar problems, [2] and it is possible to use for them similar principles.

When the time changes dramatically, the situation of shopping centres can be one day similar

139

---

2   There is a waste of very fertile soils, poor pedestrian permeability area, increase of crime in these areas, the mono-function of the area and poor quality of public spaces.

Figure 3-17 Three big unregulated shopping malls on the edge of Prague. Red: buildings, Yellow: occupied area. Source: maps.google.cz, processed by Anna Háblová.

FARM   GALLERY LIBRARY   RETIRE   JAIL

Figure 3-18 Proposals for a new use of existing big shopping centres at the edge of Prague. Source: workshop U6 2012, processed by Anna Háblová.

with processes of abandoned factories and former brownfields. Mentioned student proposals are some kind of vision of the coming 'retail fields'.

CONCLUSION

'People already refer to the near future in months instead of years, and to the distant future in years instead of decades or centuries. What may happen decades from now is treated not only as unknown, but unknowable' (Brand, 1991:21). We are living in the moment, without much consideration or understanding of our relationship to the future, as we remove mile after mile of green space, open space, public space. According to the oral tradition of the 'Great Law of the Iroguis', in every deliberation, we must consider the impact on the next seven generations. Even seven generations is not long enough really. We must consider the impact of today on time´s passing into forever.

References

Bauzá, M. (2009) The mall in the online shopping era, The 4th IFoU.
Brand, S. (1991) The Clock of the Long Now: The time and Responsibility, New York: BasicBooks.
Christensen, J. (2008) Big box reuse, Cambridge: Massachusetts Institute of Technology.
Koolhaas, R. (2002) The Harvard Design School Guide to Shopping, Cambridge: Actar.
Marcuse, P., Kempen, R. (2000) Globalizing cities: a new spatial order?, Oxford: Blackwell.
Paquet, L. (2003) The urge to Splurge: A social history of Shopping. Toronto: ECW Press.
Spilková, J. (2012) Geography of retail, Prague: Karolinum.
Starzyczná, H. (2005) Moderníobchod, Karviná: Su Opf
Sýkora, L. (2000) Globalizace a jejíspolečenské a geografickédůsledky, Prague: Přírodovědeckáfakulta UK.
Weidhofer, T. (2010) Vývojovétendence v maloobchoděporoce 2000, Prague: Masarykova univerzitaEkonomicko-správnífakulta.

TRANSURBANISM: TOWARDS A NEW TRANSDISCIPLINARY APPROACH IN URBAN PLANNING

Agatino Rizzo, Michail Galanakis

The on-going financial crisis is having a negative impact on post-communist European countries of the Baltic Sea Region. In Estonia, for instance, recent data [1] related to annual population growth reveal a loss of 0.2% while at the same time Tallinn, the capital city, has gained 0.6%. Thus a double layer dynamic affects the country whereby Estonia loses population to wealthier European states and other countries, while Tallinn drains the remaining population from the countryside.

Similar dynamics affect other post-communist Baltic States (the once labelled 'Baltic Tigers') so much so that while 30% of Estonian residents live in Tallinn, 32% of Latvian residents live in Riga, and 26% of Lithuanian residents live in Vilnius. Comparing this data with the northern sector of the Baltic Region (Finland and Sweden) we find that 11% of residents in Finland live in Helsinki and 9% of residents in Sweden live in Stockholm.

However, in this paper we argue that while the urban population imbalances (i.e. urban primacy versus shrinking countryside) of shrinking Baltic states (i.e. Estonia, Latvia, and Lithuania) put pressures on the land uses and social milieus of their capitals (e.g. Tallinn in Estonia) the same is true for Scandinavian capitals whereby rising international migration is putting pressure on their welfare states (see the case of Helsinki in Haila 2005: 20).

Maimone (2004: 6) explains that while for cultural reasons the Russian-speaking minority in Estonia has been generally urbanised, Estonians, on the other hand, disperse in the countryside. The recent urban migration in Tallinn has thus increased the chances for social conflict between Estonians, independent from USSR since 1991, and their rivals Russians. The latter are perceived as intruders and never fully integrated in post-communist Estonia (Maimone 2004: 4). In 2007 a conflict between these two groups revolved over the issue of the relocation of a soviet memorial (the so called 'Bronze Soldier') from the city centre to the periphery of Tallinn. For weeks, tensions at the political and social level (Estonia vs. Russia and Estonians vs. Estonians of Russian origin) resulted in urban riots and demonstrations.

Finland does not share a similar past with Estonia, having been an independent and liberal country since 1917; however, recent immigration inflows from European, African and Asian countries have put some strains in its social tissue - particularly in Helsinki where the share of foreigners in 2011 was above 10% (with Estonians being the largest minority) while in the rest of

---

1   Source citypopulation.de, 2010-2012.

the country this share was little above 2% [2]. The dynamic contexts above and their social, cultural and economic developments cannot but affect urban development as well.

In this paper we analyse two projects and we present our approach in planning and research practice that we have called TransUrbanism, a term previously used by Arjen Mulder (2002) to describe the contemporary state of urbanisation in which continuous transformations produce a 'multiplication of information'. In section two we further explain our theoretical and methodological baselines while in sections three and four we present, in a chronological order, two projects we were involved in Tallinn and Helsinki. These were to various degrees collaborative projects carried out by the authors together with professionals, activists, and agencies [3]. We have documented and reported on the projects elsewhere; however, by collecting here these experiences and practices our aim is to exemplify TransUrbanism. In the conclusions we summarise the results of the two projects, their significance for contemporary urbanism, and suggest paths for future applications and research inquiries.

THEORETICAL FRAMEWORK AND METHODOLOGY

In recent years the financial crisis and rising xenophobia in Greece have caused an increase of protests by autochthonous residents against refugee centres in their neighbourhoods. Once again foreigners become the Other who contaminate national space and devalue local real estate. Sandercock (2003: 112) writes about the sense of loss and even fear we experience when 'others' seem to invade and appropriate 'our' space. Urban change is often feared when the familiar is threatened to turn into something else, something that we don't know and that is causing us uncertainty and anxiety. How many instances haven't been documented of changes authorities impose without involving us (and those with less power) who will be affected? How many times don't people protest about changes that are planned for their neighbourhoods? Current socio-economic and political negotiations take place within a framework of diversity and global movements that are important factors for challenging social, political and cultural norms. Changes in our living environments while fear inducing are often necessary, therefore, we propose that, when possible, we better test (simulate) changes through the medium of Urban Art Interventions, before such changes become irreversible.

Planning for a diversity of people – autochthonous and not – requires that in order to deal with our fear of socio-spatial change we need to systematically practice pro-activeness and intentionality, as well as open-endedness. In this framework research into urban phenomena and certain foreseeable changes is recommendable when and where it is possible. Concerted research efforts could develop into open source knowledge that would contribute to the betterment of life for all. The fact that individual actors, grass roots and NGOs develop initiatives and interventions to claim urban space makes it a pressing need to study such phenomena and analyse their potentials for community engagement and sustainable development. The various formal and informal appropriations of public spaces taking place around the world are telling.

Hou (2010: 2) explains that while the idea of public space in western societies evokes the practice of 'democracy, openness, and publicity of debate', today's European public space, is mostly the result of the efforts of pre-democratic states to display their military power and to control social life. Recently, particularly after 9/11, over-control and display of power once again

2   Source: City of Helsinki, Helsinki Urban fact.
3   For more information about our collaborations see Cityleft Network at www.cityleft.blogspot.com

suppress the rights to demonstrate and of freedom of speech. Against this trend, inspired by the seemingly un-organised and informal use of public space typical of Asia and Latin America (e.g. informal markets, favelas, etc.), non-governmental urban activists around the world have sought to peacefully re-contest public space through their presence, uses, and practices such as urban art interventions. From Rebar's Park(ing) intervention in San Francisco (see Merker 2010: 45) – planting parking lots with trees and grass – to Guerrilla Benching – installing benches in empty public space – or Circle Lane Party – in London's underground - of Space Hijackers(the first staged in 1999), to the Stalker group/OsservatorioNomade's TV(2005) interventions in the periphery of Rome, artists, urban activists, and architecture practitioners have joined their forces to re-discuss, engage, and re-imagine city's public space.

In a recent conference at Bauhaus-University Weimar, Alain Bourdin (2012) has highlighted the tensions between the fields of 'Urban Studies' and 'Planning', the latter being a procedural line of inquiry while the former being a substantial one. While planning, says Bourdin, '... has not found its ways to innovate itself...', urban studies, on the other hand, have not been engaged '...in finding solid concepts for the notions deriving from action'. While planners usually answer to questions and urban researchers pose questions, local actors, say Bourdin, also formulate questions - thus urban researchers should additionally be more involved in creating tools to solve urban problems, rather than to merely contest injustice (perpetually opposing but rarely constructively proposing).

In the 'Empire of Meaning. The humanization of the social Sciences' Francois Dosse (1999) advocates for a reconciliation of the relations between exact sciences, social sciences, and philosophy based on a new transdisciplinary paradigm. Dosse notes that the social sciences are witnessing '... a genuine transformation: the terms structure, reproduction, static, combinatory, invariant, universal, and binary logic are being effaced, in favour of the notions of organizing chaos, fractal, event, process, meaning, complexity, self-organization, construction, strategy, convention, autonomy, enaction' (Ibid. 1999). Thus for Dosse the task of the new, transdisciplinary-scholar is to conduct a more modest 'clarification' rather than an artificial separation between 'judgements of fact' and 'judgments of value'. In this way he continues a '... a third way between the prevalence of pure lived experience and the priority of conceptualization...' can be sought.

Inspired by these ideas, we call Transdisciplinary Urbanism (or TransUrbanism) a new, emerging field of study/intervention in which social and action researchers, artists, animators, performers, and activists come together to contest space and to openly re-negotiate power structures in urban space. The social aspects of urbanism connect different practices, ideological frameworks and disciplines in order to address issues of everyday life. Disciplinary crossovers are central in researching and planning urban space and potentially facilitate city inhabitants and professionals to even temporarily leave their comfort zones, co-design their interactions and communication and work together in non-predetermined ways. Within TransUrbanism we advocate to industriously work with uncertainty, chance and open-endedness. TransUrbanism with its participatory and transdisciplinary approach may help us to re-think polarized European cities, such as Tallinn for its strong urban primacy in a shrinking Estonian economy and Helsinki for its increasing diversity undermining its long-established welfare state, towards a more just urbanism.

For us TransUrbanism concerns socio-spatial issues of multi-layered urban phenomena. Independently, sociology and spatial design merely provide the theoretical context of what our objective is with TransUrbanism, namely the proactive (but not pre-determined) investigation of the implications of change in urban space. TransUrbanism is our approach regarding research into socio-spatial change in urban space. We endorse the idea of researchers/activists who conduct what Hoggart et al. (2002: 292) describe as action research: 'Action Research is associated with learning about society through efforts to change it.' With TransUrbanism thus we recognize that urban research does not need to be only and always reflective; researchers may also aspire to bring social change.

Whether looking through literature, media and the press, conducting discussions and interviews, or setting up urban artistic interventions such as in Tallinn in Helsinki, our aim has been to find arguments that support our advocacy for change regarding the ways we deal with socio-spatiality. Research without such a quest for change is valuable albeit not necessarily impartial or socially relevant. In New Strategies for Social Research, Layder (1996: 45) talks about the kind of research that generates 'theory that fits the data,' rather than 'data to fit the theory'. This is called the grounded theory approach, and offers another perspective on the issue of the relationship between the researcher and the field of research. According to TransUrbanism fieldwork guides researchers to theories that assist critical understanding of the field and its actors as well as the theories themselves. It is not necessarily the aim of urban research to develop a grounded theory; however, it is part of our contribution to knowledge to make certain links between theorised practise and theory in practice, which may shed more light on socio-spatial phenomena.

In what follows we briefly present and analyse two cases that have helped us form our understanding of TransUrbanism as a practice. It is important to clarify that our attempt to formulate TransUrbanism came after these examples, and our formulation is not finite but a work in progress.

PROJECT I: ARCHIPELAGO-TALLINN

As part of an international group of young urban researchers based at the Bauhaus Dessau Foundation, in 2008 we were asked to explore the complex dynamics of trans-national urbanism in the Baltic Sea Region (Rizzo, 2009a). Our research tested the notion of an integrated regional identity formation as desired by region makers to determine whether this model or alternate emergent forms better describe the situation of the Helsinki-Tallinn-Region. Dialogue with local stakeholders and region makers as well as local inhabitants provided both a top down and bottom up view on the development of both cities and the interconnections -and imbalances- that existed between them. When considering the distribution of services, jobs and business activities our group recognized a complex area of overlapping networks without clear borders, mainly based on informal and flexible relations rather than politically governed ones.

Observing that most of the implications of this relationship appeared manifest in the urban form of Tallinn led the group to further research here. This process of rapid urbanization and modernization has had both positive and negative impact on the city and its people. Estonian Independence, declared in 1991, and the subsequent interest and influence from Finland and Sweden gave rise to a process of modernization of the region through economic growth, better living conditions, increase in wages and global connections.

The results of this rapid development have affected the demographics of Tallinn, leaving different sections of the population outside this framework. Estonians with lower income or education, or with limited Estonian language skills (such as Tallinn's sizable Russian speaking population) had more difficulty adapting to the sudden shift of internal market and governance rules. This economic disparity in the social structure plays out in the urban form of Tallinn, creating spatial segregation in certain parts of the city. Kopli, Mustamäe and Lasnamäe are

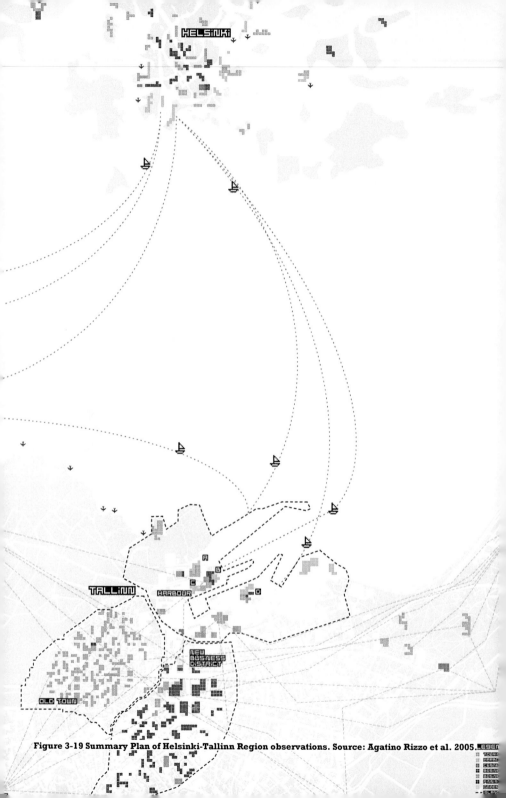

Figure 3-19 Summary Plan of Helsinki-Tallinn Region observations. Source: Agatino Rizzo et al. 2005.

examples; despite their proximity to developed or developing areas, they remain disconnected from the overall development surge of the city.

The cross border effects as well as historical pre-conditions manifest in the urban fabric of Tallinn appeared to the group as an 'Archipelago of Islands' (seeFigure 3 19- Rizzo 2009b), each with different economic, social, and cultural milieus: the unfinished harbour dotted of commercial malls catering for Scandinavian visitors; the old, medieval city centre crowded with hotels, restaurants and clubs for wealthy locals and European tourists; the socialist residential peripheries populated by the Russian speaking minority; and so forth. The model of the archipelago also drawn the group's attention on the in-between space made of semi-abandoned spaces, parking lots, roads, and other infrastructures.

After carrying out a SWOT analysis for the city of Tallinn the group discussed and generated qualitative scenarios, trying to sketch the urban future of Tallinn - within the Helsinki-Tallinn Region - against the most uncertain and important driving forces (e.g. technological, social, environmental, economic, political, etc.). The scenarios pointed to two main hypotheses (Rizzo et al. 2008): the need to deal with material and immaterial borders defining the Archipelago as a way to denounce social segregation and urban fragmentation and the opportunity given by the in-between space to negotiate diversity in the city. These latter hypotheses were tested in Tallinn through a series of urban art interventions in May 2008, concluding with a discussion between city planners, architects, art critics and general public. Tallinn urban art interventions were highly interactive and intuitive, suggesting and collecting social-local feedbacks.

'Porta de Viru' at Tammsaare Park (Figure 3 20) was a performance aimed to explore the spatial concept 'Archipelago' by visualizing the boarders of Tallinn 'urban islands' with stripes, banners, and gates. All material was acquired in the second hand market in Tallinn and deployed with the help of local NGO 'UusMaailm'. The setting was a busy area in the centre of the city (Tammsaare Park), between the old fortifications and the socialist business district. 'Tallinn Re-told' at the harbour aimed instead at building a more intimate relation between the research group and the inhabitants. Discussions with tourists and locals took place about the potential of the spatial structure of Tallinn; people were encouraged to visit different parts of the city and exchange stories about meaningful places. Another public performance ('Wind-up') helped to explore in-between space potentials. Many areas at the harbour are waiting for transformation but seem abandoned at the moment. Through temporary structures installed in the space the group wanted to show that a different use of urban space is possible. Related projects used these spaces for breakfast and dinner gatherings as well as an area next to Linnahall for a temporary beach.

Two very different areas, Rotterman district and BaltiJaam Market, were chosen for integrative projects (Figure 3 21); while Rotterman is a well designed new urban site with expensive high brands but few social interaction, BaltiJaam Market is a very cheap informal area that is very important for economically less fortunate locals. The group's project consisted of building up small market stands where participants distributed goods from the contrasting area in exchange for people's desires. The intent was to get local opinion about what has value in the further development of the city. In a subsequent project in the evening, a projection regarding real estate speculation in UusMaailm community started a discussion about the topic of future city development and whose city it is to develop.

The results of the group's interventions were not definitive but they helped to build platforms to discuss regional and local challenges with local stakeholders of both sides of the Gulf of Finland. Despite the small budget made available by the Bauhaus Dessau Foundation, the urban art

Figure 3-20 PlayTallinn, Urban Art Intervention Week: 'Porta de Viru'. Source: Agatino Rizzo et al. 2008.

Figure 3-21 PlayTallinn, Urban Art Intervention Week: 'Wind Up'. Source: Agatino Rizzo et al. 2008.

interventions helped strengthening links between the group and local stakeholders beyond the duration of the research project: a member of the group seasonally works with students of a local university on issues about landscape and identity; others have taken part in workshops and other interventions this time organized by local NGOs in Estonia.

PROJECT II: MEIDÄN-OURCITY - HELSINKI

Under the auspices of the foundation of the World Design Capital Helsinki 2012 (http://wdchelsinki2012.fi/en), a group of architects, designers, and community workers, including Galanakis, planned and realized a multifaceted project titled Ourcity (https://meidankaupunki.wordpress.com/). The members of Ourcity strived to bring forward the richness of diversity by promoting cultures present in Helsinki and by creating opportunities for intercultural dialogue to occur. Design, architecture and urban design were the main tools, while a transdisciplinary approach guided Ourcity group to focus geographically and enter into negotiations with local communities. The aim was to reach out to the people who had the least access to the design processes shaping what was their city too. The strategy was to mobilize the existing human resources in the focus neighbourhood of Meri-Rastila in the suburb of Vuosaari, in the more multicultural East part of Helsinki.

The neighbourhood of Meri-Rastila, was selected as the focus area of Ourcity project because:
1 In Helsinki, MeriRastila has one of the highest concentrations of people of ethnocultural background since immigrants tend to gravitate towards Meri-Rastila (Vilkama 2011). In 2010 in Meri-Rastila area lived 5,224 inhabitants of which 3,539 were Finnish speakers, 175 were Swedish speakers and 1,446 spoke other languages (Helsinki City Urban Facts 2011)

Figure 3-22 Ourcity presented the alternative master plan to the people of MeriRastila. Here at the annual Rastori event in the main square of Meri-Rastila. Source: MichailGalanakis 2012.

2   The City of Helsinki has plans to build private housing for 2500 new inhabitants in the area by appropriating part of forest land in Meri-Rastila. A group of active residents lobby against this plan.

By focusing on Meri-Rastila and the design challenges posed by the decision of the City of Helsinki, Ourcity group materialized what originally was the theoretical aim of the whole project; namely, to democratize design by facilitating people who are not involved in such processes to articulate their voices and concerns in ways that the authorities would find difficult to ignore. Design was the main medium with which Ourcity worked because this was a requirement from the World Design Capital Helsinki 2012 in order to secure funding that allowed the project proposal to be realised. Community engagement was a component of Ourcity project that soon became crucial in order to fulfil the promises of the project, however, it also turned out to be more challenging than anticipated.

Community engagement was challenging because Meri-Rastila has attracted a lot of stigma in Finnish media and the public opinion is rather negative or indifferent at best (Galanakis 2008). Therefore there was justifiable resistance from local ethnocultural groups to liaise with Ourcity group, an outsider. However, the group of active citizens who had a pressing need and concern quickly took advantage of the opportunity Ourcity represented. The pro-Meri-Rastila group of residents, asked Ourcity group to help them to constructively challenge the decision of the City of Helsinki to build in the forest that they considered being an invaluable asset of their area. Ourcity group members decided to offer expertise and networks to pro-Meri-Rastila people. Together with six students of architecture and planning geography a work team was formed that drafted an alternative master plan for Meri-Rastila providing housing for approximately 2,500 new inhabitants while leaving intact the forest (Ourcity 2012).

Ourcity group members pull together their knowledge and skills in order to open up the discussion regarding the area of Meri-Rastila in general, and in order to engage the local residents in planning their living environment in participatory ways. Expertise on interaction design (Figure 3-22) as well as community engagement allied design to produce a dynamic conversation and ultimately a plan that adhered to the requirements that the City of Helsinki planning office had set. A dynamic conversation spread into virtual forums on the Internet and members of the green party embraced the alternative master plan for Meri-Rastila as more environmentally friendly and socially sustainable. The alternative master plan was presented at the same time as the plan by the city's planning office in spring 2012 and was considered by the City Council, which eventually voted in favour of the official plan but only with one vote difference.

One of the strengths of Ourcity's alternative master plan was that it was built upon the results of two university courses (OURcourse) held in autumn 2011 in which students from disciplines, such as business management and geography, conducted fieldwork in the area of Meri-Rastila and came up with scenarios for new services and socio-spatial strategies based on direct observations and interviews of local residents. The results of these two courses were publicly presented in Meri-Rastila. After the courses had concluded, Ourcity group organised workshops to bring together all those working on the alternative master plan and pro Meri-Rastila people as well as other local residents.

The alternative master plan (Figure 3-23) in its entirety demonstrates that although design is an important component of urban development and planning, it needs to be effectively linked with local communities in order to represent their needs and aspirations. Ourcity also demonstrates that for an effort like the drafting of the alternative master plan to be an effective challenger of

SUUNNITTELUPERIAATTEET

| YHDISTÄÄ JA INTEGROIDA ALUEEN KAUPUNKIMAISET SEKÄ HARVAANASUTUT OSAT, JA VÄHENTÄÄ SOSIAALISEN ERIYTYMISEN RISKIÄ | KASVATTAA ALUEEN ASUNTOKANTAA JA PARANTAA ALUEEN MAINETTA | SÄILYTTÄÄ JA HYÖDYNTÄÄ ALUEEN LUONNONYMPÄRISTÖÄ JA LUODA AIDOSTI KESTÄVÄ LÄHTÖKOHTA SEN KÄYTÖLLE | ELVYTTÄÄ JA HYÖDYNTÄÄ OLEMASSA OLEVA ASUINALUE SEKÄ VAHVISTAA SEN ERITYISLUONNETTA | HYÖDYNTÄÄ PAIKALLISTEN ASUKKAIDEN TIETÄMYS ASUINALUEESTAAN OTTAMALLA HEIDÄT MUKAAN SUUNNITTELU-PROSESSIIN |

TÄYDENNYSRAKENTAMISEN ALUEET   TOIMINNOT   OMISTUSMUODOT

VAIHTOEHTOINEN ASEMAKAAVA MERI-RASTILAAN 2012
EIN ALTERNATIVER MASTERPLAN FÜR MERI-RASTILA, HELSINKI

Tristan Hughes, Marcelo Díez Gutiérrez, Martina Jerima, Petteri Kosonen, Elsi Lehto, Maija Parviainen, Heini-Emilia Saari, Sonja Sahlsten

3 / 8

Figure 3-23 Ourcity master plan for MeriRastila.

Source: http://meidankaupunki.wordpress.com/alternative-master-plan/

top-down decision-making then concerted community engagement is necessary. Intercultural competence is a key in building bridges of communication in-between cultures unaware of the common grounds they may be sharing and of the improvement they may bring to their lives if they were to negotiate and act together (See Sandercock and Attili 2009).

The outreach that Ourcity group members conducted before and while working on the alternative master plan reaffirmed to all stake holders including the architecture and planning geography students, that planning the urban development of an area cannot ignore the people in that area. On the contrary any sustainable process must in its very early stages engage as many diverse people and groups as possible. Experts thus become facilitators. As Netami Stuart (2011), a young park planner in Toronto who believed in planning for diversity put it:

'the best way to do it is to have planning done by a diversity of people. So to be as consultative as possible... I think it's really about dedicating enough resources to identifying voices and listening to them, and spending the time to understand how you should communicate with people who have different needs than you.'

We think that one of the most substantial contributions of the alternative master plan was that it created a platform for discussion amongst the residents of Meri-Rastila. Not all local residents shared the conviction of the pro Meri-Rastila group regarding the untouchability of the forest; however, through the workshops and discussions organized by Ourcity more residents had the opportunity to engage in the debate. Even if this debate was at times mainly driven by the agenda of the pro Meri-Rastila group, more stakeholders had the opportunity to realise for themselves the different perspectives, interests and some of the arguments for and against building in the forest. This was the case not only for the active residents who participated in the process of drafting the alternative master plan but also the members of the planning team as well as all the members of Ourcity.

Ourcity did not manage to carry out the community engagement it initially aspired to. The fixed time of the project (one year), its voluntary and multifaceted nature and open-endedness made many stakeholders in Meri-Rastila to be reserved. This unfortunately was the case regarding some of the crucial social service providers in the area whom the instigators of Ourcity didn't have the foresight to involve when planning the project. These stakeholders at times acted as gatekeepers of Meri-Rastila and resisted facilitating Ourcity's community outreach fearing that the project interfered too much with their work. A weakness of Ourcity was that the community outreach wasn't extensive enough to make the alternative master plan representative of most of the local residents. It did however expand the discussion of the planning agenda to more residents and managed to engage a few at least of the residents with ethnocultural background.

All these and more realizations wouldn't have been reached had not Ourcity created opportunities for multifaceted interaction with the various stakeholders in Meri-Rastila, from fliers inviting for residents' opinions about their area, to participatory design workshops, exhibitions and physical and virtual discussion forums. While the alternative master plan started as an experiment with unforeseeable results but serious investment in time, energy and resources, it progressed into a real life planning process that generated substantial media and public interest. Ourcity and the planning team that worked on the alternative master plan offered the results of their labour to the public domain and the active pro Meri-Rastila people. The alternative master plan, at the time of writing, has entered a new phase where an independent body of experts assesses the environmental impact of both the city's official plan and the alternative master plan for Meri-Rastila. There are still hopes that the City of Helsinki might reconsider their plan. The alternative master plan equipped the active pro Meri-Rastila people with confidence and a conviction that their cause is not lost and the forest of Meri-Rastila shouldn't be reduced either. Ourcity project aligns to principles of TransUrbanism by providing a testing ground for socio-spatial change, and by transforming the process of planning into a platform for community engagement and community building. As such processes are open-ended mistakes are unavoidable but even they are beneficial as part of shared knowledge.

CONCLUSIONS

The recent geo-economic crises have affected immigration flows in such a way that in post-communist countries of the Baltic Sea Region such as Estonia, capital cities have drained inhabitants from shrinking country-towns while in traditional liberal countries such as Finland, capital cities have attracted transnational workers often from the former countries (Estonians are the largest minority in Finland).

As results of these dynamics, social conflicts have been rising in both Tallinn and Helsinki. While the socio-economic-political context of these two cities are different, on the other hand, their symptoms are similar: in Tallinn as in Helsinki minorities challenge regions makers for what Lefebvre (1968) has called the 'right to the city', a right that in the interpretation of Harvey (2008: 23), is:

'... far more than the individual liberty to access urban resources: it is a right to change ourselves by changing the city. It is, moreover, a common rather than an individual right since this transformation inevitably depends upon the exercise of a collective power to reshape the processes of urbanization. The freedom to make and remake our cities and ourselves is, I want to argue, one of the most precious yet most neglected of our human rights'

Inspired by recent studies in the fields of multiculturalism, urban activism, and action research we propose 'TransUrbanism' as a practice with methodological implications in the field of Urban Studies and Planning. TransUrbanism is an emerging field of study/intervention in which social and action researchers, artistic performers, activists, architects and planners come together to contest space and to openly re-negotiate power structures in public space.

Within this framework, we briefly reviewed two research projects in Tallinn and in Helsinki. Ourcity as well as Tallinn's interventions were Urban Artistic Interventions open for public use and abuse. Both practices constituted a soft urban design approach that paid off. The empirical data retrieved during Ourcity as well as Tallinn's interventions was the biggest return, along with the trust that both authors gained regarding the unknown public. Ourcity and the alternative master plan for Meri-Rastila in East Helsinki provided a testing ground for socio-spatial development by opening up the planning debate to more local people.

As Europe is in a phase of de-growth and decline, Trans-Urbanism could help us conduct research while livening up our cities on limited resources. Trans-Urbanism also may represent an excellent framework for urban planning to regenerate itself, shifting from its procedural/technocratic origins (Bourdin, 2012) to capitalise on emergent urban activism (i.e. DIY urbanism, public space activism) that often better advocate public interests.

References

Bourdin, A. (2012) Metapolis: A Challenge for the Invention of New Categories. Conference The Media of the Metapolis. Bauhaus-University Weimar. 24-26 May, Weimar.

Dosse, F. (1999) Empire of Meaning.The humanization of the social Sciences. University of Minnesota Press, USA.

Garfinkel, H. (1967). Studies in Ethnomethodology. New Jersey: Prentice-Hall.

Haila, A. (2005) 'The coming of age of metropolitan governance in Helsinki ?'Cahiers/Working Papers dupôleVille/Métropolis/Cosmopolis 05/05.Centre d' d'Etudes Etudes Européennes de Sciences Po Paris.

Harvey, D. (2008) 'The Right to the City'.New Left Review. 53: 23–40.

Helsinki City Urban Facts (2011). Available in http://www.hel.fi/palvelukartta/ accessed July 1, 2012. [English]

Hoggart, K., Lees, L. & Davies, A. (2002) Researching Human Geography. London: Arnold.

Hou, J. (2010) '(Not) your everyday public space'.In J. Hou (ed.) Insurgent Public Space – Guerrilla urbanism and the remaking of contemporary cities (pp. 1-18). New York: Routledge, Abingdon.

Layder, D. (1996) New Strategy in Social Research. Polity Press, Cambridge.

Lefebvre, H. (1968) Le Droit à la ville. Paris: Economica.

Maimone, C. (2004) 'The Estonian Russian Divide: Examining Social Diversity in Estonia with Cross-National Survey Data'. Department of Political Science Stanford University.April 6, US.

Merker, B. (2010) Taking Place.Rebar's absurd tactics in generous urbanism.In Hou, J. (2010) (Not) your everyday public space.In J. Hou (ed.) Insurgent Public Space – Guerrilla urbanism and the remaking of contemporary cities (pp. 1-18). New York: Routledge, Abingdon, 45-58.

Mulder, A. (2002) 'TransUrbanism/Introduction'. In Brouwer, J., Brookman, P., Mulder, A. (eds.) Transurbanism. The Netherlands: NAi Publishers.

Ourcity (2012) Available at http://meidankaupunki.wordpress.com/alternative-master-plan/ accessed February 7, 2013.

Rizzo, A., Micheller, R., Jonsson, T., Kryshnamurty, S., Bajraktari, E., Santacruz, R. (2008) Helsinki-Tallinn Region.Tracing networks in an archipelago of islands. Dessau: Bauhaus Dessau Foundation.

Rizzo, A. (2009a) 'Border Cities in the Baltic Sea'.Urbanistica-INU. 140, 36-41.

Rizzo, A. (2009b). 'The Multiple City.Tallinn as playground to test new paradigms in urban studies'.In T. Ilmavirta (Ed.), Regenerating Urban Core.Publication of the YTK/IFHP Urban Planning and Design Summer School. (pp. 44-57). Espoo, Finland: C-series of CURS. Espoo, Finland: Helsinki University of Technology.

Sandercock, L. (2003) Cosmopolis II Mongrel Cities in the 21st Century. London, New York: Continuum.

Sandercock, L. &Attili, G. (2009) Where Strangers Become Neighbours. New York: Springer.

Stuart, Netami. (2011) 'Urban planner'.Interviewed by M. Galanakis. Toronto, June 13.

Vilkama, K. (2011). 'Moving in or moving out? Development of spatial concentrations of immigrants in Helsinki'. In Eckardt, F. & J. Eade (eds.) Ethnically Diverse City, pp. 421–444. Berlin: Verlag.

INNOVATION

Poplar HARCA
working with local
Police to make
Stroudley Walk
safer by design

POPLAR
HARCA

Stroudley Walk: once a vibrant market street. Source: Deljana Iossifova/SCIBE

TOTAL COMMUNITY RETROFIT
The Institute for Sustainability

IMAGINE THIS...

It's 2030 and local people are planning, designing, delivering, owning and managing a range of local projects, which are stimulated by the transition to a low carbon economy.

There has been a tremendous growth in social enterprise, small businesses and jobs for local people as a result of delivering a more sustainable environment; from local people being trained to refurbish the homes of their friends and neighbours or encouraged to set up a new local logistics company delivering goods using bicycles and electric vehicles. This activity has been funded by a mix of traditional government and private investment and innovative local micro financing initiatives and social investment bonds.

Underused and derelict buildings and land brought back into use have, amongst other things, led to an explosion of local food growing initiatives. New not-for-profit organisations have found a home in underused council buildings and a new business that 'upcycles' waste has found premises in a vacant private building.

People are behaving more sustainably - they own or have a share in local energy generation assets and can see how saving energy benefits them financially as well as the local environment. The local council and housing association have teamed up to create a 'community benefits' funding pot, using a proportion of their Feed In Tariff and Renewable Heat Incentive revenues, which local people can bid into to support their favourite project.

A local group made up of students, digital champions and industry computer programmers has been making their own sensors to measure everything from noise and park usage to when their vegetables need watering. The online Community Dashboard is a one-stop source for travel advice, local community activities and news.

...and there has been a massive reduction in CO2 emissions and fuel poverty.

TOTAL COMMUNITY RETROFIT

'The neighbourhood is a geography and a scale that resonates with people. Neighbourhoods have always been a powerful and important part of how we view city-building, and how we view ourselves as citizens.' (Hanscom, 2011)

The Institute for Sustainability is developing and delivering a demonstrator project in the London Borough of Tower Hamlets, in the Bromley-by-Bow and Poplar areas. This project will

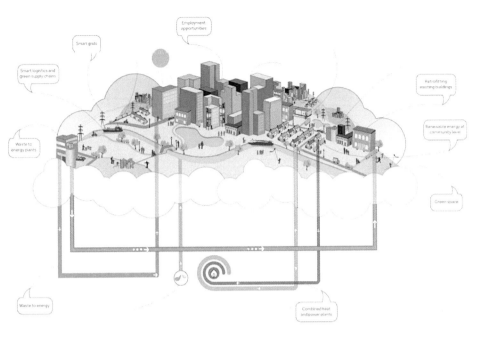

Figure 4-1 The Institute's Total Community Retrofit (TCR) aspiration starts with the premise that to deliver sustainable cities we need large-scale and systemic innovation. Source: Institute for Sustainability.

involve local partners and local people in transforming the area into a thriving community ready for the world of 2050. Local partners are working together to start to deliver that vision in 2013.

By approaching the challenge at neighbourhood scale – approximately 50,000 people in this case - and addressing all the elements of a sustainable community together, it is possible to create a more optimal solution that improves community cohesion, health, well-being, employment levels and fuel poverty, as well as quality of the environment. The traditional individual programme approach often misses opportunities for synergies and efficiencies. However, activities in Bromley-by-Bow and Poplar are being designed and delivered in a systemic and joined up way. They include:

* **Building retrofit** – residential, commercial, industrial and municipal properties
* **Decentralised, smart, clean energy** – solar photovoltaic energy generation; combined heat and power plants
* **Connected Community** – linking people, technology and services; empowering local people to use data for informed decision-making
* **Closed Loop Community** – upcycling; waste to energy plants; reclaiming and reusing resources locally
* **Green initiatives** – local food growing on unused space; sustainable behaviour programmes
* **Green jobs and skills** – jobs, skills and enterprise training for local people and businesses
* **Sustainable transport** – electric vehicle car clubs; local walking and cycling schemes; sustainable last mile logistics.

Two schemes currently in progress in Bromley-by-Bow and Poplar are summarised below.

CASE STUDY – CLOSED LOOP COMMUNITY DEMONSTRATOR

To increase self-sufficiency and resilience, cities of the future will need to transform their approach from 'disposing of waste' to 'maintaining and recovering resources'. Cities that manage resources well will accrue economic, environmental and social advantages, especially when the approach is integrated with other city systems. The Closed Loop Community Demonstrator will focus on resource retention and recovery creating local economic opportunities and value, building self-sufficiency and resilience, and reducing greenhouse gas emissions.

What it is?

Currently the London Borough of Tower Hamlets has a contract with Veolia for the collection and disposal of refuse and recycling and cleaning. The local Registered Social Landlords (RSLs) also have a responsibility to remove bulky goods or waste from their property. All the waste currently collected goes outside the borough for treatment or is taken to landfill. This project presents the opportunity to deliver better environmental services to the local area while creating employment and business opportunities for local people. Over time, the project will lead to savings which could be reinvested in the community to help deliver on other, new initiatives, which will help ensure on-going, local community buy-in for the project.

The benefits include:

* Reduction in greenhouse gas emissions and carbon footprint; optimised energy capture; minimised embodied and imported energy
* Increased local jobs, skills and educational opportunities; revitalised local markets and shops; a self-sufficient, empowered and sustainable community; improved resource efficiency and avoidance of resource scarcity
* Targeted increase in recycling rates from 26% to 80%.

The initial phase of the project will focus primarily on bulky goods, waste electric and electronic equipment (WEEE) and food collection pilots. More generally, the project will result in increased local awareness of the value of waste, particularly recyclable waste, which will help achieve an overall increase in local recycling rates.

Bulky waste - Furniture and other large items tends to be fly-tipped in local estates where they become damaged and unusable. They are subsequently collected and disposed of as waste. A simple, local scheme that involves collecting, storing, repairing and re-distributing within the community will provide huge benefits.

Waste electric and electronic equipment (WEEE) - This relates mainly to computers, laptops, washing machines, fridges and other white goods. WEEE is not currently collected and is a significant source of pollution in the area. There is a good market for metals as long as components are separated properly. Setting up enterprise locally to reclaim valuable components or identify WEEE with resale value will create skills, training and job opportunities for local people.

Pilot estate based collection models for food waste and other materials – Innovative collection models particularly for tower blocks could significantly increase recycling rates. Identifying new ways to deal with food waste particularly could have a number of positive impacts locally. One initiative considering an anaerobic digestion plant would mean food waste would be collected and then used to produce compost (possibly for local food production schemes) and energy for local homes. The plant would attract investment and create new jobs in the area.

Current project development:

* Initial scoping work to assess how WEEE and bulky goods are currently collected

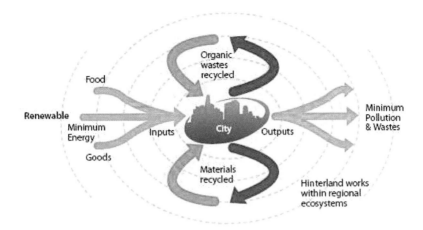

Figure 4-2 The Institute's Total Community Retrofit (TCR) aspiration starts with the premise that to deliver sustainable cities we need large-scale and systemic innovation. Source: Institute for Sustainability.

* Determine the scope and volume of waste needed to make the proposition viable
* Plan communications to attract and engage residents to use the collection services
* Identify which businesses to engage with the project to provide materials and generate revenue as the project starts
* Identify which electronic companies could be interested in partnering on the project
* Initial scoping work around the creation of a local facility including development of a business plan, and identifying potential sites and funding streams
* Exploratory work underway to identify how to engage and attract innovative SMEs to the area.

CASE STUDY – CONNECTED COMMUNITIES

Changes in government, business models, technology and demographics present new opportunities and challenges to deliver sustainable cities and communities. Residents are presented with a bewildering array of choices for accessing essential services, including health care, home energy, and council services. These services are often not joined up, increasingly complex, and internet-based. While some residents have the means to take advantage of this changing landscape, many others may not. In many cases residents may be in vulnerable situations – perhaps due to heath, income or disability challenges, for example.

At the same time, exciting opportunities are emerging to use technology in a way that can empower residents. By taking advantage of planned investments, in activities such as building retrofitting and new smart energy grids, we have the opportunity to develop innovative new approaches to providing community services while, at the same time, providing better personal and community information. These innovations can help individuals save money, live more sustainably, and enjoy a healthier and more resilient lifestyle.

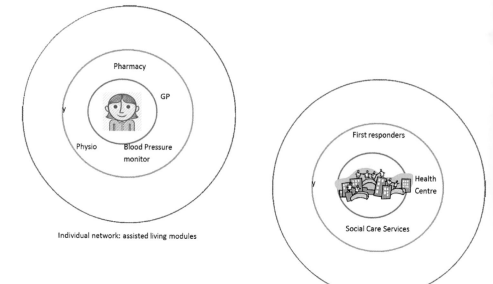

Figure 4-3 Putting people at the centre of local services. Source: Institute for Sustainability.

What it is?

The Connected Communities project will involve developing a flexible platform to link people, services and technology, providing a holistic approach to community resilience, health and well-being. The early phases will be built on the twin platforms of buildings resource efficiency (home energy management systems and smart meters) and health services (telemedicine and assisted living). Work has started on both elements locally. The Connected Communities demonstrator will include the following key components:

* **Technology** – a personalised hub that brings together various websites, data devices, sensors (e.g. HEMS, medical devices, communication and scheduling tools) and delivers information to users through an appropriate user-friendly interface
* **Services** – a 'community concierge' support organisation that focuses on integrating and matching service provision to user needs, providing efficient delivery of community services (health care, security, energy management, financial planning, outreach, etc.)
* **People** – networks for promoting knowledge sharing, community collaboration and real-world interaction

The system will provide seamless, active information for local people through supplementing their own data with local information.

Current project development

* Building a partnership with technology providers, local community groups, GPs and others to start a process of co-designing the connected communities platform
* Identifying data sources including energy meters, room sensors, appliances, health aids, medical records and banks

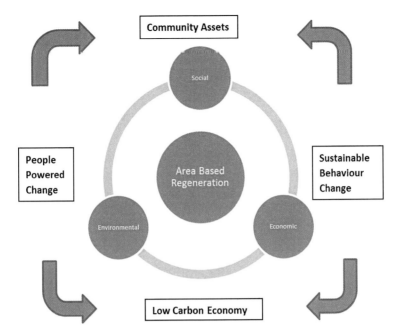

Figure 4-4 People powered change. Source: Institute for Sustainability.

* Planning for local, contextual and service information will be fed in directly from support services or indirectly via the management envelope.

CONCLUSION

Current approaches to making our existing cities more efficient often focus on taking isolated easy-to-implement measures, such as insulating homes, encouraging the switch to energy efficient products and promoting public transport usage. A step-change is required to make the transition to sustainable cities that makes the most of limited public funds, attracts institutional investment and secures the passionate engagement of communities. To do this we have to approach the challenge of transforming our cities in a different way. Total Community Retrofit is an integrated whole-system approach to renewing homes, businesses and communities so they are resilient, productive and low carbon.

This is not a radically new approach. It is the next increment step towards 2050 cities building on best practice in area-based regeneration with new innovations. As with all good area-based regeneration schemes, a systemic approach is critical – the aim should be to create economic, social and environmental value in a sustainable manner.

However, a failing of previous schemes has been a lack of deep engagement and ownership by local people. It is not enough to consult; change powered by local people is the only change that is likely to be sustained and sustainable. Every community facing problems contains within it people and groups who step forward as the solution. People cannot be the passive recipients of change; they must own the change and be its beneficiaries.

165

References

Hanscom, G. (2011) The next small thing: How sustainable neighborhoods could reshape cities. Grist, [blog] 30 November, Available at: http://grist.org/cities/2011-11-29-the-next-small-thing-how-neighborhood-level-sustainability-effor/ [Accessed: 18 February 2013].

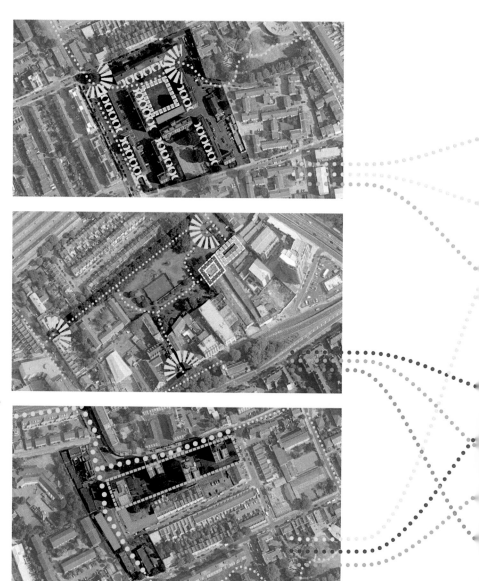

TEAM 2: URBAN ACUPUNCTURE

Students: Annalisa Lodigiani, Clenn Kustermans, Farinaz Falaki, Seppe de Blust

Tutors: Teresa Franchini and Judith Ryser

CULTIVATE IT

OPEN IT

FILL IT

LEARN IT

SELL IT

FIND IT

TEAM 6: SOFTWARE UPDATE FOR BROMLEY-BY-BOW

Students: BjörnBracke, DominikaDudek, Matteo Basso, Rui Santos

Tutor: Fotis Grammatikopoulos

BUILD RESILIENT COMMUNITIES!

* Complete dependence on external capital carries the threat of disequilibrium: revenue 'flows out' of the region
* Community based development is likely to give rise to a self-sustained system with revenue staying in the region
* Governmental institution/regulations should be cautious of business models which allow to transfer the revenue outside of districts
* Local leaders should press for profit re-investment in the region
* Policies should support the establishment of small scale cooperative housing with appropriate financing and regulatory mechanisms

FOR INSTANCE...GAMIFICATION

Collective 'green' action provides benefits for neighbourhoods:
* More natural and pleasant living environment
* Common goals (to become sustainable!) empower people
* Possibility to generate savings (generating own energy, etc...)

The main challenge in raising public awareness of environmental issues is to restore the understanding of how the use of space and resources is related to environmental and social consequences. Therefore we have to connect technical and behavioural aspects to social and ecological value chains. By using technological developments in the built environment we could provoke a shift towards ecological perception. In order to encourage people to adopt technological devices (e.g., 'ecometers') in an urban context, technological devices could be implemented through the concept of gamification.

Gamification is the use of game mechanics and game design techniques in non-game contexts. Technological devices in combination with smartphone apps and social networks to connect citizens to institutions and (public) services result in hyper-connected environments that harness the network effects and increase the involvement and understanding of citizens.

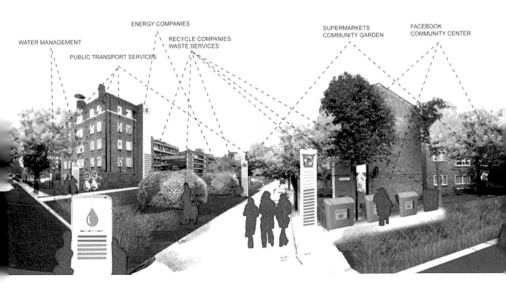

WATER MANAGEMENT

PUBLIC TRANSPORT SERVICES

ENERGY COMPANIES

RECYCLE COMPANIES
WASTE SERVICES

SUPERMARKETS
COMMUNITY GARDEN

FACEBOOK
COMMUNITY CENTER

SENSITISATION

Stroudley Walk
as it could look from
here

POPLAR
HARCA

READ & CAKES
RISPS & SNACKS
IRY PRODUCTS
USEHOLD
T FOODS

OFF LICENCE

• BEER & CIDERS
• WINE & SPIRITS
• CIGARETTES
• GROCERY
• MEDICINES

WHOSE SCARCITY? WHOSE ABUNDANCE?
ISSUES IN MOTIVATING (RE-)MAKING THE CITY
Peter B. Meyer

This essay, a reworking of the presentation made at the Third European Urban Summer School in September, 2012, addresses the policy and planning pitfalls associated with imposing externally-derived standards of scarcity (in the case of this example, scarcity of space). Whatever the recorded conditions of 'objective' scarcity existent in Bromley-upon-Bow or any other neighbourhood, it is necessary to address the issues associated with applying society-wide standards on a neighbourhood or community. The problems in such attribution of nominally objective standards arise on several levels, including:

* The 'need'to address scarcity in meeting minimum physical standards for well-being, possibly most importantly with respect to conditions contributing to health conditions.

* The dangers in terms of exploitation of 'scarce' urban land of imposing external standards to define blight and thus provide entry for nonlocal investors to gentrify an area and displace its residents. (Another US case is illustrative here: the 'scarcity' – actually absence - of closet space in an Italian-American neighbourhood in Boston once created the legal basis for razing the homes, though the residents were all using large wardrobes, many imported by their families, for their clothing, rather than the closets required under more modern building codes.)

* The economic imperatives associated with the minimum qualifications requirements for some employment outside the neighbourhood and the implications the scarcity of such qualifications for local economic well-being.

* The barriers to cooperation and collaboration with community residents in making a more supportive neighbourhood that are raised by outsiders' articulation of standards of scarcity that they do not share. (A highly likely scenario in Bromley-upon-Bow given Bangladeshis' view of their needs for space and the UK standards for overcrowded housing.)

My objective here is two-fold: (a) to sensitize readers to the difference between planning with a community and planning for residents, and (b) to highlight the risks that any forms of planning 'for' may result in an excess emphasis on planning for places rather than people. To achieve these ends, this essay addresses the question of the bases for judgment used by analysts – and in turn policy-makers – in defining urban problems and thus responses. The argument proceeds through four steps, comprising my major sections:

* Personal Context – Sources of Bias
* Standards – Good or Bad Bases for Planning?

* Looking at Some Examples
* Concluding Remarks on Method and Process

There are no firm conclusions, simply recommended methodological and logical processes intended to assist outsiders in understanding the perceived and experienced problems and proposed solutions of communities of which they are not members. The objective of the exercise here is to assist policy-makers in their efforts to work with, rather than for or on members of communities experiencing urban ills. In a subsequent essay, I turn to some issues of method, mostly focusing on the processes and pitfalls of data collection and interpretation in 'alien' environments.

PERSONAL CONTEXT – SOURCES OF BIAS

Bias is inevitable. There is no such thing as an objective analysis. While some comparisons and measurements may be recorded and the numbers used for decision-making, the fact that there is reliance on such measures does not produce objectivity since the process of deciding what to measure and how to do so is itself biased.

Most bias emerges first from the characteristics and perspectives of the analyst. For illustrative purposes, let us look at me as an example of a bundle of sources of bias. I am:

Male – No matter how hard I try, I am not capable of fully reflecting – or perhaps even absorbing and reflecting, a woman's view of problems, scarcities or other issues.

American – My cultural background includes a set of values and an analytical perspective that leads me to both a set of expectations about social processes and a tendency to value different phenomena and outcomes in ways that are consistent with my nation's societal norms.

'Elderly' – I am over 65. Depending on their cultural backgrounds, residents of neighbourhoods in which I attempt to work may want to please me and thus give answers that they think I expect, or they may dismiss me as irrelevant and not bother to provide me with data that require some thought or effort to generate. Either way, my understanding of others' perceived needs and concerns would be distorted.

Economist – My disciplinary training induces me to adopt a methodology that leads to measuring certain phenomena and not bothering with others. That is certainly a biasing tendency, especially when combined with the socio-cultural biases of my nationality.

Multi-Disciplinarian – To the extent that I spent my academic career among faculty from different academic disciplines, this source of bias has been weakened. This broadening of perspective has come not merely from exposure to other disciplines, but from participation in interdisciplinary research. (For a different personality, however, the reaction to challenges to one's methods from other disciplines could take the form of a hardening one's posture as an economist.)

Experienced in diverse cultures – I am a rarity among Americans in this regard. Europeans by and large are more broadly exposed to other cultures than citizens of the United States since they live with much narrower national boundaries. But 'other cultures' does not necessarily reflect experience in cultures steeped in different religious and social traditions, such as those of Latin America, Africa or Asia. I have spent time in depth in all three areas.

Relatively affluent – Globally, this label applies to all residents of the 'developed world' – including those perceived as 'poor'. More important to an outsider's ability to work with a neighbourhood in his/her own country is the prospect that the individual is of a higher socio-economic status than local residents. This difference produces barriers, raised on both sides, to acquisition of an understanding of the locals' actual conditions and their attitudes towards them.

Politically left of centre – Labels on such perspectives do not work well, with the majority of Democrats, the left side of the national political array in the US, arguably to the right of the Conservatives in the UK and other EU member states on social issues. Personally, I am so are to the left relative to US political norms that I find much of the Labour posture in the UK to be conservative. I am biased toward pursuit of community and minority empowerment and poverty alleviation.

Religious or moral perspective of a non-practicing Jew – Religious beliefs may form the basis for a perspective on the world, the importance of different 'social problems' and the role of different institutions in addressing those issues. The stronger the adherence to a religion-based moral perspective, the more that grounding may overcome any political leanings. My political outlook reflects my morality. But that is because I have no strong religious beliefs.

'Recovering economist' – Obviously, this is not a common source of bias. It is a label my wife, a PhD in Sociology, applied to me. I reference it her to highlight the final point to be made in considering bias: the potential errors made in measuring and labelling the sources of biases themselves.

In effect, this is a warning akin to the old adage that 'you can't tell a book by its cover.' The 'obvious biases' of an observer of – or participant in – a community or social process may not in fact, be operational in reality. We should not attribute all differences in observations to the apparent differences in the perspectives of the observers.

STANDARDS - GOOD OR BAD BASES FOR PLANNING?

Arguably, the real issue is not whether reliance on standards is good or bad. There is no potential for planning without some objectives and intents, and these ends can only be expressed in terms of some sort of standards. The important question, then, is the quality of the bases for planning that is, the nature of the standards themselves, not the reliance on them. We thus need to consider the typical origins of standards and then some issues associated with any reliance on them.

Some Origins of Standards

Cultural Norms – Standards almost inevitably emerge in part from social norms and a culture's perceptions of reality and what is valued in life. Cultures can be extremely local, as evidenced by language dialects and accents, so standards emerging from such norms can vary from city to city – or neighbourhood to neighbourhood.

Economic Myths – The myth of the marketplace as the 'accurate' measure of what anything that can be bought or sold is worth underlies many standards. In the case of property development, there is often reference to 'highest and best uses' as a desirable standard for the appropriate use of land, meaning the use that would bring the highest price. But what produces the highest use for a private landowner may not be the appropriate standard to guide decisions on the uses of publicly owned or controlled land.

Political Systems – The role of politics in setting standards is, perhaps, most obvious in the determination of what the standard should be for public participation in a planning process, with democracies valuing high participation and authoritarian regimes rejecting such a process. On a finer scale, however, democracies can differ drastically on their degrees of political centralization, which affects the standards for local control of – or even participation in – planning processes and decisions.

Economic 'Realities' – This term is used most frequently to refer to the constraints under which planning decisions must be made. The standard imposed by constraints is, of course, that they should not be violated. However, nor all perceived constraints are real, and those that are may be subject to modification If effort is expended, so standards based on assumptions that current limits on alternatives remain in place may be misguided.

Some Issues with Standards

Extent of Acceptance – However rational and appropriate a standard may be for a planning decision, the finding on the course of action to take will be suspect if the standard is not widely accepted as appropriate. Planners who assume that the communities on which they act will share their acceptance of guiding standards for action may be in for a rude shock in the real world of divergent cultures, political perspectives and economic constraints, all of which can undermine acceptance of some standards.

Costs of Compliance – Lip-service to a standard may not constitute adherence to it, if the costs of complying with a set of constraints are too high. Those costs need not be monetary in order to significantly constrain compliance. Standards that challenge local cultural norms can result in community-wide cooperation in noncompliance as an assertion of cultural identity. The failure of nonlocal planners to understand local norms thus can distort the impacts of any plans.

Malleability / Rigidity – The ability of national planning standards to adapt to local norms and perceived economic realities may be the key factor in their effectiveness on the ground. Thus the rigidity of a standard may be a negative, despite the risk that malleability leaves standards subject to the political influence of powerful interest groups. Within a local community, especially one with cultural norms and political traditions that differ from those of a nation, state/region or city imposing externally-driven standards, the most powerful interests may be those of the distinct society. This issue may be especially salient in areas with a single dominant immigrant or other distinctive population.

Potential for Change by Affected Parties – Potential for change is obviously associated with malleability. The issue here is the ability of those at the local level to modify inappropriate standards through their own interventions. A distinct population group may be the most powerful local interest, but it may still not have sufficient influence to be able to act on non-local decision-makers that have been influenced by economic power blocks that have shaped a malleable standard in their self-interest. A standard may stand in the way of responsive planning if, for example, a local low income immigrant group may not be able to modify the standard to preserve preferred uses of space while a national property development association has that power and acts in its own self-interest.

Aside on an Economist's Language

Demand – This has very special meaning in economics. It is not synonymous to 'need' or 'want' but refers to the monetary expression of perceived needs and wants in a marketplace. Thus a need experienced by a population with little money may never arise as a demand in a market economy, even if the need is for a resource such as food that may be required for survival.

Deprivation – This term refers to the scarcity of access to some resource by a population. That scarcity might be considered relative to the access available to others in a society or relative to some minimum. For our purposes here we shall use the term to refer to 'absolute' deprivation – access at a level below some accepted standard.

Poverty – This is the term we shall use for relative scarcity, to distinguish access to resources at levels below societal norms but above accepted minimum standards.

Growth – This means what one would expect – and expansion is size or quantity.

Development – By contrast to growth, which can happen in local property values or a community economy, many use this term to refer to those forms of change, sometimes including growth, that increase the power of a community, neighbourhood, or other social unit to influence events and shape a desired future.

Cost and Benefit – These terms, used in policy-makers' cost benefit analyses may include a range of factors beyond those readily measured or exchanged and thus reducible to a monetary measure.

LOOKING AT SOME EXAMPLES OF STANDARDS AND PLANNING

Four examples serve to make my point here, two from the United States and two from London itself. Before offering US examples, it is necessary to provide some perspective on the legal bases – and limits – for action in the country, since public planning has a very different status in the US than elsewhere.

'Urban Renewal' in the US is the process of clearing land and/or buildings in order to, in principle, permit regeneration. Under the laws of most of the US states, this process permits compulsory taking of property for independently determined prices (labelled as 'exercise of eminent domain'). Exercise of this power, however, requires a finding of 'Blight' in the designated setting in order to permit action. The standard may have the effect of promoting displacement and gentrification (and may be intended to do so). Ambiguity and uncertainty – and conflict – arise from the definition of what constitutes a blighted condition.

Blight, arguably, involves the failure to meet some societal standard, But that standard could be: (a) aesthetic ('it is ugly'!), (b) economic ('they are impoverished' or 'the site is underutilized'), (c) 'cultural' ('they don't conform to our norms'!), or (d) some combination of these and other subjective judgments. Not surprisingly, where norms differ, poor planning outcomes may result.

Boston, Massachusetts, USA

Boston's old 'South End' is now a major financial centre of high rise office buildings. But it was once a thriving Italian-American working class neighbourhood. The city has garnered increased property values (and thus revenues from taxation of that property) and, arguably, attracted more financial sector jobs as the result of displacing the residents who once lived in the South End. Whether the social costs imposed are worth the economic gain was certainly an issue when the planning decision to acquire and raze the neighbourhood was made.

The process was a perfect example of the undemocratic application of a rigid societal standard. The South End was not impoverished: as working class it had below median incomes on average, but that does not mean 'poor.' It was not immigrant: it was ethnically almost completely Italian-American, but most of the residents were second or third generation native-born. It was only marginally 'crowded' by then current standards of appropriate area per person in dwelling units, reflecting the somewhat lower than average household incomes. The area became visibly dirty, but only after Boston reduced its frequency of waste collection in the neighbourhood. The dirt could not hide the fact that the buildings themselves were structurally sound and well maintained, wither owner occupied or used for apartment rental.

So the city was hard pressed to find any sort of 'blight.' It turned to the letter of the current standards for residential occupancy. Those requirements, mandatory for new construction but arely applied to existing occupied buildings, specified the number and size of closets relative to bedrooms and intended occupants.

The South End had old buildings and a paucity of closets. The residents used the huge wardrobes that their immigrant families had brought over with them from Italy and were not inconvenienced by that 'flaw' in their housing provision.

Violation of the closet standard, however, was sufficient to produce a finding of blight and resulted in the forced destruction of a fully functional urban neighbourhood. Did that rigid standard contribute to good planning?

Louisville, Kentucky, USA

Louisville, home to the Kentucky Derby and the largest city in its region, once built itself an airport just outside of the city limits. The city surrounded the airport as it expanded spatially. Later, United Parcel Service (UPS) began overnight delivery using air transportation – and chose Louisville as its US national air hub. By the 1990s, the airport needed to expand. The three surrounding neighbourhoods had income levels slightly above, but educational attainment slightly below the local medians. They were, unusually for the city, racially integrated, and had dwelling units built in the 1950s that were small, only 65 per cent of the then current norm. They suffered from severe environmental problems, with noise level double that of city median and air quality significantly lower than that of the city (which itself was below US Environmental Protection Agency standards).

Since the time the homes in the area had been built, they had become hedged in on all sides by noisy, polluting transportation systems: rail along one side, the airport on another, and along all other boundaries wide thoroughfares and motorways carrying diesel truck as well as automobile traffic. The city claimed the area was blighted by its environmental factors and took it by eminent domain.

However, market economic measures of blight were absent. Home owner-occupancy rates in the area exceeded those city-wide. Property generally sold by word of mouth, if homes were not passed down in families. Over a 20-year period leading up to the declaration of blight, local property values in the three neighbourhoods, as measured by sale prices rose significantly more than those in the city as a whole. Obviously, the residents viewed their community and homes by standards that differed from those applied by the city.

In a society that measures vale by market prices, how could the neighbourhoods be considered blighted? In fact, the top court of appeals in the State of Kentucky ruled that the finding of blight was unjustified and required the city to pay additional compensation to the residents that they had displaced. That ruling, however, took place after the fact and failed to preserve the neighbourhoods. The reliance on a standard to justify an intended planning action clearly can lead to both distorted application of the standard and to bad planning decisions.

Bromley-by-Bow, London, UK

Turning from the US to the UK, we can look at the contrasting assessments of Bromley-by-Bow reflected in official statistics and residents' responses to questions. The local data collection by the Scarcity and Creativity in the Built Environment (SCIBE) project team underscores the differences in perceptions and reflects vastly different standards applied to the quality of the physical environment by British and London public assessments on the one hand and the residents of the neighbourhood on the other.

By National Standards, Bromley-by-Bow is acutely overcrowded, with five times the residential population density than the level prescribed by national housing standards. The residents are predominantly low income. Not surprisingly, given their incomes, they are far more state-dependent for the resources needed to survive than most communities in Britain. Culturally, they are overwhelmingly immigrant, with household heads, if not children, born in Bangladesh; they are perceived as ghettoized, especially those that speak little or no English. (Their language barrier reflects the low educational attainment of the immigrants, since English is the language of higher secondary and all tertiary education in Bangladesh; the lack of schooling also implies minimal exposure to the modern economy prior to arrival in the UK.) The area is also seen as a 'food desert' with no large food stores in the community, though access is available just outside the neighbourhood. Green space is not seen as a major issue, given proximity of a major park and small green areas scattered in the neighbourhood.

By the Community, however, life in Bromley-by-Bow is seen very differently. Housing density is actually far lower than the Bangladeshi norm. The housing provision is faulted not on unit size, but on the number of bedrooms for families that are far larger than the UK median. The residents feel they have economic security that was unattainable in their home country, where there was no state provision for the needy. That said: they feel they lack opportunity for economic advancement, which to them often involves the ability to form their own businesses, not to seek employment by others (which would be the expectation of most of the poor in England). They find their setting physically secure (which is not outsiders' perception), but alien and they miss access to more outdoor space despite the parks.

Given these different perceptions of the conditions in Bromley-by-Bow, there is little likelihood that planning decisions based on national and/or London-wide standards will be seen as appropriate by members of the community. The contrasting perspectives virtually assure that what would be 'good' planning from the perspective of even the London Borough of Tower Hamlets, the governing local authority which tends to accept the national standards, would be seen as inappropriate by a large fraction of the community residents in Bromley-by-Bow. Planning based on national standards for a setting in which they are not appropriate may well do more local harm than good.

Applying national standards and ignoring local insights can, moreover, result in planning outcomes that may be 'poor' even by national standards. One excellent example of such an outcome exists in another London neighbourhood close to Bromley-by-Bow on which the full force of national planning and economic powers has already acted: the London Docklands.

London Docklands, UK

The Conservative Government of Mgrs. Thatcher created the London Docklands Development Corporation (LDDC), with a board appointed by the Government and responsible only to Parliament for its decisions and actions. The LDDC was given full planning powers, including exceptional rights of compulsory purchase, along with substantial budgetary resources.

The remit to the LDDC was the economic revitalization and regeneration of the derelict and abandoned enclosed East London docks and the surrounding neighbourhoods. While the docks were no longer international transport centres and many buildings adjacent to them were deteriorating, the area as a whole was not abandoned. Myriad small business enterprises used pockets of space along the docks. They were surrounded by residents living in mostly council housing estates to whom they provided employment and who constituted the customers for their retail marketing.

The rationale for the LDDC, however, was the attainment of the 'highest and best use' of the docklands property. They were expected to apply a national standard predicated on economic mythology – the accuracy of market valuations as measures of the social benefit to be gained from use of land. With the financial centre of London ('The City') adjacent, it was appropriate under this standard for the LDDC to look market its land assets to financial firms rather than the current users and occupants simply because the former could pay more.

This turn to non-local demand to shape decisions on new land uses, however, had the effect of muting the voices of the local community. The loss of input from the locals, in turn, led to decisions about retention and demolition of buildings that ignored many of their current or future potentials. This was especially glaring in the case of large open structures associated with the docks that could have served as recreational centres. Despite the objections of, and detailed documented plans offered by, the London Docklands Consultative Body (LDCB), those structures were demolished ... and later new recreational facilities were built to serve both new residents in riverfront housing and the workers in the new high-rises of the Canary Wharf.

The LDCB was grounded in the docklands communities and had local expertise and knowledge. It offered information from a source that the LDDC, because of its structure and remit, could not tap efficiently: local people and organizations. In ignoring the information available from the LDCB because its interest in neighbourhood preservation, however, the LDDC failed to accurately measure many of the impacts of its actions.

Using national standards for the number of employees per unit area in different businesses, the LDDC underestimated the number of jobs it would affect by displacing local businesses since Dockland employers used more workers in smaller spaces. Applying national data on the number of firm closures associated with relocations, the LDDC failed to recognize the impact of displacement on the very tenuous and fragile Docklands-located firms: the vast majority closed their doors when they lost their premises. Similar errors were made with respect to employability of local residents in the new businesses attracted to the area and with regard to residents' willingness to relocate or to commute to work when the previously walked to their jobs.

The result was very expensive regeneration with massive displacement and all the social and economic costs that entailed. New premises for the City might, alternatively, have been provided at lower overall costs on some of the underutilized docklands while retaining and refurbishing existing buildings rather than building new and while still providing for revitalization that served people already in the locality.

CONCLUDING REMARKS

We first must confront the planning methods and objectives to be brought to bear on a neighbourhood. Is the objective broad strategic or is it narrow community-focused planning? That may determine the appropriate consultative or participatory processes to be employed.

Planners and the planning process brought to bear on a community need to be examined for their ability to address locally-specific factors in any case. That capacity will vary with:

* Sources of standards (and the dialectics of their creation and modification), including those for (a) Physical elements or (b) Socio-Economic elements of the plans.

* Sources of the planning body's power to act – and sources of local organizations' potentially countervailing powers, which may be derived from (a) Legal, (b) Economic, or (c) Political / Moral / Cultural foundations, or some combination of them

* The extent to which the powers to act can be exercised by both external and internal

institutions. That is, the extent to which the powers are, or may become, complementary o competing.

Even if community enhancement is the defined objective of the planning process, the organizational context of the planning body involved remains crucial. In the US, there has been a great emphasis on planning through, with or by so-called 'community-Based organizations' but the label of 'CBO' has been found to be a misnomer.

An organization may be located in, that is placed, in a community, but not based in it. Local residents, businesses and property owners (not absentee landlords) may have apparent power in terms of their participation, but that is insufficient. Do the planning staff and those with power to make decisions see their roles as 'doing for' neighbourhood stakeholders rather than 'working with' them? If so, they are not really community-based. Even if planners see themselves as collaborators, not providers, they may still fail to serve specific sub-communities within a larger neighbourhood, such as the ultra-religious, the disabled or other group with special needs o interests.

Immigrants may, as in the case of Bromley-by-bow, constitute such a special group. They may have extensive self-help organizations, but may be reliant on external funding since immigrants typically have limited resources. That dependency, however, may constrain their ability to fully reflect idiosyncratic interests out of fear of alienating their funders. The organizations' capacity to represent the special constituency as a whole may further depend on their inclusivity.

Thus reliance on planning participation by even specialized interest organizations may fail to reflect all relevant interest. The US 'War on Poverty' of the 1960s and 1970s pursued 'maximum feasible participation' of those being served in the management and administration of public programs. A similar logic might be appropriately applied to individual residents' participation in planning processes and decision-making.

Such an approach is not particularly revolutionary for planning practice. The increasing reliance on open-access charrettes in US planning reflects an effort to provide individuals with an opportunity to participate in both problem definition and development of responsive plans. The charrette process is not new, but borrowed from long-standing practice in architecture. It can of course, provide only limited participation access and may be structured to only make plans to address pre-defined issues. The process can, however, be made open and be employed to define as well as respond to planning problems.

But even an open access problem-defining charrette has to either start from or begin by defining some set of standards participants can agree are appropriate for decision-making. Those structuring and participating in the process need to determine the degree to which planning decisions that have long term consequences for the physical environment can be based on idiosyncratic factors and considerations.

This need then leads inexorably to a requirement that locally-specific judgments about the applicability of nominally objective standards to the problem at hand. Even the UN's Millennial Development Goals, crafted with an eye to global cultural and economic diversity, may be too narrow and prescriptive for individual countries, let alone communities. Private business standards such as those developed by the ISO (International Organization for Standardization) similarly need to have malleability to fit individual enterprises.

Planning to respond to a particular community's scarcities need not distinguish between the 'real' and the 'perceived' since such a judgment imposes a rigid external standard. It does, however, need to derive its own internally consistent definitions of the problem(s) to be addressed and the bases for assessing the costs and benefits associated with alternative responses to the identified problem issue(s). Global standards are not inherently bad, but the absence of conscious adaptation of those criteria to local issues cannot be good.

TEAM 3: LET THE PEOPLE TALK!
Students: Anna Háblová, Katia Pimenova, Mateus Lira da Matta Machado,
Rony Hobeika, Tuba Dogu

Tutor: Peter B. Meyer

I WISH THIS WAS

YOUTH CLUB

I WISH THIS WAS

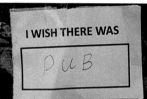

I WISH THERE WAS

PUB

I WISH THERE WAS

BIG MARKET
ON WEEKEND

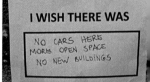

I WISH THERE WAS

NO CARS HERE
MORE OPEN SPACE
NO NEW BUILDINGS

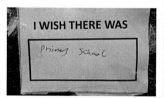

I WISH THERE WAS

Primary School

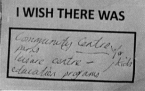

I WISH THERE WAS

Community Centre
parks
leisure centre —
education programs

I WISH THERE WAS

Parks

I WISH THERE WAS

BIG MARKET
ON WEEKEND

I WISH THIS WAS

PUNK Rock BP

I WISH THIS WAS

SHOP

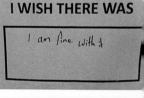

I WISH THERE WAS

I am fine with it

I WISH THERE WAS

More plants, trees, flowers and
benches.

I WISH THIS WAS

YOUTH CLUB

THE RULES OF THE GAME: SCARCITY, REGULATORY REGIMES AND OPEN SPACE IN BROMLEY-BY-BOW

Naznin Chowdhury, Carlos Manns, Nick Wolff, Alison Killing

In a plan of Swan Housing Association's recent development at Rainhill Way, external areas are shaded in three colours. The light green, spread around the refurbished and new build housing blocks, denotes 'Green Space'. A few darker green areas are 'Formal Playspace'. Somewhere in between the two is a swathe of orange marking 'Incidental Playspace'.

These coloured lines on maps tell a lot. Within five minutes' walk of Rainhill Way are numerous open spaces managed by other housing associations, private developers and Tower Hamlets Homes (the council housing management organisation), each with their own terms of classification and regulation. If we zoom out to the Bromley-by-Bow ward borders and plot all the nine areas recognised as open space by Tower Hamlets council, we find none of the open space at Rainhill Way on the map we produce. Mapping everything the council calls a park produces an even smaller cluster - just five spaces within the ward.

These simple maps take us directly to significant questions about how urban space is being produced, classified, measured and regulated in Bromley-by-Bow - and how this relates to its use, interpretation and meaning by those who live there. The curiously precise delineation and classification of open space in a new housing development suggests considerable thought went into its provision. But what thought, by whom, under what influences? And what does it mean to someone living at Rainhill Way or the surrounding areas in Bromley-by-Bow as they unwittingly chase a football across Incidental Play Space and into Green Space?

REGULATORY REGIMES

At one level, it is helpful to consider these questions in terms of institutions and how they work together in different circumstances to take and implement decisions. We can call the dynamic and complex interactions between powerful institutions that get exercised through governance structures and codified in policy and regulations 'regulatory regimes'. If we use the concept of regulatory regimes as a loose framework, it is helpful also to acknowledge regime theory, which places our context in the neo-liberal philosophy that has so shaped London's planning and regeneration policies since the early 1980s.

The collapse of municipal approaches to development over this period, the growth in public private partnerships, fragmentation of council housing and expansion of housing associations are reflected in the range of institutional actors involved in producing urban space in Bromley-by-Bow. Poplar HARCA, Swan, Barratt and Circle Anglia are all currently developing land or buildings, which will provide new or re-shaped public open space. Development finance brings its own heavy influence to bear on what gets built and to what standards. A mixture of private financial institutions and the post-crisis remnants of Greater London Authority and local authority regeneration budgets are currently supporting various developments to a point of precarious 'viability' (with amenity and non-market elements such as playspace the first to give way in the face of any balance-sheet squeeze). As the state has reduced its role as a direct producer of urban space through building or finance, in favour of a regulatory and influencing role on the market, so the regulatory agencies have come to the forefront as the main lever of publically accountable control over urban transformation. London's complex planning and design guidance operates at a minimum three levels simultaneously, national, city-wide and local authority, with the London Legacy Development Corporation also holding planning and land assembly powers in part of Bromley-by-Bow and exerting its influence from the east. Wider government agencies, such as the police, contribute their own influence, as do bodies such as RTPI and RIBA in shaping professional practice and philosophy.

We find that in Bromley-by-Bow the regulatory regimes concerning the production and regulation of the built environment are as fragmented and complex as the space they produce. Yet the picture becomes complicated further by internal tensions in the multiple functions of institutions, not least the local authority, as the main regulator of day-to-day use of open space in the area. The management of Council owned trees is currently shared between several departments (66% Parks and Highways, 10% Housing, 2% other municipal areas). (Tower Hamlets Council, 2006)

The Tower Hamlets open space strategy lists nine areas in the ward which are classified as open space. These are areas that benefit from some planning protection and local authority interest in their preservation and good use. They are not all under council ownership and management, yet the council has laudably produced a document (London Borough of Tower Hamlets, 2012) to assist groups or organisations that wish to hold an event on any of these spaces. Tellingly the advisory note runs to 22 pages, lists 19 parts to an event plan, 11 suggested further readings, no fewer than 11 'key contacts' and 20 health and safety considerations. This is not to imply a criticism of those who produced the document but it illustrates the complexities generated by large organisations' external obligations and internal diversity of function, ironically highlighted when trying to simplify the public's free and creative use of open space in the borough.

The recently reviewed by-laws for Tower Hamlets parks are another case in point. Acknowledging the difficulties in coming up with an all-encompassing set of regulations through a democratic local body, and which need to retain their relevance decades into the future, the outcomes are, perhaps inevitably, curious. (The banning of a range of highly-specific activities can be productively seen in its inverse: If I cannot practise javelin, discuss, hammer or shot, could I pole vault and hurdle? What else can I do here?). However, it is perhaps more telling to look once again at where these regulations apply. They apply only in the parks. Or rather, the designated Parks of which there are just five locally. In this fraction of all the open space in Bromley-by-Bow, legalised regulations have been put in place that apply neither across other council recognised open space nor the extensive green and open spaces that surround the estates, be they marked on a map as Formal Playspace, Incidental Playspace, Green Space or simply unnamed and underused 'amenity space' looked after by one of the several housing providers in the ward.

This cuts to the core of the challenge of understanding how influence and decision making over public space in Bromley-by-Bow has been consolidated within institutional standards, that have been made impenetrable by the fragmented and complex inter and intra-institutional structures, influences, interests roles and functions that shape them. The implications are significant at the institutional level - In terms of how space is planned and provided, how space is classified and measured (as adequate or inadequate) and how it is protected and regulated.

But it is at the lived level, the social and the street, where we need to reflect on how scarcities are constructed by this complexity of regulation. The institutional map is illegible on the ground, it only makes itself known when the boundaries of regulation are accidentally transgressed or challenged. How do people assign value and meaning to their open space and take ownership over it in this context? And how can they find strategies to engage with this institutional complexity of regulation to make it more meaningful or even change it?

ACCESS TO ALL - USEFUL TO ALL?

Sharon Zukin says that the essential characteristics of public space in urban environments are 'proximity, diversity and accessibility' (Zukin, 1995: 262). These features are important particularly as we are looking at public space in a diverse, densely populated area of east London. Moreover, we need to establish a definition of public space which goes beyond 'access to all', and looks to draw in principles which make public space enabling and useful to those who access it.

The characteristics outlined by Zukin are important in our analysis of public space provision in Bromley-by-Bow for two reasons: firstly, to consider whether the provision of public space meets the needs of the community living in the area, and secondly to conceptualise scarcity in how regulatory regimes affect both the provision and the use of public space. One of our main areas of interest has been whether a sense of ownership and belonging could be fostered without a person or the community owning or having the private right to access space. Public space exists to be shaped by those who use it; people have a right to the space and should have a sense of belonging but equally a level of ownership of the space.

'OPEN' SPACE?

Research conducted by Tower Hamlets Council suggests there is a significant deficit in open space. The statistic which is applied to this assertion is 0.4ha of public open space is available per 1000 residents in the area, compared to a 2.43ha standard set by the Mayor of London. This deficit in open space is reported in 2006 and again in the 2012 area Master Plan. But how this deficiency presents itself is as important as the deficiency itself; the vagaries in the way that open space is institutionally labelled, and hence measured, present an apparent physical lack of free public space that is not necessarily recognisable when walking through the area. But we also wanted to pay attention to the apparent limitations of the space that is available. We wanted to identify the missing elements that lead to public space not maximising its potential as meaningful and dynamic space.

The importance of open space/public space should not be overlooked. Numerous studies (Green Alliance/Demos) have concluded that those living in disadvantaged and deprived urban environments like Bromley-by-Bow, are negatively impacted by the lack of access to natural and open space. However, in assessing how public space could maximise its potential we looked beyond just a lack in terms of provision sufficient to the population, to how well space is being utilised by local people and whether it truly empowers them. Through the project we identified large amounts of open public space scattered throughout Bromley-by-Bow. This was 'un-designated' space, spaces of potential which were un-used, un-discovered and ignored in assessments of 'designated' open space by the council.

In order to gain a good understanding of the Bromley-by-Bow area within the context of the research we carried out interviews with youth and community workers groups as well as making general observations when we visited the area. We identified the following as a series of circumstances around social regulation of open space produced in the community, by people, irrespective of the instructions in guidelines and regulations.

* Surveillance: promoting a sense of safety through connection, such as parents sharing the tasks of keeping an eye on young children when they went outside to play.

* Spatial ranges: determining where young people interacted and agreeing safe distances with their parents on how far they could travel to play, how this influenced the places where children chose to congregate and how what was allowed by one parent might influence an overall group.

* Sacred places: discovering places through exploration; the young people discovered their 'own' special place which they visited regularly to play and look for foxes and named this place 'Bamboo' They associated 'Bamboo' with a certain level of possibility and danger which made it more attractive to them. This idea of discovering sacred places resonates in Anna Minton's (2009) book Ground Control where she writes about a lack of open space for young people to discover.

* Negotiation: the potential of negotiation to forge creativity and shared interest; this was illustrated by an example given in Bob's Park where a woman with a young child negotiated sharing space with a group of young boys who were playing football. There is an assumption that this very rarely occurs - due in part to the expectation that institutionalised authority will step into disputes - however if encouraged it could happen more frequently helping those using public spaces to interrelate.

* Territoriality: claiming spaces and appropriating ownership; young people had many stories of being chased out of areas or told off by adults for activities such as drawing on pavements with chalk, suggesting regular small tussles over ownership and meaning of spaces that hint towards potential for a more dynamic view of meaning in public space.

These features, we suggest, are co-created by the community but under-utilised through a lack of encouragement and opportunity. Strategy and governance documents currently underestimate the worth of these circumstances of social interactions. They allow people to explore the sphere of possibility and engage with others to negotiate the use of space in a way that lets it be defined by them, and not for them. How can we get to Lefebvre's idealisation of social space as a 'means of human reappropriation through the development of counter space forged through artistic expression and social resistance' (Lefebvre in Butler, 2009; 11)? How public space is viewed and the understanding of social space needs to be adjusted or redressed to mould it in such a way that it allows for space to represent a creation/ensemble of interaction and social relations by users and those who provide public space. We can argue that the use of space in this way is utilised and produced more effectively and frequently by those with wealth or access to provision and resources. For those living in deprived areas where there is an obvious lack of resources there are barriers to this realisation, and the empowerment to act can take longer. Naturally this is more complicated than simply those who have wealth and those who do not but what is being emphasised here is that public space is always under construction by its users, therefore re-appropriation of space for those who may not have a strong sense of ownership needs to be assisted through a grassroots or community led strategy.

In the interest of health & safety please do not
bring dogs, glass or Alchohol into this area.
Smoking is strictly prohibited.

This is your play area, please help us to keep
this site in good Condition.

Figure 5-1 'Formal Playspace' - Rainhill Way. Source: Carlos Manns.

The purpose then of an open space or play space strategy should be to go beyond a set of guidelines and regulations that define and portion the amount of space available to local people. It needs to list a set of apparatus that allows social action to be envisioned or realised. This is an approach to thinking about the provision and arrangement of space as enabling, and as a socially dynamic concept as well as a physical construction. Making the important distinction between use of public space as currently measured and highlighting why it is crucial to define or redefine uses. Communities are diverse, consisting of a collection of identities expressing and co-existing together, therefore it is logical that public space will need to be negotiated. Although commonality and establishing common features is useful, it can be more useful to explore the differences that need negotiation and encourage a more relational perception of open space, making a case for strategies for a public space always under construction and reconstruction by its users, open to possibilities, diversity of meaning and shifting moments of ownership.

STRATEGIES WITHIN INSTITUTIONAL STANDARDS AND WITHIN SPACE

When it comes to possible strategies it might be necessary to take a double approach: as observer and as practitioner, allowing as much reflection on the discoveries as action on the ground. The importance of strategies - besides the shape - includes the capacity of a middle-man to integrate purposes and resources, to allow the coexistence of a diversity of visions and to navigate in the politics of the intra-institutional structures as well as the spatial and social of lived space.

'THIS IS YOUR PLAY AREA'. MEANING AND VALUE OF OPEN SPACES

In Bromley-by-Bow, under the private-public institutional mechanisms of 'public space' provision which are set under pre-existing scarcities - financial and land constraints among others - resources are maximised and redistributed as an institutional provision of 'benefit', within a financially sound solution-making approach from developers. This structured institutional provision transforms the perceived value of common areas of space and finds its legitimacy on a label where space use and function is determined beforehand. Spatial outcomes in the shape of community assets are then value-modified through these forces.

Written boards on pitches and playground will put emphasis on phrases such as 'this is yours', insisting on the 'right to use'; typological use will promote mono-activity and lack of variability, as well as fragmentation of space and territorial adaptation40 especially from younger groups.

Kids will inherently challenge boundaries and concepts, especially those that have been imposed on them. A fence that has been removed, or a space that finds another use will challenge the regulatory regime, but not at the policy level of control apparatus which retrofits - in a vicious cycle - the imposition of institutional regulation in design and regulates behaviour in space through estates regulation and guidelines.

These dynamics rarely promote a sense of belonging in changing a sense of private ownership. From early design phases processes have not been properly set in place that can allow others' interpretations on what and how these provisions can be, nor allow instances of future adaptation. Under the existing regulatory regime design has little room for other possibilities since design practices are exercised under constraints that reinforce structured institutional mechanisms of regulation which promote ownership, functionality and object-based outcomes.

RULES OF THE GAME. DEFINING STRATEGIC ACTIONS FOR OPEN SPACES IN BROMLEY-BY-BOW

A strategy could draw possibilities of working mainly at spatial and regulatory level, drawing on Brian Massumi's (1997) idea that an 'emergence of codes of rules follows the emergence of an unformalized proto-sport'. This understands the game as a constant process of emergence and evolution, where 'circumstances arise that force modification of the rules' (Ibid). This process allows a wide range of variation of events, uses, activities and actions to appear which are endemic to a game.

For Massumi, regulation 'has all the reality of a formation of power' and 'will then capture and contain the variation'. We see this formation of power and further containment of variation as a potentially inclusive and open process. A further codification is a framing derivative that a regulatory code can arrogate to itself the 'role of foundation', setting only precedence for further game play.

In the context of Bromley-by-Bow a strategy could have as its main objectives:

* Redefine value of open space;
* Unlock common areas and public space for other uses and other interpretations;
* Promote challenging regulatory regimes by enabling groups to establish their 'rules of the game'; and
* Build sense of belonging, allowing flexible and inclusive processes and common-sense.
* Give access to open space and facilitate spatial resources as common assets for a more comprehensive approach to the area.

This might be achieved by:

Figure 5-2 New rules of the game? Community art, Bromley-by-Bow. Source: Carlos Manns.

* Allowing more variability of possible activities that can take place. Variability can allow space for experimentation; for negotiated design processes where pre-conceived rules can be superseded by grassroots regulation and common sense;
* Enabling future residents as well as architects and planners, associations and other actors to access decision making and to participate in the role of foundation of any code or regulation;
* Participation and evolving negotiations: these can open up other meanings of space provision, meaning and values. It can bring a possibility of less dependency on institutional determinacy in favour of more socially driven regulatory scopes with their potential for an enhanced range of meaning and value for spaces.
* These opportunities for participation and evolving negotiations must stay open to circumstances where community surveillance, spatial ranges, discovery of new places, negotiations and territoriality among other circumstances can happen.

Some initial exploration with grassroots groups reveal many that are already encouraging young people to exercise different activities that are in an indirect way challenging the standard use of spaces. Others are seeking to implement new community-led activities in restricted open areas. Working strategically at the grassroots level offers the observer and practitioner opportunity to explore with users the impact of a top-down provision and regulation of public open space on such aspirations. This role can then evolve to assisting in identifying entry-points to interventions that can both reveal existing regulatory structures to scrutiny and open up the possibility of change.

Acknowledgements

The work that has informed this text was carried out under the Scarce Times: Alternative Future project, through the SCIBE programme. Alison Killing of Killing Architects also partnered with the authors in this project and contributed to the ideas presented at the EUSS.

References

Butler, C. (2009) 'Critical Legal Studies and the Politics of Space', Social Legal Studies, 18 (3 313-33.

Massumi, B. (1997) 'The Political Economy of Belonging and the Logic of Relation' in: Davidson C. (Ed.) Anybody, Cambridge: MIT Press. 174-189.

Minton, A. (2009) Ground Control: Fear and happiness in the twenty-first-century city, London Penguin

Tower Hamlets Council (2006) An Open Spaces Strategy for theLondon Borough of Towe Hamlets 2006 - 2016. Last accessed online 18 February 2013, http://www.towerhamlets gov.uk/lgsl/451-500/465_open_space_strategy.aspx

Tower Hamlets Council (2012) Advisory Notes for Events 1st January 2012 – 31st December 2012 Last accessed online 6 November 2012, www.towerhamletsarts.org.uk

Zukin, S. (1995) The Cultures of Cities, Oxford: Blackwell.

EMBRACE ME WHEN I'M WALKING: SOME PERSONAL NOTES IN NON-JARGON

Clenn Kustermans

After being in school benches for a couple of days and listening to a dozen people saying that Bromley-by-Bow is the most deprived area in the UK, I went out for a walk in Bromley-by-Bow. Because I couldn't confirm or deny what was said. Because I wanted to see it myself.Because I have always been attracted to deprived areas.To swap jeans in a butcher shop downtown Joburg. To walk and eat in Belsunce, Marseille.Parts of New Orleans.Real-life scarcities, daily scarcities. I had great expectations.

And Bromley-by-Bow showed its sad side that rainy day. Sad houses, sad shops, sad people walking by, sad cars on wet streets. A sad breakfast with beans swimming down Stroudley Walk. Poor whites gambling their bits of money at Ladbrokes.Women with burkas and tender but discrete eyes walking out the beauty salon.A post office with an ATM, a vegetable shop, some women wearing plastic bags with whatever. No real British English but English as a mix of many tongues. Something beautiful. And it actually wasn't too bad at all; despite the rain Bromley-by-Bow actually looked alright that rainy afternoon. No beggars, no hustlers, no streetwalkers, no kids scraping for food. People with families and houses and yes, possibly poor and with hard lives in bad working and housing circumstances, but it didn't seem to be too bad...

Met Henry in a pub. He wore a jacket of the Belgian army and he had a four day beard. He wasn't Belgian and he wasn't very well-mannered but he was alright. A bit of a disappointed socialist.Unemployed, divorced twice, accumulation of things. Henry told me some things about Bromley-by-Bow, a place where he has lived since twenty years. You know, pub talk, not too personal and not too subtle. About East London, that it is poor, that it has always been poor and that it will always be poor. It's a matter of geography. East London was boggy and thus unused and thus cheap land outside the city walls, where the industry was placed when the factories became bigger and unhealthier. Moreover, East London was downstream and the prevailing wind direction in the UK is southwest so the rich in the city wouldn't have the stink of the industry in their gardens. But the working-class was placed close to the factories too. And although the industry is disappearing in London, the social structure has been laid and that won't change. A few pints later I thanked Henry for his interesting evaluation and evolution of a place over time. Time to hit the road.

I walked on, caught a bus that took ages to Central London. Hopped off, walked through the rain-rainer-rainst and saw the speculative side of London, cold modern buildings and unappealing Victorian buildings (was Victoria a relative of Dracula?) and I crossed the Thames

and the undefined colour reminded me of the Scheldt back home and I walked on and London wasn't very nice to me and I begged her to embrace me because I have longed for her (London is female to me, but a cold one) but she didn't and finally she wouldn't and stinking tube corridors and two tubes brought me to my hotel where I dried up.

A few days later I walked through Bromley-by-Bow again. The sun shone and the neighbourhood wasn't bad at all, in fact, it looked alright, I mean, it was a nice place to be. Shops with market stalls in front, locals knowing each other and chatting and flirting, gentle double-deckers stylishly dancing down Bow Road.Et cetera. I met John who ran a coffee shop in an alley north of Bow Road (his name probably isn't really John, but he looked like a John to me in such convincing way that it could have been his own nickname too). 'You're not from around, are you?' he asked me when I studied a map. Some words later I explained him I'm an urban planner attending a summer school with scarcity as its theme. John didn't really understand. I told him I was interested in how Bromley-by-Bow could be improved. Spatially, socially et cetera. 'Ah yeah, I see', he replied. He then told me he had just started his coffee shop a few weeks ago. Why here? Because it is 'affordable in London terms'. John also told me about the London climate of so-called gentrification developments that jumped up like mushrooms all over the city. 'You know, those private developments for the wealthy few who want to engage in relationships to afford their overpriced homes'. Gated blocks, anonymous apartments that could be anywhere. I stirred my coffee. 'I saw gentrification as a more or less spontaneous development', I told him, 'creative minds settling in poor neighbourhoods and attracting shops, bars and so forth, as in Berlin for example'. John said there where areas like that in London too - and actually he is one of the

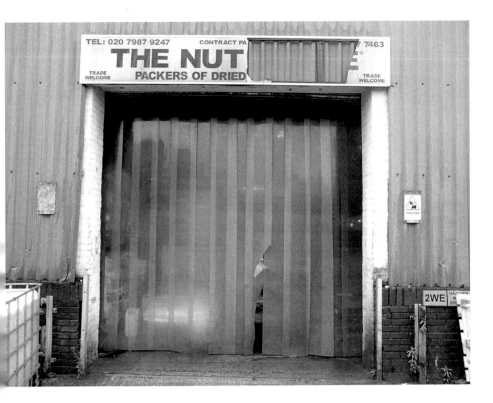

pioneers in Bromley-by-Bow himself, you know, with his fancy coffee and all that. Some more words later John said there might be a lack of shops and bars in the neighbourhood. He referred to Hackney as a place where the creative minds have gentrified the area. 'But behind the lively main streets in Hackney there are blocks of social housing too'. As I went out I saw Bromley-by-Bow differently. Does it have potential to become a liveable place?

Scarcity. I looked at that word in July 2012 when I tried to write an article. What did it mean, a lack? Less supply than demand? Or scar city as in a city with scars? Eureka! I started to write about a city I had visited a few times, a city with scars of a certain period in its lifetime, a city where money is scarce and where people are getting scarcer, a city that had riveted me from the first time I saw it: Chemnitz in East Germany. A shrinking city where creative thinking might create liveable space.Fast forward to October 2012. London isn't shrinking. But London does have areas where creative thinking is also needed to create liveable space. Especially in times of scarcity. Although I still can't define scarcity. But I do know that scarcity means more than lack and that it means more than just a supply and demand thing. I am working on it.

So.Bromley-by-Bow.

Generally spoken people leave if there is no work. But in cities it is different. There are always places where people will live if they do not have any other possibilities. The cheapest places close to factories and motorways.Where parks are scarce and ugly et cetera.To commute every day.Long days. To get depressed, drunk and divorced. Bromley-by-Bow apparently is one of those places (although I still can't confirm or deny it). I walked around a bit, sat in bars and I spoke to some people.

Now there are a lot of things to do around Bromley-by-Bow and there is nothing to do within Bromley-by-Bow. Is that bad? Might be. Around Bromley-by-Bow you can shop, eat and drink, meet people, spend time, spend money. Bow Road in the north has big and small shops, bus and tube stations, religious facilities, administrative amenities, monuments, office spaces to let and so on. There's a park and playground down the coffee shop alley as well. In the east, beyond the motorway A12 and in the Lea River valley there's Tesco and there are businesses and parks and housing developments. Further east there's the Olympic park, although I still cannot believe this would contribute to the regeneration of Bromley-by-Bow specifically or East London generally. South of Bromley-by-Bow there's a quasi-industrial zone with wholesalers, mosques, a concrete mixing company with many trucks, an artist colony, a sandwich bar with a friendly lady and a pub with a man in a Belgian army jacket. In the west there's something beautiful too: small car handlers' shops have settled in the brick arches underneath the DLR railway track - you wouldn't dare to make a picture and economically it's very marginal but very entrepreneurial. Very fascinating, indeed.

But within Bromley-by-Bow there's hardly anything to do. And therefore it could be a nice place to live, to stroll with your kids, to enjoy a quiet atmosphere. But it isn't. It's a place where nobody wants to live (apparently). Stroudley Walk is a local centre like there are many in Europe: a handful small shops ran by struggling locals, a health centre where you do not want to be brought to if you may choose, a lot of unused space (you can't call it a square) and an overall depressing atmosphere. And although you can't really see it, Stroudley Walk is only a stone's throw from Bow Road...

So here's the deal: add things that attract people to Stroudley Walk. Because then the area becomes lively, safer, shops can flourish, people are happier. Build units that can be used to run a business. Create a mix of smaller and larger-scaled enterprises (beside John's coffee bar it would be good to have one or two bigger attractors like a supermarket or a chain shop). Just to get some locals in the streets permanently. Urban designers can think about the improvement of the spatial/ physical connection to Bow Road so that people walk in and out almost automatically. And if the London condition of so-called free market is of that sort that large-scaled gentrification projects are being built, then let that be. You can't fight that, and you don't have to. Look at the bright side: there are more people living in the area, that's good for safety and local enterprises. But I still believe that a city can ask something in return for real estate development. The development company can invest in local amenities too, in public space, in big things that actually cost little money for those who have a lot of money but that are of great use for those who have little money.

I do not have a concluding sentence because my work in Bromley-by-Bow is not finished yet. I must talk a bit more to Henry, who will still live there for another twenty years, and to John, who might stay there a bit longer, too.

PROGNOSTICATION

Summer School/RIBA Student Charrette participants in Sugerhouse Studios. Source: Jeremy Till/SCIBE.

SCIENCE FICTIONALITY
Bodhisattva Chattopadhyay

LET'S FACE IT

DYSTOPIAS ARE EASIER

TO CREATE

TO PREDICT

TO PRESENT

THAN UTOPIAS (APOCALYPSES ARE EVEN EASIER)

THAN UTOPIAS (A PLACE TO BUILD OUR DREAMS)

UTOPIAS (OUR DREAMS)

What is science fictionality? It is not science fiction, not an envelope for literary or aesthetic artefact, however economical or extravagant. Science fictionality is the way in which we narrativise possibilities, whereby the experienced reality of our lives as individual and as species is temporally directed towards the future and conditionally bound to technoscientific change. Take for example the narrative of 'planetary boundaries', perhaps the quintessential science fictional narrative of our times in the dystopian vein. In 2009, Johan Rockström from Stockholm University and colleagues in a small article in Nature wrote about these 'nine boundaries that define the safe operating space for humanity with respect to the Earth system and are associated with the planet's biophysical subsystems or processes'. This was followed by the usual apocalyptic rhetoric: 'If these thresholds are crossed, then important subsystems, such as the monsoon system, could shift into a new state, often with deleterious or potentially even disastrous consequences for humans.' (Rockström et al., 2009) There were the terms that have in contemporary time become media watchwords: phosphorus, ozone depletion, climate change. There was also the usual cluster of allied associations: sustainability, conservation. Et cetera. In the humanities, GayatriSpivak, half a decade before, with her usual boldness, had proposed the acceptance of a new concept: 'planetarity': the recognition that we existed as a species, on a planet loaned to us. (Spivak 2003)

The same vocabulary, with the humanities inflection, watered the plant of her interdisciplinarity. We are running short of essentials, and time is running out. This narrative of planetary boundaries, itself an amalgam of ideas that have their origins in the industrial revolution, and even in their present sense since at least the first atomic weapon, transforms the future from an infinite field of mysteries to a dimly lit blind alley. A general alarmism maintains the industries of despair, and rightly so, and ensures continued funding for concerned activity: some of us need to fix the lamps on that blind alley.

Like all narratives, there is a villain in this story: the city. The city, with its vastness, networked impersonality, randomness, sewers and waste, represents at once the pinnacle of human industry and the cornerstone of its modernity, and its exact opposite, a wasteland symptomatic of human wastefulness and degeneracy. If artists are to be believed, we are heading straight towards the anarchy of McCool and Templesmith's 'Shotgun City':

'devo-fucking-lution: how we have embraced you. We're living in one big melting pot of futility and folly, and somehow it continues to flourish. There's not a thing I can do about it. Not anymore. Mutiny has ravaged the ship and we are slowly sinking. Note even the sharks will want to eat us.' (McCool and Templesmith, 2010)

I wanted to explore here the relation of the city of London to science fictionality, to see in particular the ways in which the narrative of degeneration and decay pervades a representation of the city in science fiction literature. This is because science fictionality, although more than the genre of science fiction, is certainly allied to it. It is in fact it is the defining characteristic of the latter, for we cannot have something called science fiction that is not science fictional. For IstvanCsicsery-Ronay, Jr. Science fictionality is characteristic of all of what he calls technologiade, 'the epic of the struggle surrounding the transformation of the cosmos into a technological regime' (Csicsery-Ronay 2008). Science fictionality is what allows us to understand the mechanisms by which the science fiction text engages in world-building and constructs the relations internal to that world.

London, as a megalopolis, has all the attributes of a city one can imagine. Or maybe one can say, like Disraeli in Lothair, that London is a nation, not a city (Moorcock 2012: 33). It had those attributes in the time of William Blake when he wrote about chartered streets and mind forged manacles, and things just kept getting more city-like. Fin-de-siècle alarmists spoke of outcast London, a theme that has recurred at various points since then, including, recently, China Mieville's 2009 novel The City and the City. Herbert Spencer and Francis Galton weighed in with their science fictional opinions on eugenic manipulation of the race in order to nip the degeneracy and decadence in the bud. Stoker came up with Dracula, a Romanian undead feudal lord let loose in London to terrify its wealthy bourgeoisie that had grown with colonial trade. The novel bloomed in Victorian England.

And then a certain kind of literature began to be written, which introduced a speculative element into the mix. This speculative element was of at least two different kinds. One was analogical, in which the speculative was an extension of the present, and the other metaphorical, in which the speculative mirrored the present. H. G. Wells, the father of the British tradition of this literature, wrote examples of both, and stretched the limits of the future state of London. The War of the Worlds recreated British colonialism in Tasmania and placed it in London where the Martians became the colonisers ruthlessly eradicating the 'natives':

'And before we judge of them too harshly we must remember what ruthless and utter destruction our own species has wrought, not only upon animals, such as the vanished bison and the dodo, but upon its inferior races. The Tasmanians, in spite of their human likeness, were entirely swept out of existence in a war of extermination waged by European immigrants, in the space of fifty years. Are we such apostles of mercy as to complain if the Martians warred in the same spirit?' (Wells 1898: 4-5)

The Time Machine (1895) stretched class divisions to a point where humanity evolved into two distinct species. The workers became the industrious yet cannibalistic Morlocks, while the bourgeoise became the beautiful, 'consumptive', infantile Eloi. The Time Machine story was set in Surrey, not London, although a number of sequels have been set in London.

'But at first, starting from the problems of our own age, it seemed as clear as daylight to me that the gradual widening of the present merely temporary and social difference of the capitalist from the labourer was the key to the explanation. No doubt it will seem grotesque enough to you and wildly incredible, and yet even now there are circumstances that point in the way things have gone. There is a tendency plainly enough to utilize underground space for the less ornamental purposes of civilization; there is the Metropolitan Railway in London, for instance, and all these new electric railways ; there are subways, and underground workrooms, restaurants, and so forth. Evidently, I thought, this tendency had increased until industry had gradually lost sight of the day, going into larger and larger underground factories, in which the workers would spend an increasing amount of their time. Even now, an East End worker lives in such artificial conditions as practically to be cut off from the natural surface of the earth and the clear sky altogether... So, in the end, you would have above ground the Haves, pursuing health, comfort, and beauty, and below ground the Have-nots; the workers, getting continually adapted to their labour.' (Wells 1922: 114-117)

Richard Jefferies wrote After London in 1885, and it is one of the first examples of postapocalyptic fiction in Britain. A catastrophe decimates the population, and the few survivors try to adapt to the new surroundings. The novel is in two parts; in the first we are given a description of the new London, which is a swampland and the second is the adventure that makes it science fiction instead of a future history. There is a subtle distinction between future history and the science fiction. The future history plays with the notion of truth; that incidents recorded in such a history will be realised in the future, like prognostics or what is now called foresight studies. Wells had a good phrase for it in his own future history: 'the shape of things to come.' Science fiction does not claim historicity as a vector; it claims its truth from science. Although a few utopias did come up, particularly socialist utopias like William Morris' News from Nowhere (1890), a majority of the works dealt with chaos. And after the chaos, the dissatisfaction of a society and civilization that has crumbled. Lord Dunsany's Joseph Jorkens, world explorer, in the nineteen thirties and forties, tells fantastic stories in a London club about the Empire in an Empire coming to an end, trying to restore magic to a world with no more dark places. By mid-twentieth century, it all became part of one big story, the story of what we call science fiction. And when the 60s new wave with writers like J. G. Ballard and Michael Moorcock came on the scene, post world war trauma, cold war threat, and psychedelic drugs mingled in the surreality of their vertical cities and flying cars. Moorcock described his fantasy landscapes as the product of war-time experiences, specifically, wartime London.

'The metamorphosis of Blitzed London became the chaotic landscape of Elric the Albino. As in need of his soul-drinking sword as Chet Baker was in need of his junk, he witnessed the death of his Empire, even conspired in it. The adrenaline rushes of aerial bombardment and imminent death informed the Jerry Cornelius stories where London's ruins were recreated and disaster had a celebratory face.' (Moorcock 2012: 21)

His New Worlds colleague, J. G. Ballard, probably the most important science fiction writer of the last half of the twentieth century, whose ideas on science fiction also gave rise to the term 'architecture fiction' as an equivalent of science fiction, wrote:

'The world is continuing to grow more surreal. The external world is now a kind of huge surrealist novel that we all inhabit, and we look more and more to our own imaginations to find reality. That's a complete reversal, of course, since the heyday of surrealists in the 1930's. The surrealists set out to remake the external world using the interior world of fantasy, and that's been reversed. You treat reality now as if it's a huge dream. That's the way you can make sense of, let's say, somebody like Ronald Reagan. You've got to treat the landscape of television, of advertising, of politics conducted as a branch of advertising, of your friends and the way they furnish their homes, and yourself, as if you're a figment in a dream. That's the classic surrealist approach.

I can't see this trend reversing itself, simply because as the prosperity of the world increases people have more leisure time, so we're moving into what will be a wholly entertainment culture. And the world of work, in the traditional sense, will have passed into oblivion. People will live for the hours of recreation and entertainment. Increasingly, everything in life begins to mimic the entertainment industries. We see the traditionally serious professions such as medicine and architecture moving into the realms of show business, with show business lawyers who behave like film stars. The whole of postmodernist architecture is an off-shoot of surrealism: the use of architectural forms to express fantasy. .. But now these surrealist jokes are now in the form of hundred-million dollar office blocks.' (Ballard 1988)

From technofutures they retreated to the 'inner space' of the Ballardian world, trying to define a new aesthetic for a new generation where hope was a luxury, and ultimate redemption, impossible. From there to a nostalgic return that we find in British steampunk, usually based in London, is but a small step, even when the works are deliberately subversive, like the Luther Arkwright graphic novels by Bryan Talbot. They imbue the far future with Victorian sentimentality.
This is, in most ways, the state of contemporary British science fiction. Or what is British in it anyway. Some authors have all but abandoned Britain for stories of the far future, for example, Ian M Banks sets his novels in 'Culture', similar to Star Trek in that it is set in a post-scarcity (and in some ways post-national) galaxy, but different in its technological framing, and different in that Culture is about colonialism at a galactic and universal scale whereas Star Trek is not. In some ways both universes are conservative: both revisit the old idea of the expanding frontier in the Western but for a completely different purpose. In the western the characters need to expand in order to find and create better places for themselves, in a post-scarcity world characters need to expand because they are bored with having everything, and must therefore seek adventure 'boldly' out there. There is nothing recognizably British in Banks. An occasional exception to the rule are

episodes of the British television series Dr Who. But the most exciting exception to this is the work of China Mieville. Although most of his work is set in the alternate universe of Bas Lag, Mieville has consistently focused on the city of London (in books such as King Rat and UnLondon) in his work, although the London he describes is very much in the same tradition.

Yes, that is what I wanted to explore. But then I realised I would not. Not because of shortage of material, for London has been the focal point of much science fiction (and also, of fantasy) since its inception, and the history of London in science fiction is yet to be written. But I wouldn't for two reasons.

One, dystopias are easy. And British science fiction, or, if I were to follow the author and critic Brian Stableford, British scientific romance, has always loved dystopias. In fact, Nicholas Ruddick, trying to identify the existence of such a thing as British science fiction in order to distinguish it from its American counterpart, identifies pessimism as one of the chief characteristics of the British tradition. Everywhere in British science fiction, we find things coming to an end. To a certain extent this is due to an obsession with the twin tropes of Empire and biological determinism, and since the nineteenth century, the laws of thermodynamics, which Barri J. Gold calls 'thermopoetics' (consider for instance a play as recent as Tom Stoppard's Arcadia.)

Two, depending on your scale, uniqueness of a city is an artefact of its past and present, and a footnote of its future. The future city, for anyone willing to look past the geographical tyranny of the present, is not a unique location. The future city is a space altered by globalitarian forces into a dispersed homogeneity; every city in that future is 'The City', and all that existed before it will have uniqueness catalogued and displayed as in a cabinet of curiosities or an exotic zoo, peddled for tourist smiles and the picture postcard.

The reason then that I chose to alter the focus of my talk slightly is that we can take any city and sample its uniqueness alongside its familiarity. We can do so even now. The speculative tendencies of a futurist run along the lines of familiarity rather than uniqueness. And because I did not want to speak of dystopias. It is science fictionality; but what I refer to specifically is an unvarnished belief in the magic of the future, and our capacity to not merely survive it, but find our way to the stars. Space cities if you like. That would be a good beginning.

Warren Ellis, the prominent English transhumanist and graphic novelist, in his keynote speech at the 2012 Improving Reality Conference, 'How To See The Future' engages in a similar thought process. Ellis's point is simple. He takes issue with VentakeshRao's term 'manufactured normalcy': 'the idea is that things are designed to activate a psychological predisposition to believe that we're in a static and dull continuous present.' This is because, Ellis explains, a loss of wonder. Science fiction ideas of the future seem to have either been realised in tiny gadgets (the table and the Star Trek TNG PADD – personal access display device for example), and a sense of living in the science fiction condition itself has become a symptom of banality, so much so that people explore everything through a 'rear-view mirror'. Where are those magical inventions that were promised to us in the 1920s? And when something is invented, we try to discover its origins. We have our face turned either backwards or upstream, and we have stopped perceiving the present as magical, where every moment new ideas, concepts and technologies are coming to life. Ellis asks us to restore our faith in the science fiction condition, and the magic of the present.

'Reality as we know it is exploding with novelty every day. Not all of it's good. It's a strange and not entirely comfortable time to be alive. But I want you to feel the future as present in the room. I want you to understand, before you start the day here, that the invisible thing in the room is the felt presence of living in future time, not in the years behind us.

To be a futurist, In pursuit of improving reality, is not to have your face continually turned upstream, waiting for the future to come. To improve reality is to clearly see where you are, and then wonder how to make that better.

Act like you live in the Science Fiction Condition. Act like you can do magic and hold séances for the future and build a brightness control for the sky.

Act like you live in a place where you could walk into space if you wanted. Think big. And then make it better' (Ellis 2012)

Science Fiction condition.Science Fiction.Science Fictionality. Ellis' point is a valid and a subtle one, but there are more problems in the Science Fiction condition than Ellis has space for in his very short keynote. This is not because humanity always looks at things through a rear-view mirror, or is not caught in the charm of novelty; it is because novelty itself is considered an inevitable product of living in the science fiction condition. Science is the eugenics of ideas. As 'science,' however defined, comes to refine our ideas and our picture of the universe, what is novel therefore, and how society develops, is considered bound to linearity, the linearity, that is, of technoscientific development. The idea of innovation, a product of the marketability of ideas, defines our movement across this linearity, and what we perceive is a constant connection between the future to come and the present, even as we give it shape. It is not the rear view mirror, nor is that face turned upstream 'waiting for a future to come'; we act as if we live in a future, but what that future is like, has already been defined. Like Isaac Asimov's psychohistory in the Foundation universe, where thousands of years into the future have been mapped out by telepathic sages, the future is a knowable quantity. If the future is the absolute unknown, then we have a right to know about it. Science fictionality is our heuristic playpen, our way of inscribing possibility on the palimpsest of perception. What I have tried to demonstrate, is that from authors Jefferies, Wells and Wyndham to Banks, Ellis and Mieville, there is a certain way of extrapolating that works with either analogy or metaphor. These two in turn are premised on two methodological assumptions about the future, epistemological, by which one means that the present state of knowledge and the future state of knowledge are connected, and therefore the future to be designed requires a better modelling of the ways in which we know and can know, and technological futurism, by which one means that one can extrapolate future technologies from current one. But we need to look beyond a dystopia that we have come to accept. Even cosy dystopias. The ultimate unpredictability of the future is a precondition for restoring the magic that Ellis speaks of.

Predictables are too easy; how we deal with unpredictability is the true test of our foresight - and that is not a tautology. Can we be ready for eutopia?

References

Johan Rockstrom et al, 'A safe operating space for humanity.' Nature, Vol. 461, 24 September 2009.
Spivak, Gayatri Chakravarty. Death of a Discipline. New York: Columbia, 2003
Moorcock, Michael. London Peculiar and Other Nonfiction.Michael Moorcock and Allan Kausch, eds. Oakland, CA: PM Press, 2012.

Ballard, J. G. More Stories about Buildings and Mood'. Interview by Richard Kadrey, in Science Fiction Eye, no. 6 February 1990. 54-55 (http://www.jgballard.ca/media/1988_jan_science_fiction_eye_magazine.html). Accessed 15 Nov 2012.

Wells, H. G. The Time Machine. New York: Henry Holt & Company, 1922. 114-117.

Wells, H. G. The War of the Worlds. London: William Heinemann, 1898. 4-5.

McCool, Brian and Brian Templesmith. Choker. Vol. 1. Berkeley, CA: Image Comics, 2010 (February)

Ellis, Warren. 'How to See The Future'. 2012. (http://www.warrenellis.com/?p=14314). Accessed 15 Nov 2012.

Csicsery-Ronay, Istvan.The Seven Beauties of Science Fiction, Middletown, CT: Wesleyan University Press, 2008. 217

Stableford, Brian. Scientific Romance in Britain 1890-1950. New York: St. Martin's Press, 1985.

Ruddick, Nicholas. Ultimate Island: On the Nature of British Science Fiction. Westport, CT and London: Greenwood Press, 1993.

Gold, Barri J. Thermopoetics: Energy in Victorian Literature and Science. Cambridge, MA and London: The MIT Press, 2010.

URBAN FUTURES: SCENARIO-BASED TECHNIQUES

Silvio Caputo

In his recently published book 'Design Futuring', Tony Fry (2009) outlines a design methodology that includes the use of scenarios as a way to encompass within the design scope considerations (and concerns) about the future. Society is on course for an environmental meltdown and cities are largely responsible for this threat. If the future must be secured, we must learn to design with the future in mind and redirect design practice accordingly. The idea of a change of direction implies that to date designers have predominantly acted in response to the here-and-now, ignoring the future consequences of their decisions. In a way, this pattern of behaviour can be regarded as entrenched in contemporary (and maybe past) culture. Fry maintains that 'while the inability to project our action in time seems to be a structural limitation of our mode of being, overcoming this condition and acquiring much greater futuring capability will become an increasingly vital factor for securing our on-going being... Unless this is done, later events can make earlier decisions redundant, or expose them as inappropriate'.

It would seem that today the human species possesses an excessive tendency to restrict the time scope of actions and focus predominantly on the preoccupations of the moment. Yet, such a tendency seems not to conflict with its opposite. History is scattered with utopian visions of the future, ambitious paradigm shifts whose physical and theoretical marks (or scars) are still with us, and to which we still knowingly or unknowingly reference. Ebenezer Howard's garden city model, for example, (2009 [1902]) is still influencing the urban design debate and is the urban form that some associate with eco-cities. Peter Kropotkin's dream of a delocalised and diffused pattern of urbanisation integrating work, live and play, and nature (1994 [1912]) resonates in, say, much of the transition towns' philosophy. It can therefore be assumed that in the face of the capacity to imagine, outline, and appreciate options that could lead to a better future, the present has the power to obliterate our long-term dreams and dictate a more pragmatic, often short-sighted line of action. These two impulses can coexist in society and still be decoupled: while there is an aspiration to change for the greater good, personal conditions and value systems lock in day-to-day decisions and professional choices, gearing them up to the often unsustainable necessities (either induced or real) of the present.

History provides sufficient evidence that contingencies can push towards very unsustainable directions. In his seminal study on the collapse of societies, Diamond (2005) cogently reconstructs the dynamics that brought mighty civilisations to extinction. In spite of their sophisticated cultural and social architecture (in itself a visionary project in constant evolution: a cultural construct regulating social aspirations and relationships), their relentlessly increasing daily needs and wants proved irreconcilable with their long-term ambitions. That is why, as Fry asserts, today design practice must be redirected. It is not sufficient to envision our future. In order to substantiate it we must change our design methodology abandoning a schizoid attitude of envisioning bold shifts of society and still operating professionally with a business-as-usual approach. A new methodological approach can remind us of the impact our current choices will have on the future, thus reconciling the future with the present.

The process of designing in itself can be defined as 'the planning and patterning of any act towards a desirable, foreseeable end' (Papanek 1984). Thus implicit within the concept of designing or planning is the idea of the future (Conroy 2006). Still, what motivates designers in taking their decisions? As students, architects and urban designers are encouraged to nurture and express their particular views, using space to mould places. At a higher level, they are taught to think of these spaces as vessels for cultural values. The resulting process is one that morphs aesthetics and function, appearance and performance. Nevertheless it is undeniable that the fascination with form comes with the risk of an undue reliance on its potential for conveying and transmitting contents that can divert the design focus away from that of the building programme and its effective performance. Over the last three decades there has been much formal experimentation. Nevertheless form for the sake of form can produce consumable objects. In a sort of 'the media is the message' logic, formal experimentation can become self-referential: 'architecture talking about architecture' (Hagan 2009). Much experimentation, however, has focused also on the building and city programmes, namely the conditions and the modalities with which buildings and spaces can perform. This new fertile ground of design investigation inevitably takes the time factor to centre stage, since it deals with the multiplicity of uses the built environment will support over its lifetime. This is important since as professionals we tend to crystallize buildings at a point in time, expressions of a cultural milieu and collective aspirations. Be it the Garden City utopia or the modernist's 'city of towers' dream, the paradigm of the moment always dictates how buildings and cities are designed. But how do we ensure that current visions of a brighter future will succeed? And even so, how do we ensure the future we dream is a positive future?

It is a fact, however, that we are experiencing the beginning of an age of scarcity, although scarcity should be defined. Is it induced or is it real (see Goodbun et al. 2012)? Does it stem from an excessive concentration of resources for the few, or is it the result of overexploitation? There is no univocal answer, although that which is known through science evidences the finite nature of resources and the critical deterioration of ecosystems. It demonstrates that excessive consumption entails high environmental bills. Designing in an age of scarcity becomes therefore the opportunity for a paradigm shift in design thinking, with political and methodological implications. Implications are political because designing for scarcity is concerned with the disadvantaged. The social landscape is rapidly mutating. Low-income groups today are swiftly increasing in number, including the educated young as well as professionals. Skills and education are no longer a guarantee of economic success and opportunities are increasingly limited. It is for this majority with scarce economic possibilities that designers will probably be called more and more frequently to work in the future, developing new architectural approaches and exploring innovation (so far predominantly focused on the wealthy) within tight constraints. The implications are also methodological: tight resource constraints impose thrift, ingenuity, and a particular attention to the long-term, so as to ensure resources are well allocated, and the built environment we design adapts to future aspirations and needs, thus lasting longer. Since this is not conventional professional and/or didactic approach, students and professionals will inevitably need to go through a learning curve (see Fisher 2008), possibly facilitated by new methods and tools.

Concerns about the future, the scarcity of resources, and about the sustainability of present lifestyle are a call to arms for designers. Still the question remains of methodological approaches fit for purpose. The last decade has witnessed designers engaging in participative experiments, co-design, and more. Fisher (2008) defines this practice 'public-interest architecture' as opposed to one that concentrates its efforts for those who have ample means. It is also in this context that the research developed by the Urban Futures team can find a useful application within design practice. The research has produced a method to analyse the long-term efficacy of that which is designed today using an explorative form of scenario analysis.

Scenarios have been and are used to explore the challenges and risks that lie ahead. They were first utilised in war games during the first years of cold war, with Herman Kahn and his colleagues being some of the main experts in this field (for an account on scenarios techniques see Ruskin 2005). Only in the 70s was this approach developed into a stream of future studies, which were particularly appropriate to explore consequences of environmental degradation and excessive resource exploitation, at a point in time in which they were coming to public attention. 'Limits to Growth' for example (Meadows et al. 1979; Meadows et al. 2004), is one of the most famous studies utilising scenarios developed with mathematical models. In parallel to quantitative approaches, scenario techniques were developed using qualitative ones. For example, Royal Dutch/Shell used them as a strategic management technique to explore the probable evolution of markets and the consequent impact on their business. This type of analysis implies projecting a plan of action (any plan of action) considered for implementation against the backdrop of a set of conditions that may happen in the mid/long-term. In so doing, the plan of action can be modified to be valid under all possible future conditions considered. Modern scenario techniques tend to merge quantitative and qualitative models. The development of a storyline, a narrative that can convey the several nested levels in which the future unravels, is a precious tool for discussions at a strategic level. Datasets generated through mathematic models provide the evidence base supporting the reasoning developed through the exercise of scenario analysis. Scenarios are extensively used at a macro scale to probe the long-term efficacy of national and global systems (e.g. energy systems, food systems, climate change etc.). The merit of the Urban Futures methodology is to provide a tool that can be used to assess a smaller scale of intervention (i.e. urban development), which can enable professionals operating within the built environment domain to utilise a scenario-based techniques without possessing any particular futuring skills.

Scenario analysis can be normative if the exploration of one or more desirable futures is functional to gain an understanding of pathways for the accomplishment of a desired end point (e.g. an aspirational vision of urban development); it can be exploratory (or descriptive) if diverse future scenarios are used to interrogate plausible developments of the present in order to understand the significance of potential impacts (IEA 2003). It is from this second approach that the Urban Futures41 method originates. Eschewing the temptation to outline a desirable future of the world, designers can focus on the performance of the built environment and on its intended programme. Thus, to an extent, the method is neutral, in that it does not interfere with design aspirations and objectives although by questioning a field of possibilities, it identifies vulnerabilities that may undermine performance, so inevitably impinging on design choices. More importantly, the method can be used as a strategic approach to direct the attention within the design process towards the future.

In the Urban Futures method, scenarios that are used to test the resilience of design options portray four diverging but plausible urban conditions in 2050. They are based on the work of the Global Scenario Group (see Gallopinet al. 1997) although the original scenarios developed by that group were enriched by the Urban Futures research team so as to better capture the conditions of the urban context. Scenarios are determined by the different evolution of the world's drivers of change. These include: society, technology, economy, environment and policy. Internally consistent variations of the drivers influence the unravelling of the present towards different directions. Deploying the scenarios on the imaginary axes of social equity (i.e. self-interest/solidarity) and political structure (i.e. global/national); it is possible to visualise scenarios covering a wide range of alternatives. The analysis is therefore developed by comparing design options against sufficient amplitude of plausible evolutions of the present so as to identify all possible adverse factors to the good performance of the option considered. As a result risks will be elicited that need to be addressed to ensure the functioning of the design option whatever the future holds.

This multiple evaluation has similarities with the concept of different 'trajectories or visions of the longer term future' introduced by Hillier (2011) as opposed to a future envisioned in continuity with the present, or as a path-dependent repetition of the past, which tends to form the (unreliable) basis for traditional urban design and planning. Arguably the future is uncertain, and design and planning methods based on a linear evolution of the present are inevitably predicated on flawed assumptions. Hillier argues for a 'cartographic method' to develop planning, in which potentialities are traced, and maps of the forces' interplay are drawn up. The resulting map can be a valuable instrument for taking decisions informed by future risks and challenges. Likewise, rather than relying on a determined design strategy to attain the desired aim, the map of possibilities resulting from the Urban Futures method of analysis can represent a rich tool of exploration, in which possible design pathways can be compared, considered, or even merged in a non-linear process.

An exhaustive presentation of scenarios, characteristics, and the methodology can be found in the BRE publication 'Designing resilient cities' (Lombardi et al. 2012). The method has been also formatted into a free web-based tool (see www.urban-futures.org). What follows is a brief description of the scenarios:

New Sustainability Paradigm – Society moves towards an ethos of 'one planet living' and embraces equity and sustainability values. New socio-economic arrangements change the character of urban industrial civilization, rather than its replacement;

Policy Reform – Policy attempts to regulate the market so as to mitigate its impact on economic imbalances, social equity and environmental degradation, although the public domain resists change. Tensions between continuity of dominant values and greater equity for addressing key sustainability goals ensue;

Market Forces - Free market doctrine dominates, with individualism and materialism as core society values. The 21st century global system evolves without major surprise, in the belief that incremental market adjustments are able to cope with social, economic and environmental problems as they arise;

Fortress World - The world is divided, with the rich minority living in interconnected, protected enclaves and an impoverished majority outside. Armed forces impose order and prevent collapse.

The method can be used in many ways. A comprehensive list of urban characteristics (i.e.

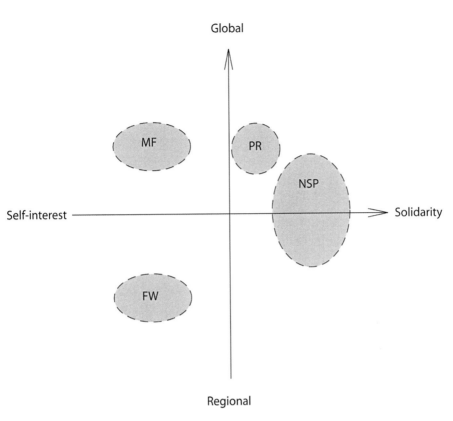

Figure 6-1 The four scenarios deployed on a diagram with axes Global/Regional and Self-interest/Solidarity. Key for the four scenarios: NSP = New Sustainability Paradigm; PR = Policy Reform; MF = Market Forces; FW = Fortress World (modified from Hunt et al. 2011).

indicators of urban sustainability such as domestic energy use, water quality, dwelling density, etc.) supports a rigorous and detailed evaluation that can be both quantitative and qualitative. In addition to this type of analysis, a 'light touch' version that is more appropriate for short workshops or brainstorming sessions can be utilised. In this format, it is sufficient to grasp the dynamics behind scenario narratives (i.e. how the drivers of change behave) and discuss the consequences of these dynamics on the design options examined. It is an evaluation that lends itself to be developed discursively and that can be easily performed within small design teams or in isolation, thus facilitating its use even for small scale design projects. It was trialled, for example, in the course of a short workshop within the European Urban Summer School 2012 (EUSS), in which a brief description of the method was presented to an audience of postgraduate architects, urban designers, and young professionals with diverse backgrounds. Subsequently, teams that were developing design projects for the summer school were asked to quickly trial the method on their design schemes.

The Urban Futures method is structured in five steps (see Figure 6-2). The sequence is designed to be circular and iterative rather than linear. It allows the analysis of single particular aspects (e.g. materials, technologies, strategies, policies, etc.) of urban development. Findings can be used to modify the initial design and make it more resilient to future events, thus closing the loop. The first step consists in the identification of the intended purpose of a 'solution for sustainability'. It prompts answering questions such as: is this solution fit for the purpose stated? Has it really the potential to attain it? This is an important step, since it brings the focus to the design programme and the benefits this is supposed to deliver, thus taking the finality of the project rather than the solution examined or its form to centre stage. For example, one of the groups testing their initial design scheme in the course of the EUSS workshop described their plan of installing an over-sized billboard on the wall of an existing building as a means to encourage interaction of passers-by and therefore community building. Bromley-by-Bow, the area for this project, is a degraded London neighbourhood inhabited by low-income groups. Expressing thoughts on the billboard and possibly exchanging opinions with those standing by the billboard could constitute an occasion to facilitate interaction and a much needed community cohesion. The identification of the intended benefit of the design concept leads to some questions such as: Is the billboard an effective media and its position ideal for luring people to express themselves? Will the billboard be vandalised thus failing its objective? Such questions help scrutinize the actual effectiveness of the design concept. Their formulation leads to the second step, aimed at detecting the 'necessary conditions' for delivering the initially stated benefit, not only now but, more importantly, over the potential lifetime of the design scheme. For example, owners of the buildings must allow the use of the external wall for a sufficiently long period to attain the intended results (i.e. community building). This poses an issue of ownership. Passers-by must be willing to use the wall for communicating their thoughts, which poses an issue of communicating effectively to them the purpose of the billboard. It also poses an issue of community engagement of each individual. The third step consists of assessing these 'necessary conditions' against the four scenarios. This can be done consulting characteristics and performance of relevant indicators or, in the light version, deducing some risks implicit in the nature of each scenario. For example, in a Market Forces world the external wall of the building may be reclaimed by the owners that have little interest in community issues. Can we think of a way to protect the billboard? In a New Sustainability Paradigm world, a community is likely to be well established even in currently disadvantaged areas. Can we think of a way the billboard can be adapted so as to be utilised in this scenario too? In the fourth step, findings are aggregated to determine the degree of resilience of the solution. Finally, in the last step a decision informed by the analysis results can be taken. If conditions are supported in all futures, the 'solution for sustainability' is robust. Conversely, causes of adversity must be identified so as to address them, or another solution must be selected.

In the workshop the analysis was not entirely completed, and the last steps were not developed. Nevertheless, the initial and brief evaluation indicated a few factors that can help reinforce the initial conceptual design. First, the scheme must encompass factors such as community and building owners' involvement. Second, the solution must be adaptable enough to be used also under social circumstances different from today. This can imply many things: an effective integration with the building envelope that can enhance the formal qualities of the building (thus circumventing the owner's reluctance to make the wall available); the planning of a series of community events as an integral part of the design scheme; and the design of a multifunctional surface that can be used, say, as a local notice board in a New Sustainability Paradigm scenario.

Inevitably, large scale projects will require more sophisticated appraisals when using the Urban Futures method. Nevertheless, in its simplicity the example presented here captures well

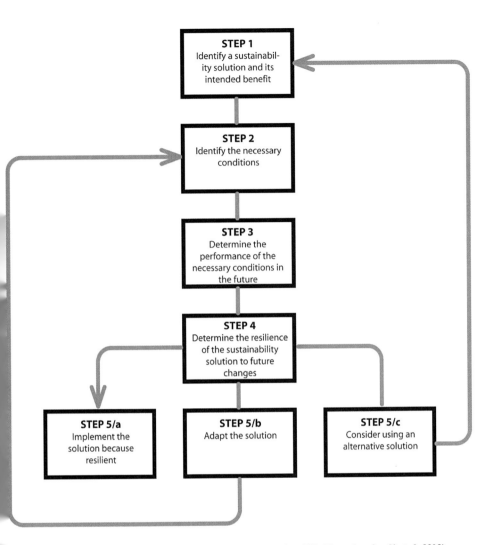

Figure 6-2 Diagram of the five-step sequence of the UF method (modified from Lombardi et al. 2012).

the potential of the method to change conventional design processes and integrate a particular attention to long-term factors within them. Ultimately the method is meant to be a tool to facilitate a change of attitude. It clearly represents only one of the possible structured approaches for such a purpose. Still its novelty lies in the use of scenarios as a way to capture the several dimensions of the city. Their narratives encapsulate the social, the economic, and the environmental showing how these interact. This way, users are prompted to an integrated appraisal of their projects. It is hoped that this structured approach can facilitate change. It certainly changed the attitude to design of those who developed it.

References

Conroy, M. M. (2006). 'Moving the Middle Ahead: Challenges and Opportunities of Sustainability in Indiana, Kentucky, and Ohio', Journal of Planning Education and Research, 26(1), 18-27

Diamond, J. (2005) Collapse – How societies choose to fail or survive, London: Penguin Books

Fisher, T. (2008) 'Public-interest architecture: a needed and inevitable change' in: Bell, B. and Wakeford, K., eds., Expanding architecture: design as activism, New York: Metropolis Books

Fry, T. (2009) Design Futuring: Sustainability, Ethics and New Practice, New York: Berg

Gallopin, G., Hammond, A., Ruskin, P. and Swart, R. (1997) Branch Points: Global Scenarios and Human Choice, Stockholm: PoleStar Series Report n 7 Stockholm Environment Institute,

Goodbun, J., Till, J. and Iossifova, D. (2012) 'Themes of scarcity' In 'Scarcity – Architecture in an age of depleting resources', Architectural Design 218, Wiley

Hagan, S. (2001) Taking shape – A new contract between architecture and nature, Oxford: Architectural Press

Hillier, J. (2011) 'Strategic navigation across multiple planes -Towards a Deleuzean-inspired methodology for strategic spatial planning' Town Planning Review, 82 (5), 503-527

Howard, E (2009 [1902]) Garden cities of to-morrow, Dodo Press

Hunt, D.V.L., Lombardi, D.R., Atkinson, S, Barber, A., Barnes, A. M, Boyko, C.T, Brown, J., Bryson, J., Butler, D., Caputo, S., Caserio, M., Coles, R., Cooper, R., Farmani, R., Gaterell, M., Hale, J., Hales, C., Hewitt, N., Jankovic, L., Jefferson, I., Leach3, J., MacKenzie, A.R., Memon, F., Pugh, T., Rogers, C.D.F., Sadler, J.P., Weingaertner, C. and Whyatt, D. (2012) 'Scenario Archetypes: Converging rather than Diverging Themes', Sustainability, 4(4), 740-772

International Energy Agency (2003) Energy to 2050 – Scenarios for a Sustainable Future. Paris: IEA Publications

Kropotkin, P (1994 [1912]) Fields, factories and workshops, Montreal: Black Rose Books

Lombardi, D.R., Leach, J. M., Rogers, C.D.F., Atkinson, S, Barber, Barnes, A. M, Boyko, C.T, Brown, J., Bryson, J., Butler, D., Caputo, S., Caserio, M., Coles, R., Cooper, R., Farmani, R., Gaterell, M., Hale, J., Hales, C., Hewitt, N., Hunt, D.V.L., Jankovic, L., Jefferson, I., Leach3, J., MacKenzie, A.R., Memon, F., Pugh, T., Sadler, J.P., Weingaertner, C. and Whyatt, D. (2012) Designing Resilient Cities: a guide to good practice, Bracknell: BRE Press,

Meadows, D. H., Club of Rome and Potomac Associates (1979) The Limits to Growth: A Report for the Club of Rome's Project on the Predicament of Mankind, Macmillan

Meadows, D. H., Randers, J and Meadows, D L (2004) The limits to growth – the thirty-year update, London: Earthscan

Papanek, v (1981) Design for the real world – Human ecology and social change. London: Thames and Hudson

Raskin P, Monks F, Ribeiro T, van Vuuren D and Zurek M (2005) 'Global Scenarios in Historical Perspective' in Carpenter, S. R. Pingali, P. L., Bennett, E. M. and Zurek, M. B., eds., Ecosystems and Human Well-being: Scenarios, Volume 2- Findings of the Scenarios Working Group of the Millennium Ecosystem Assessment, Washington: Island Press

ACKNOWLEDGING COMPLEXITY AND CONTINUOUS URBAN CHANGE

Ulysses Sengupta and Eric Cheung

Current practices of urban planning and spatial design have shown an inability to cope adequately with, and successfully intervene in the complex spatio-temporal nature of our cities. With current trends of urbanisation indicating increasing speed of change, the European Urban Summer School event was an opportunity to engage young planners with complex systems and digital tool based approaches aimed at the growing necessity to address temporal and morphological urban systems. Non-deterministic computational modelling techniques simulating complex urban territories in states of rapid change provide the potential to observe, comprehend and test the relative possibilities of spatial and policy based interventions while working with unknown futures and trans-scalar influences (Sengupta, U. 2011). In order to situate spatial design methodologies within current discourses in planning theory, the wide existing gap between theory and practice in urban planning, i.e. between rationale spatial implementation and communicative theoretical intention, must be addressed (De Roo et al. 2012). We believe the potential for bringing spatial and social issues back together, and thus addressing the space of action, lies in the ability to understand the forward projected impact of political, spatial and regulatory interventions on the identifiable trajectories and trends of existing socio-spatial evolutionary conditions.

MULTIPLE FUTURES AND DIAGRAMMING COMPLEX RELATIONSHIPS

The conceptual framework for urban change over time if based on evolutionary theory (Weinstock 2010), requires that one accepts the idea of a singular, fixed or predictable future as a fallacy. If things are constantly changing, and this includes emergent complex behaviours, and the possibility of new or external influences, then it follows that new futures based on tangents to existing directions of change are potentially created at every moment. The idea of working with multiplicity, complexity and change over time can be illustrated in a simple diagram (Figure 01), where the point of intervention on the timeline, and the type of intervention are subject to change and testing based on projections into the future. The diagram below was originally produced as a teaching aid for architecture students at the University of Nottingham, and subsequently reused for the EUSS young planners hosted by the University of Westminster in London.

The principle of working with multiple trajectories and identified social, spatial, economic, political and environmental issues remained important to the tutor group of young planning students with whom we worked directly for the remainder of the summer school. Instead of prioritising a preferred or singular future vision and aiming to take actions towards this singular

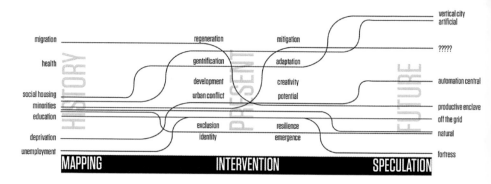

Figure 6-3 This figure illustrates the idea of considering multiple urban futures as part of change over time. Source: Ulysses Sengupta.

goal, or helplessly ignoring the larger issues in favour of small scale interventions with limited transcalar effects, the idea of multiplicity and complex overlapping relationships was further explored through a new diagramming exercise which the students developed in conjunction with us. They called this network graph diagram the SAG (ScarcityActionGoal) tool, and used it to illustrate the networked and looped nature of scarcities, actions and goals (an expansion of SAG), including the impossibility of predicting pure causal relationships by transversing the network both forwards and backwards from scarcities through actions to goals and vice versa (see Figure 6-4, Figure 6-5, Figure 6-6 and Figure 6-7).

The 'scarcity-action-goals' diagram tool created by students for the 2012 European Urban Summer School demonstrates the potential of a network graph diagram where the key issues identified by students are classified in terms of the situation (scarcity) of Bromley-By-Bow, possible actions, and intended outcome. When these are drawn up in a diagrammatic form, we can start to understand and revisit each of the issues and find its relationships within the network by traversing the connections. The main advantage of using such a diagram is to allow one to identify and communicate the key components and possible process of a system that can be readjusted by discussion and negotiation between stakeholders, thus adjusting the diagram and network to incorporate new information and lose out of date aspects, both before and during the actual processes of implementation.

COMMUNICATING SPACE TIME DEPENDENCY: PLAY SIMCITY

The initial condition that must be acknowledged for any planning implementation to take effect is change. However, it is essential to consider change as an on-going process over time with or without the intervention of planners, designers or governance. Too often, planners and spatial designers tend to work from the position of someone who believes it is their job to initiate urban change, and we would like to deconstruct this notion, by introducing the idea that urban change is both inevitable and continuous. Here continuous does not refer to any continuity of speed or constancy, but rather to the idea that 'change' itself is on-going. Hence, the idea of intervening

Figure 6-4 Network graph of identified scarcities/risks, potential actions and ideal goals. Source: Ulysses Sengupta, Eric Cheung.

within a stable system or situation must be rethought to engage with the possibilities of working with constant spatial change and multiple tipping points leading to new systems (Holling 1996).

In order to communicate the idea of spatiality as a morphological phenomenon to a generation of young planners educated on a diet of transactive, advocacy, bargaining and communicative planning methods, focused on socio-economic aspects rather than socio-spatial relationships, we thought it useful to run a live exercise in which the computer and console video game SimCity 4 would be used to design, sustain and grow a small city. SimCity is an open ended game in which the player is asked to take the role of the mayor or master-planner whose responsibility it is to initiate, grow and maintain a visually represented city. The first version of the game was published in 1989 and designed by Will Wright. The game works on the basis of controlled top-down interventions by the player, such as housing, factories, schools, roads and services, becoming part of a complex causal network within the virtual city environment, where demands for meeting the requirements of the residents of the city evolve over time based on phenomena such as industrial pollution creating lower living conditions, lack of higher education resulting in a lower skills labour market etc. As the mayor of the city, it is the player's responsibility to keep residents happy, to generate income through taxation and to use this income to intervene with new and additional functions and services, attracting more people, and hence growing the population of the city and the space of the city itself over time.

During gameplay, which took place on screen with audience participation from the EUSS students, in the form of suggestions for interventions, the discussed controllable aspects of the game were the possibility to add housing, schools, power generation, road networks, sewage networks etc. to the city that had grown. However, what was emphasised was the ability to influence these and other specific parameters through particular actions without having any direct control over other changing aspects such as population demographics, industrial pollution, migration, happiness of residents and/or any control over the whole situation/system. Another aspect that was clearly identified was the fact that the various changeable, influenceable and uncontrollable

221

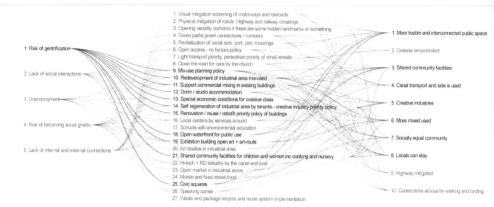

Figure 6-5 Transversing the risk of gentrification through mediating actions to ideal goals. Source: Ulysses Sengupta, Eric Cheung.

aspects of the game actually worked on the basis of a complex network of interdependencies (as seen with the SAG network graph developed by the students subsequently), which created a non-linear experience. Without these interdependencies, the game would have been linear with a set of right and wrong decisions at every stage.

DEVELOPING NEW TOOLS FOR BROMLEY-BY-BOW

In order to demonstrate the possibility of direct spatial engagement with Bromley-by-Bow, following the conceptual discussions above, a simplified digital tool, called the BBB Generator, which was developed specifically for the EUSS, was unveiled. This tool allows the translation and exploration of limited (see control layers below) policy and governance decisions regarding density, height, mix of uses etc. into a virtual 3D environment. The base map or starting point of the BBB Generator tool reflects the existing networks and urban topography in Bromley-by-Bow, creating a starting point where the primary structural elements such as roads and railway lines provide a basic grounded pattern from which to work. The logic behind this is that these elements are less likely to change quickly in this context than the buildings and urban spaces. This tool is simpler than SimCity in terms of the interdependencies defined and number of elements available. It allows a greater degree of spatial relation to the actual site conditions as it is not based on a regular underlying grid like SimCity, but instead on a closer representation of the existing urban parcellation of Bromley-by-Bow, with buildings and spaces defined to work with these realistic constraints. While there are some overlapping parameters such as the height, plot ratio and plot size, uncontrolled change was not built into the model. Hence, the functionality of the model is aimed at the idea of working with intuitive decisions that affect spatiality, through visual understanding of projected future scenarios. Additional examples shown to the students such as previous work with Cellular Automata, agent based systems and complex adaptive systems, were used to demonstrate and emphasise how more complex relationships and systems would function as models, following multi-scalar studies of specific urban topographies (but these remain outside

SCARCITY   ACTION   GOAL

Figure 6-6 Transversing the goal of new pedestrian and cycling connections backwards through possible related actions and effected risks/scarcities. Source: Ulysses Sengupta, Eric Cheung.

the scope of this article). The functionality, parameters, controllable elements and underlying logic of the BBB Generator are discussed below.

TYPES AS PARAMETERS

Existing common and likely building typologies are defined through a study of the existing urban topography and recent changes, resulting in the tool being based around four primary 'types' of urban object, where a type is a basic genetic form which can adapt or react to the environmental conditions it is placed in, making it more flexible than the more strictly defined typologies:

1. Houses (terraces, semi-detached or detached)
2. Courtyard/perimeter blocks
3. Low rise/industrial/warehouse blocks
4. Tower/slab blocks

USER CONTROL

The user controls provided consist of four basic colour and value maps which can be changed easily using common software such as Photoshop, reflecting the possibility of changing control parameters and constraints on development in a similar manner to changing planning policies. The resultant change from all the overlapping maps is displayed in a 3D visual output model. The four maps allow the user to control the aspects listed below. (SeeFigure 6 8)

1. Function (residential vs. commercial vs. open green/space)
2. Plot Area (relative size of plots)
3. Height limit (number of storeys)
4. Plot Ratio (height to footprint)

TOOL DEVELOPMENT FOR BROMLEY-BY-BOW

The process of using the BBB Generator to visualise projected futures (25 years?) of Bromley-by-

Figure 6-7 Transversing the action of introducing a new speakers corner through the potential scarcities effected and goals contributed to. Source: Ulysses Sengupta, Eric Cheung.

Bow can be described as a series of algorithmic design stages, including the choice and data taken into the model, and the process applied to this data. The final output of the tool is both visual and statistical, providing a read out of the actual available floor areas etc. once the model based on intuitive decisions is generated.

1 Base Map: Bromley-by-Bow was studied using maps, aerial and street level photographs in order to create a base layer which is split into urban blocks by inputting all observable major boundaries such as roads or railways, with defined widths.

2 Plot Divisions: For each block a similar plot division operation to the Ersi City Engine's (Parish & Müller 2001) procedural generation of parcels by recursive oriented bounding box method is used. The main difference is that instead of using bounding boxes, the closest point in the polygonal boundary (parcels) is used and is re-evaluated at a defined step distance, iterated until it splits the bounding polygon. This is yet to be validated but the aim is to allow more control and adaptation to n-sided irregular parcels found in London. This is a recursive process, it repeats until it reaches a threshold controlled by the user inputs acquired from the plot sizes/areas maps.

3 Building Types and Heights: The plots are then assigned a building type based on the control map for function. The image map colour red, green, blue translates to residential, green and non-residential respectively. A simple weighted random choice is implemented for gradients interpolated between the 3 base colours. A suitable building type is then placed as footprints into the plot by checks on available space. The control layer for height limit and plot ratio is used to determine the number of storeys of the building in relation to the building footprint. At this stage, a visual representation of the situation becomes possible (see Figure 6-9).

4 Report Generation: At the end of each generation, a report quantifying the total floor area produced and the total footprint area occupied by different functions and types can be generated as stack graphs with correlated aerial images and the control image maps for each execution. This provides feedback in the form of ratios of green area, open area, building

| PLOT SIZES | FUNCTIONS | PLOT RATIO = 2 TO 4 | HEIGHT LIMIT 7 - 70 |

Figure 6-8 Underlying control maps allowing manipulation of spatial policy decisions. Source: Eric Cheung.

footprints area and building areas for housing etc. allowing a comparison between multiple projections/experiments (see Figure 6-10).

LIMITATIONS AND IMPROVEMENTS

In its current state, the BBB Generator is not a simulative urban model based on evolutionary behaviour and its functionality is limited to visualising the effect of specific changing parameters within a given context. We suggest it would be possible to make use of this functionality to roughly understand the potential impacts of policy decisions before they are made, if the definable policy/value layers correlate directly to decision categories of actual policy makers, enabling a direct visualisation of the spatial effect of policy decisions in the foreseeable future. However, it should not be mistaken for a design tool incorporating emergent or evolutionary behaviours.

CONCLUSION

Our ambitious attempt was to create common ground between current planning theory and planning practice, including spatial implementation. This task was undertaken through communication of how overlapping and trans-scalar issues might be approached in an open ended non-deterministic system, through an acknowledgement of the potentials embodied in existing urban situations and constant urban change. While the students had neither the time to learn, customise or use the presented simulative systems or the BBB Generator directly within the limited length of the summer school, we believe the development and use of the SAG tool by students is a positive indicator that the aim of communicating the need to work with change and with multi-polar and trans-scalar issues was achieved, as was the incidental idea that planners can create and work with custom made tools to work with different situations. We hope that this initial exposure to complex systems, new digital planning tools/methodologies and morphological processes will continue to reverberate within the future practice of our young EUSS planners.

References

Holling, C.S., 1996. Engineering resilience versus ecological resilience.Foundations of Ecological Resilience, pp.51–66.

Parish, Y.I. & Müller, P., 2001.Procedural modeling of cities.In Proceedings of the 28th annual conference on Computer graphics and interactive techniques. ACM, pp. 301–308.

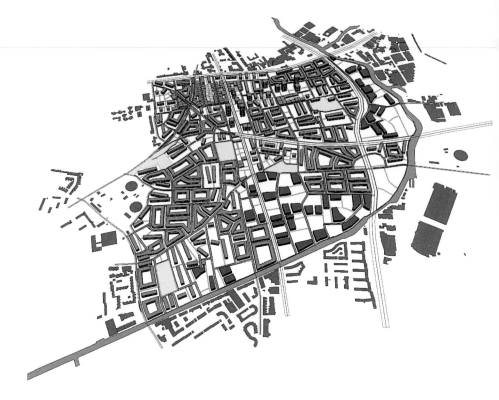

Figure 6-9 Visual representation of Bromley by Bow using the BBB Generator. Source: Eric Cheung.

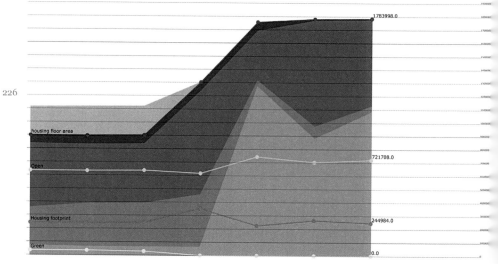

Figure 6-10 Stack graph demonstrating a comparison between seven experiments. Source: Eric Cheung.

De Roo, G., Hillier, J. & Van Wezemael, J., 2012.Complexity and Planning: Systems, Assemblages and Simulations, Ashgate Publishing.

Sengupta, U., 2011. Urban Morphology: Incorporating Complexity and Variation. In Urban change: the prospect of transformation. Wroclaw: UN-HABITAT & Wroclaw University of Technology, pp. 180–189.

Weinstock, M., 2010. The architecture of emergence: the evolution of form in nature and civilisation, Wiley.

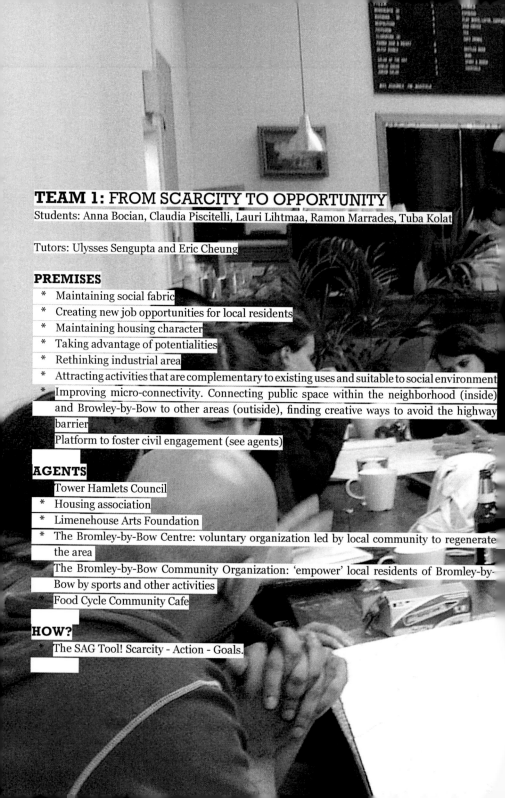

TEAM 1: FROM SCARCITY TO OPPORTUNITY

Students: Anna Bocian, Claudia Piscitelli, Lauri Lihtmaa, Ramon Marrades, Tuba Kolat

Tutors: Ulysses Sengupta and Eric Cheung

PREMISES

* Maintaining social fabric
* Creating new job opportunities for local residents
* Maintaining housing character
* Taking advantage of potentialities
* Rethinking industrial area
* Attracting activities that are complementary to existing uses and suitable to social environment
* Improving micro-connectivity. Connecting public space within the neighborhood (inside) and Browley-by-Bow to other areas (outside), finding creative ways to avoid the highway barrier
  Platform to foster civil engagement (see agents)

AGENTS

Tower Hamlets Council
* Housing association
* Limenehouse Arts Foundation
* The Bromley-by-Bow Centre: voluntary organization led by local community to regenerate the area
  The Bromley-by-Bow Community Organization: 'empower' local residents of Bromley-by-Bow by sports and other activities
* Food Cycle Community Cafe

HOW?

* The SAG Tool! Scarcity - Action - Goals.

DIRECTION

TEAM 4: THE GINGER BREAD PATH (CALORIE-BASED URBAN DESIGN)

Students: Anita Brechbühl, Joel Abumere Idaye, Nikolay Zalesskiy, Serena Maioli

Tutors: Nuala Flood, Eoghan-Conor O Shea

DISCOVERING SCARCITY: URBAN STORYTELLING. TEN DAYS OF INVENTIONS, DOUBTS, ENCOUNTERS, FALLACIES AND WORKING TOOLS

Serena Maioli

[1] SCARCITY THE SNAKE (PREMISES)

TOOL ONE: ASK YOURSELF WHY

The first day I heard about scarcity, I was primarily curious about its meaning. In ten days, I discovered that no univocal explanation is possible. We can start debunking a myth: scarcity is not just a condition that exists in the poorest countries in the world. The urban experience of scarcity is ambiguous as a snake which sneaks around us changing its shape. Scarcity, suddenly, appears as the other face of richness, the dark edge of crystal skyscrapers: in the age of endless desire related to possession, whenever we discover inequalities, we see the fail of redistribution represented by a widespread condition of scarcity.

I begin to look for a different angle, partially dark and partially shining, which allows me not to determine if I am seeing scarcity, but to understand the reason why the urban environment can be seen as scarce (just) by certain people. Now I am ready to discover when the snake changes its skin, and why.

[2] SCARCITY AND EXPECTATIONS (IN SITU

TOOL TWO: MENTAL MAPPING

Bromley-by-Bow is a question mark between Canary Wharf and the Olympic Games site: how many Londoners would be able to draw the proper limits of this wide portion of land inhabited by a 60% of Bangladeshis and few bored British?

Sugarhouse Studio is far from the metro station, especially because I have taken the wrong exit. Walking down the High Street I feel I am getting lost, drunk of the smell of motor oil melted with fast food. Not far I see the Bow Roundabout. On the opposite side of the High street, crossing the monumental traffic island where a skinny church is standing, there is a white bicycle left as a memorial, teaching me that traffic is the boss in here. Rain and cold weather cover my first impression of Bromley-by-Bow, but would it be different if it was sunny? Walking through Bow means to go up and down, crossing infrastructures and rivers, orienting through new and old landmarks. I expected an urban decay I don't see, the evidence of abandonment that I cannot proof basing on the vital industrial area, dirty and disconnected, but fascinating and populated.

Before visiting Bromley-by-Bow I read the statistics and masterplan of the area and I was, let's say, well-learned on the topic. But the topics in the field were different.

One day, Peter said that it's all about expectations: the prejudice influences our impressions, our feelings, our critiques. Sometimes, it's better not to be prepared, to be a virgin, for a spontaneous first impression.

[3] SCARCITY TALKS (PEOPLE)

TOOL THREE: CONSTANTS

Trying to get the information you want from the people you interview, never works; during ten days of talking in Bromley-by-Bow I learned three important things:

* Forget to be an architect: don't use terms like urban environment, accessibility and cityscape.
* Be transparent but not rude: never ask directly what you want to know.
* Try to find what people love and talk about it, using this argument to better understand how they live and if they are happy. Start to belong to their world.

In the industrial area close to the river Lea, Jane helps me to analyse Bromley-by-Bow in depth: she tells me she likes the neighbourhood but she doesn't remember any place which she feels attached to, except Victoria Park and Canary Wharf's restaurants, all located outside the limits of Bromley-by-Bow. She reminds me of my grand-aunt and thus I feel like I can have a more relaxed conversation with her. I come back to her workplace twice. During these talks I learn of some problems in Bow; first of all, community disconnection. Everyone I talk to seems really busy in their own everyday lives, suspended in a private microcosm. Trying to learn more about their attitudes and desires gets tougher.

Talking is never just talking: it's more like searching for a contact point. Jane becomes my constant, my personal way to go deeper.

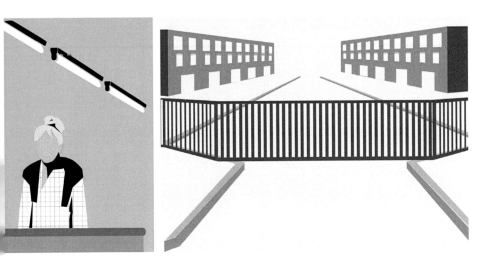

[4] SCARCITY CREATES A NEW LANDSCAPE (AT NIGHT)

TOOL FOUR: SELF-ANALYSIS

The common feeling that there is not enough space for all, that in order to improve the quality of life in our cities it is compulsory to provide them with new facilities, is a consequence of the global trend to consume rather than use. At the base of this phenomenon we find one prejudice exceptionally damaging: the idea that New as best. New is more beautiful; faster; easier to use. The truth is that cities don't need new functions and objects all the time.

The problem then moves from a lack of resources to their wrong placement. Cities are already full of stuff, but people are prevented from accessing these resources. In order to survive in times of crisis, to use differently (instead of to use less) seems important. How many territories can be used more, better, than today? Will the hyper-planning that London has in mind for Bromley-by-Bow consider the potential of spaces in-between, or will it super-impose flat-pack facilities and places?

The new landscapes created by scarcity could be an opportunity for institutional planners to involve communities in something that is different from the abused cliché of participation.

[5] GO BACK TO SCARCITY (A PROJECT)

TOOL FIVE: PURPOSE-GLASSES

Which level of intervention is still possible? The scarcity landscape forces us to reconsider the role of planning. Indeed, bottom-up planning does not just mean to ask people what they want to do with existing and future spaces; the aim of planners is not just to define rules for the production of new spaces and functions. The goal is to discover the possibility of making in the public realm with nothing but imagination.

Luckily, space is always a new discovery. Thus, when I come back to the streets and squares of Bromley-by-Bow, thinking of stimulating people's reactions I discover how surprisingly dynamic the common space becomes when you look at it with a specific purpose.

Usually we experience the urban space with a short range of uses and most of them are predetermined by an official function, because centuries of zoning prevent us to think about the multi-functionality of each space. On the contrary, we should say to ourselves 'Find a place, give new rules'. The Ginger Bread Path (below) invented by my team goes in this direction: it is a tool which helps people in recognizing the flexibility of urban space and aims to improve the observation skills of citizens and their ability to create new coloured tones in their grey neighbourhood.

[6] SCARCITY IS HAPPINESS (THE END)

TOOL SIX: POLLYANNA WAY THINKING

Walking through Bromley-by-Bow I ask myself if the missing link might be just a sparkle of happiness in the interaction between people and spaces: neither the production of new spaces nor their re-arrangement can really improve the city scene if we miss urban life.

As a rational architect, it is hard for me to define happiness as a possible tool for planning. Still this emotion, associated with memories and future perspectives, is the (most subjective and partial) marker we have to understand community satisfaction; the identity, the pride to belong to a piece of land instead of another one. We cannot quantify it, but in times of crisis it could probably be an advantage.

Under condition of scarcity, planners have to recognize the potentialities of existing built space, its capacity of generating joy, fun and intense experiences. The guys from Assemble were able to transform a petrol station into a theatre and the underpass of a highway into a playful meeting point! If scarcity is the mother of invention, happiness can be the one condition we need to deal with in order to transform contemporary urban spaces into generators of individual and social experiences.

SCARCITY THINKING AND PLANNING THEORIES

Matteo Basso

Planning contemporary cities requires new capacities of dealing with a great complexity of unexpected problems which have been challenging the established professional practices and creating an intense theoretical debate among academics.

Obviously, this is not a new issue for planning theory and practice. In fact, since the mid-fifties of the twentieth century, a lot has been written with reference to the inefficacy and the impacts of the so-called 'rational-comprehensive' models of planning. In the Anglo-Saxon context, for instance, many planning theorists – for the most belonging to the field of political science and public policy analysis – have been arguing the limitations of such a decision-making approach for a long period of time.

Among the huge amount of contributions, Lindblom (1959) and Altshuler (1965) have brilliantly pointed out the inadequacy of and the dissatisfaction with this dominant paradigm, focusing on the gap between goals and outcomes of planning policies [1]. For Lindblom such an approach, far from being concretely practiced, represents indeed only an ideal and abstract formalisation.

Planning processes – according to them – are dominated by persistent conditions of ambiguity and uncertainty concerning problems, goals and means which basically undermine the intellectual capacity of computing and dealing with them [2] . Likewise, it has become extremely difficult for experts to take into account and assess the whole range of policy alternatives.

The supposed political and technical ability of defining uniquely and unitarily the public interest is hence upset. As a consequence, the so-defined public actors are not isolated and are not the only ones entitled to take part in a decision-making process: arenas are therefore densely crowded of many actors both public and private, both formally legitimised and not. An abundance of groups of citizens protesting against projects and top-down decisions is in fact almost always part of these arenas, playing an important 'pressure role' in accelerating or curbing the whole process.

---

[1] This gap has been deeply analysed by scholars belonging to the 'implementation research' field, such as Pressman and Wildavsky (1973). According to them, planners have generally been focusing more on the phase of plans preparation rather than that of plans implementation, considering plans abstract procedures easily transferable into other contexts.

[2] For a general discussion on cognitive and informative uncertainty, unsuccessful planning experiences and the limitations of forecasting techniques see for instance Hall (1981), Friend and Jessop (1969), Flyvbjerg et al. (2003). It is worth noting that for other scholars such as Hirschman (1967), this cognitive ignorance has a positive role. In fact, if planners knew all the variables, relevant factors, difficulties and complications in advance, they would not be able to start any project (principle of the 'hiding hand').

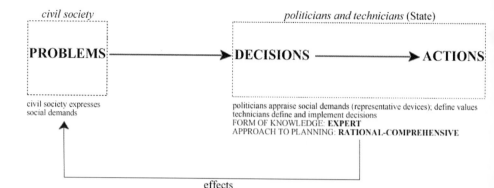

Figure 7-1 This figure represents an ideal problem-solving decision-making perspective. Source: Matteo Basso.

Yet it is useful to underline that in spite of this strong and passionate criticism, the rational-comprehensive paradigm has continued to be adopted in many fields of public policy over the years (Dalton 1986). For instance, evidences of such a persistence are recognizable in technical decisions supposed to give solution to social problems without first consulting the persons concerned, or in controversial cases of grand plans and projects implementation which regularly take place in most of our cities.

Among the many explanations, one is from my point of view the most appropriate in clearing up such a persistent situation: the difficulty – both among technicians and politicians – in abandoning a powerful approach which has been absolutely relevant in the foundation and legitimisation of the pillars of the modern urban planning profession (Sandercock 1998; Allmendinger 2001).

We are now living in overall conditions of scarcity and uncertainty that permeate any intervention on the built environment. These circumstances are therefore bringing to light again a general criticism of the established approaches to planning [3]: in particular, these are implying – I would through these notes briefly argue – a significant redefinition of the role and position of planners within the planning processes.

In fact, since cities are characterized by dynamics and social demands raised by many different populations (which are then transferred into different land-use patterns), urban policies [4] must pursue at the same time different conflicting goals. First – which is the set of goals more easily recognizable in the built environment – they produce physical outcomes in terms of new buildings and infrastructures construction, buildings refurbishment and public spaces amelioration. Secondly, they deal with social justice issues, as for instance the provision of affordable housing, public services and local initiatives aimed at taking care of specific vulnerable social groups.

240

---

3   This criticism has become today more relevant due also to the current economic, political and social crisis, which is probably creating a new 'demand' of different and more effective kinds of regulation. It is yet useful to underline that planning theory has traditionally focused more on issues of uncertainty than those of scarcity.

4   I am referring here to the definition given by Crosta (1990) who defines urban policies 'a) as the set of public activities, b) regarding (physical) territorial transformations, c) put in practice both by public actors and private [...]' (p. 260 – the translation is mine). Urban policies are hence deliberate transformations of the physical and functional organization of cities and territories.

Finally, they have to achieve local development objectives as well as the preservation of the overall environmental qualities.

As it is obvious, these goals are not automatically shared due to a floating condition of mismatch between values, point of views, interests, ideas and expectations recognizable in planning policies (Campbell 1996). Therefore, since trade-offs are not easily reducible, an interactive and conflicting dimension characterizes the whole urban policy-making process (Banfield and Wilson 1963) which in the end requires a shift of the role and the perspective of planners from that of 'solutions design' to that of 'problems investigation'.

The full comprehension of the socio-economic dynamics affecting contemporary cities and territories is therefore absolutely relevant in order to improve both the theory and the practice of urban and regional planning. As planners we must in fact be aware – from an epistemological point of view – of the origin, the nature, the limitations and validity of different kinds of human knowledge, in order to design better policies and to cope with multiple publics (Lindblom and Cohen 1979).

FROM PROBLEM-SOLVING TO PROBLEM-SETTING

Conditions of scarcity, uncertainty and complexity require therefore that planners work more deeply on the comprehension of problems rather than on solutions definition. To this end the plurality of actors in policy arenas represents an undoubtedly concrete and strategic resource in order to improve the knowledge of problems. According in fact to Schön (1978), '[...] the essential difficulties in social policy have more to do with problem setting than with problem solving, more to do with ways in which we frame the purposes to be achieved than with the selection of optimal means for achieving them' (p. 255); hence, '[...] it has become clear that we ought no longer to avoid the problem of setting the problem' (p. 262).

Since scarcity is a social construct and does not represent a given and objective situation, experts are requested to abandon the presumption of knowing in advance the whole range of its dimensions thanks to their supposed expertise. Planners must first of all understand the different representations of what is really missing, what is wrong and what ought to be done in specific contexts through a process of continuous inquiry into the stories and the cognitive frames of the many actors who actually live and use that environment [5]. A process of social involvement, hence, where technicians and politicians work with and within local communities instead of for, in order to make sense of the reality and better set the problems. This operation has obviously become absolutely relevant in our contemporary cities, where 'we need to acknowledge the many ways of knowing that exist in culturally diverse populations, and to discern which are most useful and in what circumstances' (Sandercock 1998, p. 5).

I tried to represent this change of perspective through two different schemes [6], in order to explain more clearly the concept.

Scheme A (see Figure 7-1) represents the linear problem-solving perspective, where the separation and the boundaries – in terms of competences and responsibilities – between the sphere of society and that of the State (performed by politicians and technicians) are easily identifiable,

---

5   For reference on the concept of cognitive frames see Schön and Rein (1994).
6   I got the ideas of this kind of representation from the schemes proposed by Friend and Jessop (1969), chapter 5 and Crosta (1998), chapter 1. The first scheme represents actually the traditional policy-making process: manifestation of social demands, agenda-setting, policy formulation and implementation.

with a consequent unidirectional and top-down dialogue between the two [7]. Civil society appears therefore as a passive subject who expresses social demands and dissatisfactions with an existing situation (such as scarcity of public services, interventions or conflicts regulation) and is then served and regulated by the government. On the other hand, the State acts both as a provider of services and a regulator of social practices through an interactive process between politicians and technicians in the definition of which problems at stake are to be solved [8]. In particular, politicians are supposed to be able to understand and appraise the troublesome situations and to define a priority of values through the traditional devices of representative democracy. Technicians are then requested to formulate, asses and implement technical and rational responses in accordance with the political direction and thanks to scientific techniques such as Multi-Criteria Analysis or Cost-Benefit Analysis (technical rationality). The civil society is eventually the recipient – both in a positive and in a negative way – of this specific process.

In this model of policy choice, planners search therefore for desired solutions to given social problems, which are generally considered to be completely knowable and static. The planners position within the process is hence one of separation from the rest of the society due to the greater expert knowledge that as technicians they are believed to possess

On the contrary, scheme 2 (see Figure 7-2) is a graphic representation of the problem-setting perspective which offers an immediate comprehension of the circular and intertwined process inherent in such a model.

Since problems and scarcity circumstances are not given but are constructed by human beings, a cooperation between civil society, politicians and technicians appears as the essential instrument in order to get a more realistic and pluralistic interpretation of the ambiguous and complex situations. A multiplicity of point of views about what is really missing makes it indeed '[...] dramatically apparent that we are dealing not with 'reality' but with various ways of making sense of a reality' (Schön 1978, p. 267). Hence, '[...] the design process is a social process: problem setting represents the outcome of the interaction between the actors, with their alternative, multiple and unstable definition' (Fareri 2009, p. 212 – the translation is mine).

Then, the absence of a clear separation between the sphere of society and that of the State – and the participatory devices introduced in order to reduce the distances between them – allows the different actors to explore both the problems and the choice of the decision, as well as its implementation. In an interactive and multidirectional cycle, the whole policy process aims therefore at better and continuously (re)defining the problems at stake, with feedbacks, improvisation, collective reflection, learning-by-doing and reframing processes gained through the practice (Schön 1983; Schön and Rein 1994). The stage of problems definition is hence relaunched during the whole process and a strict separation between formulation and implementation is definitely overcome. As indeed Crosta (1998) accurately asserts, there is no separation between knowledge and project, since '[...] the relation between decision and action is not much an antecedence/consequentiality relation (= first decide, then act), but a coming-

---

7 In spite of '[...] a continuing interchange of information and influence across the interface between them' (Friend and Jessop 1969, p. 102). This linear procedure requires obviously a clear separation between policy-makers and policy-takers.

8 Politicians and technicians are here believed to be able to deliberately choose the right and appropriate response to a specific situation. In particular, technicians produce an amount of expert knowledge regarding social problems that politicians then 'use'. In order for this expert advice to be really rational, technicians have yet to be neutral and separated by politicians. Conditions of scarcity refer also to the refusal, by politicians, to deal with specific social demands (political scarcity).

and-going relation, between decisions and actions. The 'stage' of decision and the 'stage' of action continually interpenetrate, are intertwined' (p. 20 – the translation is mine).

Furthermore, the State acts here more as an enabler than a provider: it creates the opportunities to involve and improve the capacities of communities to act in order to solve problems rather than simply offering them its own solutions (that is giving people the opportunity to become policy-makers as well). Planners are hence requested to be able to get this involvement started and are expected to gain more experience in fields such as mediation, negotiation, collaboration, social interaction management and participatory processes design [9]. In general terms, planners turn out to be a sort of social researchers – together with other practitioners belonging to different disciplinary orientations – committed at first in observing social contexts, listening to different voices and point of views and interacting with inhabitants. In particular, 'the reflective planner participates in these societal conversations; and in doing so, he or she helps to construct the problem to be solved' (Sandercock 1998, p. 64). According in fact to Gelli (2002), 'this requires that the researcher continually and personally reconsider himself, above all in his consolidated role of 'expert', by accepting a condition of cognitive uncertainty open to surprises and contradictions and especially to the contribution of other forms of knowledge which are not purely 'technical', 'scientific', 'professional'' (p. 3 – the translation is mine).

Monitoring and assessment devices are eventually useful to identify the manifestation of unintended consequences and events – which are perceived as problems as well – and to correct the decisions.

DIFFERENT KINDS OF USABLE KNOWLEDGE

Compared to the first one, scheme 2 introduces a clear specification and combination of three different types of knowledge all equally usable in the solution of social problems (Lindblom and Cohen 1979), as 'knowledge of various kinds, treated in different ways, are used in the formulation and implementation of urban and regional policies' (Crosta 1998, p. 15 – the translation is mine).

In a problem-setting perspective, in fact, beyond the knowledge explicitly possessed by experts – derived from professional training and practice –, the one which arises from civil society assumes a central role in exploring both the situations which public policies are intended to change and the local potentialities that should be to this specific end enhanced.

Ordinary knowledge – as discussed above – is the form of knowledge which planners can discover and activate through participatory processes and qualitative techniques such as everyday practices observation, listening and talking, as well as intuition and imagination [10]. It is a grounded knowledge which characterizes and differentiates specific contexts and results from local common sense, know-how, culture, practical wisdom and settled social capital, defined as savoirscitoyens by Yves Sintomer (quoted in Cellamare 2011, p. 205). It represents hence a fundamental resource for planning under conditions of scarcity and uncertainty, since it offers the opportunity to understand which local resources can be better used in the definition of more sustainable solutions to social demands.

There is finally another important form of knowledge that can enrich the whole policy-making process. It is called 'interactive' since it raises from the interaction between many actors

243

---

[9]   Their objective is not simply to produce a legal 'product' (documents called plans or projects), as to design and manage a political 'process' of interaction with people.
[10]   In addition to the traditional statistical approaches. Moreover, qualitative approaches are important in order to comprehend symbolic and emotional dimensions which should not be ignored.

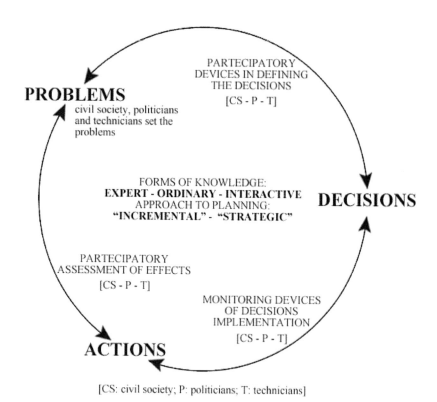

PARTECIPATORY
DEVICES IN DEFINING
THE DECISIONS
[CS - P - T]

PROBLEMS
civil society, politicians
and technicians set the
problems

FORMS OF KNOWLEDGE:
EXPERT - ORDINARY - INTERACTIVE
APPROACH TO PLANNING:
"INCREMENTAL" - "STRATEGIC"

DECISIONS

PARTECIPATORY
ASSESSMENT OF EFFECTS
[CS - P - T]

MONITORING DEVICES
OF DECISIONS
IMPLEMENTATION
[CS - P - T]

ACTIONS

[CS: civil society; P: politicians; T: technicians]

Figure 7-2 This figure represents a possible problem-setting decision-making perspective. Source: Matteo Basso.

(both experts and ordinary) during the concrete policy implementation: according again to Crosta (1998), '[...] the most useful form of knowledge for the action is created during the action, by the same actors who are involved (not, hence, by 'external' operators). I call this form of knowledge 'interactive': since it is produced by interacting actors, but above all since it is produced during the same course of action (and hence produced at the very moment in which it is used)' (p. 15 – the translation is mine).

At this point, it is worth noting that citizen involvement does not represent a pure democratic ideal. In fact, it assumes a concrete 'usable' orientation each time it allows local authorities to trust local communities (for instance associations) and empower them in the process of maintenance and reproduction of common goods such as public spaces and services. In my opinion, this interactive knowledge is therefore the most important in conditions of scarcity, as it permits – through a process of 'trial and error' and of social interaction – the creative and collective exploration of innovative alternative ways of reaching the goals that local authorities cannot easily achieve [11]. According in fact again to Schön (1978), working on problem-setting '[...] has to do with

---

11   In particular in the current condition of shortage of financial resources which local authorities must daily address

generativity. It is nothing less than the question of how we come to see things in new ways' (p. 255). This – I would suggest – means exactly the capacity of setting problems and solutions in a more creative way, since 'the social production of 'citizens knowledge' [...] is already a process and a creative and design action in itself' (Cellamare 2011, p. 214 – the translation is mine).

To conclude, the new role of planners as 'process designers' '[...] is hence appropriate for the mobilization, during the decisional process, of a field of knowledge as broad as possible – scientific, ordinary, interactive' (Fareri 2009, p. 223 – the translation is mine).

CONCLUSIONS

The aim of these short notes was to suggest a possible reflection regarding role, competence and position of planners within planning processes that seek to cope with conditions of scarcity and uncertainty.

It has been argued, for instance, that planners are requested to abandon the conventional role of 'solutions designer' for one that could be described as 'problems investigator'. New skills are hence expected, such as the capacity of designing and supervising participatory processes, the ability of facilitating and listening to different point of views, as well of negotiating and observing local contexts in depth.

As technicians, planners shift therefore from the situation of pure neutrality (with respect to politics) and separation (with respect to the society), which makes them external actors in a problem-solving perspective, to that of full immersion in the contexts where certain situations are perceived – from many different actors – as being problematic.

The consequence of such an approach is then reflected on their specific position: planners are in the situation they propose to solve, are within the communities and collaborate hence both with politicians and ordinary people in processes which are designed to shorten the distances and to be multidirectional.

This of course does not mean that planners completely lose their role and relevance as experts. On the contrary, it is expected that they gain more experience in the translation of different languages (the technical one and the language 'possessed' by citizens) in order to give a real and concrete project orientation to the different forms of knowledge above discussed [12].

Coping whit scarcity means yet revising forms and contents of traditional planning instruments, since piecemeal, symbolic and incremental approaches – against a so-called 'mega-projects' tradition – are often preferred in order to explore and test the local resources that can be activated in addressing social problems (as suggested in scheme 2) [13].

Obviously, this is not to say that planning is today completely useless but that planning practices must shift from the ordinary elaboration of land-use plans and zoning ordinances to the definition of long term flexible visions, aimed at coordinating and managing different projects, evaluating the interrelations of their outcomes, introducing feedbacks and goals reframing (this is what I call 'trial and error' processes).

To conclude, new approaches require an overall change in the technical culture which characterizes planning practices, especially in the procedure of elaboration and implementation of plans within local authorities. Such practices must recognize and valorise the potentiality of

---

12   For instance, planners have to find the optimum spatial conditions in order to place the solutions which are proposed by communities.

13   Through the implementation of small, verifiable and demonstrative actions aimed at improving the existing situation. This refers obviously to the method of 'successive limited comparisons' discussed by Lindblom (1959).

local know-how and transfer it into ordinary plans or projects. According to Healey (2010), this is needed in order to give a concrete 'planning orientation' to the creative practices put spontaneously in place by different people to address the problems of our cities.

References

Allmendinger, P. (2001) Planning in postmodern times, New York: Routledge.

Altshuler, A.A. (1965) The city planning process. A political analysis, Ithaca: Cornell University Press.

Banfield, E.C. and Wilson, Q. (1963) City politics, Cambridge, MA: Harvard University Press.

Campbell, S. (1996) 'Green cities, growing cities, just cities? Urban planning and the contradictions of sustainable development', Journal of the American Planning Association, 62 (3), 296-312.

Cellamare, C. (2011) Progettualità dell'agire urbano. Processi e pratiche urbane, Roma: Carocci Editore.

Crosta, P.L. (1990) 'La politica urbanistica', in Dente, B. ed., Le politiche pubbliche in Italia, Bologna: Il Mulino, 259-279.

Crosta, P.L. (1998) Politiche. Quale conoscenza per l'azione territoriale, Milano: Franco Angeli.

Dalton, L.C. (1986) 'Why the rational paradigm persists.The resistance of professional education and practice to alternative forms of planning', Journal of Planning Education and Research, 5(3), 147-153.

Fareri, P. (2009) Rallentare. Il disegno delle politiche urbane, ed. by Giraudi M., Milano: Franco Angeli.

Flyvbjerg, B., Bruzelius, N. and Rothengatter, W. (2003) Megaprojects and risk. An anatomy of ambition, Cambridge: Cambridge University Press.

Friend, J.K. and Jessop, W.N. (1969) Local government and strategic choice. An operational research approach to the processes of public planning, London: Tavistock Publications.

Gelli, F. (2002) Politica & politiche. Lo studio di caso? Una domanda di ricerca, Milano: Giuffrè.

Hall, P. (1981) Great planning disasters, London: Penguin Books.

Healey, P. (2010) Making better places. The planning project in the twenty-first century, Basingstoke: Palgrave Macmillan.

Hirschman, A.O. (1967) Development projects observed, Washington, D.C.: The Brookings Institution.

Lindblom, C.E. (1959) 'The science of 'muddling through'', Public Administration Review, 19(2), 79-88.

Lindblom, C.E. and Cohen, D. (1979) Usable knowledge: social science and social problem solving, New Haven: Yale University Press.

Pressman, J.L. and Wildavsky, A.B. (1973) Implementation.How great expectations in Washington are dashed in Oakland; or, why it's amazing that federal programs work at all, Berkeley: University of California Press.

Sandercock, L. (1998) Toward Cosmopolis. Planning for multicultural cities, Chichester: Wiley.

Schön, D.A. (1978) 'Generative metaphor: a perspective on problem-setting in social policy', in Ortony, A. ed., Metaphor and Thought, Cambridge, MA: Cambridge University Press, 254-283.

Schön, D.A. (1983) The reflective practitioner. How professionals think in action, New York: Basic Books.

Schön, D. A. and Rein, M. (1994) Frame reflection. Toward the resolution of intractable policy controversies, New York: Basic Books.

CHANGING CONDITIONS – CHANGING OUR ROLE

Giulia Maci, Seppe de Blust, Clenn Kustermans

After briefly discussing the changing context of urban planning, the article focusses on our experiences in Bromley-by-Bow. During the summer school we had an in-depth visit to this East London neighbourhood. Our colourful experiences are then put in a manifesto, which can help young urban planners understand their jobs. To arms!

TODAY'S CONTEXT FOR YOUNG URBAN PLANNERS

Times are changing fast. The economic crisis points out the risks and the limits of our current planning system. In times of scarcity it becomes inadequate for, let's say, three reasons.

First, traditional planning is characterized by a strong hierarchical structure, with a promoter that coordinates the actions of different urban players. This model needs a high availability of scarce public resources (financial, human resources and knowledge) and lacks the needed transparency and democracy in today's multi-actor society.

Second, traditional zoning as a tool to regulate land use is not able to manage the emerging dynamics of the transformation of the territory. Its 'catch 22' between the necessary flexibility for new win-win situations on the one hand and the stringent framework to guarantee spatial quality on the other hand leads to stagnation.

Third, the complexity of society is growing. A growing diversity and social inequality puts society under pressure. Space and spatial planning interact in this process by putting socio-spatial incongruence in focus and by making social structures spatially permanent.

EXPERIENCING BROMLEY-BY-BOW

What does this changing context mean for towns, cities and neighbourhoods? Can we actually see the changes? How does it affect people?

The summer school lead us to Bromley-by-Bow in East London. Within the wondrous world of statistics, Bromley-by-Bow is known as the most deprived area in the UK. It is primarily known for its ethnic diversity (although the Bangladeshi majority does not really imply diversity), low incomes and high unemployment rate. Within the dwellings, which are mainly 'social', living standards are low. And this makes Bromley-by-Bow a perfect place for young planning professionals who want to change the world positively.

The changing context affects this neighbourhood too. Being a focal point of social housing, the quality of life is driven by a few influential companies: the housing company Poplar HARCA, the municipality and a few private investors. To improve quality of life, these actors mainly refurbish or build new homes. Strengthening the local economy is not perceived as key policy. Result of this focus is that Bromley-by-Bow becomes a dull residential area. And that isn't necessarily a bad thing, but we believe Bromley-by-Bow has more potential.

The Olympic Park (and its planned legacy) is just a stone's throw away. Within the London context of speculative private investments, Bromley-by-Bow also undergoes gentrification. Instead of spontaneous gentrification (in which alternative lifestyles attract investments), there seems to be rather a kind of intended gentrification (planting gated middle-class apartments on strategic spots). These developments make social inequality more visible.

We were surprised that Bromley-by-Bow is the most deprived area in the UK. While walking around, we could hardly find any confirmation of that statement. I mean, it was not that bad! True, the grey buildings and the shops were depressing, but there was energy in the streets where people meet. There must be worse neighbourhoods in this country known for the gap between the rich and the poor. This brought as in an awkward situation: we couldn't confirm or deny its problematic status and therefore it was hard to find solutions.

Confronted with this lack, Bromley-by-Bow made us think differently. Instead of finding physical interventions, the problem identification behind the so-called 'problematic' status of the neighbourhood took our first attention. What are the mechanisms behind the actual community in Bromley-by-Bow? Through observation and participation we started looking at valid and possible carriers for new urban solutions. Our main focus was on new forms of decision-making, social networks, alternative production methods and new concepts of scale and progressive urban development.

We understood that, while creating spatial synergies, our task as (future) urban planners is to actively intervene in community-building. Such new ways of planning and design demand reformulating our role as urban planners. If we want to reclaim the possibility of making we have to define our role in the given socio-spatial context. Our role is to do acupunctural interventions that catalyse other interventions within the framework of the existing community, qualities and possibilities. Instead of focussing on spatial dynamics on a bigger scale (e.g. East London, Olympic legacy, gentrification), our primary goal is to strengthen existing social networks and spatial opportunities in Bromley-by-Bow. To make this role clearer we started to write a Manifesto.

MANIFESTO FOR YOUNG URBAN PLANNERS

There I am, sitting in a bar with two friends and fellow urban planners. They are discussing their jobs, their projects and their doubts. While I roll a cigarette they unveil the issue of 'the role of the young urban planner today'. While silently sipping at another beer I think there is no other job that is more questioned by its practitioners than the urban planners' job. If you are a plumber, your task is understandable. The same goes for a postman, a poet, a psychologist, a prisoner, a pet nurse. But the planners' task remains discussed. Why?

Our world has been manufactured and all we got to do is reinvent it. Our forefathers have brought us wealth, yes, but a lot of shit as well. Look at the cities we are living in! Money is scarce, new ideas are lacking, social issues are still unresolved, cities are evolving rapidly and worse, projects must be sustainable but in fact they are not, sustainability is hollow or dead. Moreover we, planners, are expected to solve global economic, social, ecological, spatial, political, philosophical problems. We ought to answer every issue, we are asked to be ambiguous but we don't have a clue where to start. Tell me, baby, why you've been gone so long. Can't you see the signs that we are heading towards new Middle Ages?

Our cities are getting dark, introvert, goalless, pointless, stupid. Ethics dissolve, barricades are being built, there is intellectual famine and philosophical incest. Today cities are not progressing or forwarding, but declining and rewinding. And indeed, we are running in circles. We must redo things. In eras of doubt, people tend to write manifestos in order to structure their thoughts and to mobilize others.

So, for what it is worth...

A MANIFESTO

Giulia Maci, Seppe de Blust, Clenn Kustermans

We must re-evaluate traditional concepts of planning. As planners and human beings we are used to growth. Growth seems (or seemed) to be natural, because there is coherence with our own lives: you are born, you grow, you sustain, you shrink, you die. But in urban terms today de-growth or shrinking does not necessarily mean decline or dying. We need to accept the fact that cities cannot and will not grow like they used to do. Moreover, in times of scarcity and shrinkage we can (at last!) focus on the parts that already exist.

We must react to rapid urban transformation. It seems necessary to go beyond theories and try practical actions to address concrete urban issues. It is time to get out our laid-backed offices and to leave our desks, digital aerial maps and other tools. Monitoring and evaluating real daily life are fundamental in our job to learn from the experiences and to *readjust* theories and strategies. An urban planner experiences local struggles personally. In East Germany, for example, a vast amount of cities is shrinking. Instead of trying to find ideas for new growth in the East, there is rather a need to fulfil local needs. And instead of building new suburban neighbourhoods (market-based thinking) and breaking down high-rise areas, planners could focus on *reshaping* the high-rise areas into positive and well-used places by new concepts. Enter the area, experience it melancholically and do something with it.

We must relocate urban functions and reorganize the metropolitan area as a network of autonomous centres. We cannot stick to our grandfathers' ideas of mono-centred cities. Many cities have grown from a core city to a core city with dead and depressing suburbs. Local centres become more important if people are working long days in another place or at home. It is time to focus on outlying neighbourhoods where most people live nowadays. For example, Berlin, London and Rotterdam are not just cities, but accumulations of different social worlds. To react on people's needs and to act democratically, a city must accept its polycentric form and attitude.

We must reuse and revitalize traditional city places adapting the spaces to old and new needs, uses and meanings. In this process it is important to identify and include all the different identities that constitute the city. What we do is not for ourselves, planners, but primarily about the other people shaping the city: plumbers, postmen, poets et cetera.

This also means that old-fashioned state tax systems should rather be reorganized: instead of luring cities and towns into growth-based income, a new concept can be introduced. As an alternative to growing and with more demographic, political and financial power, cities can be financed by other aspects (for example by stimulating projects that take away social struggles). In Belfast and Derry, for example, or in today's policy of building new Israeli settlements, there is an urgent need to answer local calls. Instead of continuing separate growth, many cities could focus on social integration of the people who already live there and not just on political or military strength.

We must redefine planning priorities and a new ethic for our profession and redistribute responsibilities for city development among different actors. The role of planner has to be redefined as a mediator who is able to listen to people's needs and expectations and translate them into right answers. This seems to be an old-fashioned phrase, and actually it is. But nonetheless it is still current. It must be understood that we can't manage a city by ourselves. It is like a dance floor. Space is limited, but people are free to dance. You can be timid and some basic steps, but you can also swing round boldly. The floor is made for people to communicate and dance or play together, not to curtail someone else. It is a collective individual happening in search of some happiness. The spatial planner is a background musician, bringing the beat and defining the pace. Just a face in a music-making crowd. Mediating such a process needs communication and ethics that do not judge the opinion or acts of the participants, but give space to their stories to become part of a bigger picture.

We must reduce and redistribute the ecological footprint of cities, plan compact cities, improve the efficiency of waste management, promote sustainable mobility and energy independence and to bring social justice to cities. One of the main qualities of the future city is climate resilience. Of course, today no one can deny it. But well-known examples of sustainable cities or neighbourhoods are out-dated. They are already in need of restoration. Moreover, sustainability nowadays is worn out by the bad examples representing it. Focussing on existing urban areas instead of growth brings a whole new dimension to sustainability. Especially in times of scarcity, social sustainability is a key issue. In Antwerp, for example, there is a huge need for improvement of social and ecological factors. Multiculturalism and transport have boosted the city since its early stages, but are now left unimportant.

We must re-imagine, too. If we want to take our responsibilities serious – solve global economic, social, ecological, spatial, political, philosophical problems – and accept that we can't do it alone; if we want to combine the ever-present utopia with concrete interventions; if we want to give space to collaboration and not get caught by ambiguity... then we will need to claim a non-contested position, the neutrality of the expert. Few people know what an urban planner is. Let us change that! It's the planner's expertise to re-imagine space, it's our first task to make this clear, communicate it, brand it and make it incontestable.

And, due to rapidly changing conditions, we must rewrite the Manifesto every year.

APPENDIX

CONTRIBUTORS

ASSEMBLE

Assemble are a young, award winning practice of artists, designers and architects based in London with a strong track record of developing successful public spaces in difficult urban situations. Their work focuses on using design as a tool to improve social and cultural life, and is committed to uncovering the extraordinary opportunities and potential pleasures that exist on the fringes of everyday life and the built environment. At the heart of Assemble's working practice is a belief in the importance of addressing the typical disconnection between the public and the process by which spaces are made. Assemble champion a working practice that is interdependent and collaborative, seeking to actively involve the public as both participant and accomplice in the on-going realization of the work.

BARBARA ELISABETH ASCHER

Barbara Elisabeth Ascher studied architecture and urbanism at Bauhaus University in Weimar and Oslo School of Architecture and Design with a scholarship from the German National Academic Foundation. She graduated from Bauhaus-University in 2006 and has worked as an architect an urban planner in Austria, Egypt and Norway as well as a guest critic at the University in Stavanger since. She recently joined the Oslo School of Architecture and Design as a PhD research fellow, where she researches on Scarcity and Creativity in the Built Environment.

MATTEO BASSO

Matteo Basso is an Italian city and regional planner. He graduated from the IUAV University of Venice in 2011, where he is currently a PhD candidate in Regional Planning and Public Policy. His main research interests are planning processes, policy-making and planning theory, with a particular attention to the main actors involved, their roles, relations, and conflicts. He is interested in the way public actors, private actors and civil society relate to each other in trying to address contemporary urban challenges, secondly in the way different point of views and practices may improve the traditional and formal process by which institutions ordinarily produce plans, projects and policies.

DUNCAN BOWIE

Duncan Bowie was a principal strategic planner for the Mayor of London and contributed to the 2004 and 2008 London plans. He was previously investment director for the London Region of the Housing Corporation (the UK government's housing investment agency) and has also worked for the London boroughs of Lambeth and Newham and for the London Docklands Development Corporation.

SILVIO CAPUTO

Silvio is an architect with a vast practioner's experience and sustainability as a main and powerful driver. He directed his design office for more than a decade working at an urban and architectural scale, acquiring broad knowledge of the design process and the construction industry. He is currently developing academic research as a member of a multidisciplinary team (Urban Futures) that investigates sustainable urban development and the conditions to make it resilient. His work focuses on energy efficiency at a building and urban scale. This research project has produced relevant outcomes which have been disseminated through academic and conference papers, as well as workshops and other events that he has conducted both individually and with the team. In parallel with the academic activity, he continues to develop design-led research and explore environmental design strategies and languages both independently and with the RED group, a collective formed by academics and professionals from different areas of expertise. He also has experience in teaching at a graduate and postgraduate level.

BODHISATTVA CHATTOPADHYAY

Bodhisattva Chattopadhyay is Kultrans Doctoral Fellow at the University of Oslo. While his doctoral work is a comparative study of colonial era scientific literature and science fiction in terms of globalisation, he has published and lectured on various aspects of science fiction, including evolution and degeneration, future histories and posthumanity. In his academic daydreams, he thinks of himself as a Vulcan-Human hybrid, caught in the magic of pure armchair speculation and fantasy yet reigned in by the quest for scientific certitude.

STEVEN CHODORIWSKY

Born in Englehart, Canada, Steven lives in Maastricht, Netherlands. Currently a design researcher at the Jan van Eyck Academie, he received degrees in architecture from the University of Waterloo and the Tokyo Institute of Technology, and took part in the CCA Kitakyushu research programme. General practice incorporates built form, installation, performance and text.

NAZNIN CHOWDHURY

Naznin Chowdhury has five years experience on urban regeneration policy and projects, including positions in central and local government in the UK. She specialises in planning and regulatory issues as they affect economic development in diverse inner London economies and also has a passion for community and youth development work. She has an MA in European Studies from King's College London.

ERIC CHEUNG

Eric Cheung is currently working as an architectural designer with a strong interest in urbanism, complex systems and computational design. He has been involved in both large and small scale mixed-use affordable housing in the UK and is currently involved in projects in China of various scales at SoftGrid UK. Eric is experienced in CAD/3D software including Maya, Rhino, Sketchup, Microstation and AutoCAD with the ability to extend their functionality through programming and scripting. He has taught Processing, Python in Maya and introduction to Rhino while co-tutoring architecture design studio units at the University of Nottingham over the past two years. As a freelance developer, he is also engaged in his own research and inquiry into multi-agent simulation, computational geometry, topology and their relevance in architecture and urbanism.

SEPPE DE BLUST

Seppe De Blust is a Sociologist (2009) and Urban Planner (2012) and currently works as an advisor on urban policy for the Flemish Minister for Energy, Housing, Social Economy and Urban Policy. Before that, he was active as a researcher at the Department of Sociology – University of Antwerp (Belgium). He has a special interest in the search for new spatial (planning) models in support of urban solidarity.

TERESA FRANCHINI

Born and educated in Argentina as architect, Teresa Franchini is currently living in Madrid, Spain. Her academic background comprises several degrees: PhD at the Madrid Polytechnic School, MSc at the University College London, and two Diplomas on City and Regional Planning. She has a long experience as lecturer in urban and regional planning, being at present Associate Professor and Coordinator of the Planning Department at CEU-San Pablo Polytechnic School in Madrid. As a researcher she collaborates with the Spanish National Council of Scientific Research. She is author of several books and articles on urban and regional issues and as a professional she has participated in the drafting of numerous regional, municipal and special plans. Between 2002 and 2005 she held one of the Vice-Presidencies of the International Society of City and Regional Planners (ISOCARP). At present she is member of ISOCARP Scientific Committee.

MICHAIL GALANAKIS

Michail Galanakis (born 1969) is concluding his postdoctoral research on intercultural public space at the Department of Geography and Geosciences of Helsinki University funded by the Finnish Academy (Decision No. 137954). Galanakis' main research interest is urban public space as social space, and his perspective revolves around issues of inclusion. Galanakis, a trained architect and designer has been living in Finland since 2001 where he has been investigating the importance of social sustainability in our increasingly diverse cities. Galanakis conducts research, writes articles, teaches and loves to discover cities and their cultures.

ANNA HÁBLOVÁ

Anna Háblová studied architecture at the Faculty of Architecture in Prague where she continues to study PhD with the theme 'Influence of globalization on cities and shopping malls'. She works as an architect and urban planner in design studio Headhand. She got experiences in SeArch and JiranKohout design studios. She has won many awards for her architectural design and urban theoretical contributions. Among others for her dissertation 'Vision for Prague' at Young Architecture Award 2010. art, performances and writing poetry.

INSTITUTE FOR SUSTAINABILITY

The Institute for Sustainability is an independent charity established in 2009 to support cross sector collaboration and innovation. The Institute's mission is to significantly accelerate the delivery of economically, environmentally and socially sustainable cities and communities. The

Institute does this by driving innovative demonstration projects and developing programmes to actively capture and share learning and best practice.

DELJANA IOSSIFOVA
Dr Deljana Iossifova is a Lecturer in Architectural Studies at the University of Manchester. She holds a PhD in Public Policy Design from Tokyo Institute of Technology and a diploma in Architecture from the Swiss Federal Institute of Technology (ETH Zurich). At the time of the EUSS, she was a Research Fellow on the project Scarcity and Creativity in the Built Environment (SCIBE) at the University of Westminster. Prior to that, she was a PhD/Postdoctoral Fellow at the United Nations University, Institute of Advanced Studies (Sustainable Urban Futures Programme). As an architect, Iossifova has practiced in Europe, the United States and East Asia. She frequently contributes to the Europe China Research and Advice Network (ECRAN) on EU-China relations around urbanisation and sustainability.

ALLISON KILLING
Alison Killing is an architect and urbanist based in Rotterdam, the Netherlands,where she runs her own design practice, Killing Architects. Before starting herown studio Alison worked for a number of international offices in the fields ofarchitecture and urban design, including BuroHappold and KeesChristiaanse.Her recent work includes an invited competition for a new building for the GerritRietveld Academy in Amsterdam; a study of financial models for temporary useprojects funded by the Dutch Architecture Fund; and a study of responses to humanitarianemergencies in cities and the ways in which urban design and urbanplanning tools could strengthen an emergency response, funded by the RIBA.

MICHAEL KLEIN
Michael Klein is an architect and researcher based in Vienna, Austria. He studied architecture at Vienna University of Technology and the EcoleSpecialed'Architecture in Paris and graduated from the Academy of Fine Arts Vienna in 2007. Since then, he has been working in the field of architecture, landscape architecture and urbanism. From 2009 on, Michael has been lecturing and teaching design classes at Vienna University of Technology. His theoretical research interest focuses on how political thinking, its theory and economic conditions affect design, architecture and the urban environment.

CLENN KUSTERMANS
Clenn Kustermans is a spatial planner for the privately held company OMGEVING in Antwerp, Belgium. Currently, he is involved in strategic spatial planning, spatial research, infrastructure planning and land use zoning. After Clenn had finished his studies in town and regional planning in 2008, he worked for the municipal boards of Breda and Roosendaal (both in the Netherlands) until 2011. Clenn is a self-proclaimed writer. Within his short writing career he has won two qualifying rounds of the writing competition Write Now. The content of his short stories and poems is often related to urban space. On short term Clenn will become a reporter on developments and exhibitions in architecture and urban planning for DeSingel, an arts campus in Antwerp.

GIULIA MACI
Giulia is an architect and urban planner. After completing her architecture degree she worked

in Italy, Macedonia, Turkey, Albania and The Netherlands. In addition, she took part in several international workshops on urban design and published a number of articles in journals and conferences, on architecture and planning in the Balkans region. She also recently graduated in Urban Planning and Management at Erasmus University, Rotterdam with a specialization in Urban and Regional Development and Housing.

SERENA MAIOLI

Serena earned her Master of Architecture in 2011 graduating magna cum laude in urban design at the Facoltà di Architettura di Ferrara, with a thesis titled 'No concept: hybrid architecture for the archipelago city' focused on public space and buildings' regeneration in the Rotterdam's former harbour. She participated in many international workshops investigating the centrality of public space in contemporary cities, such as 'ALIAS: pratiche urbane in spazialtri', in partnership with EcosistemaUrbano, and 'Think Fluid Town'collaborating with IZMO and Carlo Ratti Associates. Furthermore, she works on social communication and civic involvement in urban life.

CARLOS MANNS

Carlos Manns has 10 years of experience as Architect in his own practice and international practice such as MVRDV, Architecture Studio and Aedas among others. Carlos also has been teaching at University de Chile, Talca and Portales and worked on the organization of Students Competition for the Biennale and the curatory of the Architecture Room at the Museum of Contemporary Art in Santiago, Chile. He has an MSc from UCL in Building & Urban Design and was involved in the research of urban transformations in Dharavi, Istanbul and London.

RAMON MARRADES SEMPERE

Ramon Marrades holds a degree in Economics (University of Valencia) and MSc in Economic and Geography (Utrecht University). As a researcher he focuses on studying city resilience to economic shocks and public policy assessment on a territorial basis, being part of a multidisciplinary team (l'Ambaixada), which manage urban interventions and city consulting. He has been guest lecturer at University of Valencia and has co-authored two books about urban economics. As an entrepreneur, he leads Cien Pies to manage walking bus schemes (to gets kids walking to school).

PETER B. MEYER

Peter B. Meyer, Ph.D., is Professor Emeritus of Urban Policy and Economics, and Director Emeritus of the Centre for Environmental Policy and Management, at the University of Louisville, Kentucky, USA. He previously served as Director of the Local Economic Development Assistance Centre at The Pennsylvania State University for over a decade after participating in founding the first undergraduate program in Community Development in the country. He also is President and Chief Economist of The E.P. Systems Group, Inc., a private research firm that has conducted economic development and environmental policy analysis for over 30 years. A specialist in community and local economic development, Dr Meyer has been engaged in local area economic development research and practice since the 1970s, researching the forces shaping urban infill and spatial expansion patterns and their economic, social and environmental impacts. His experience spans the US, Western Europe, and Third World countries including Bangladesh. He is currently advising local US governments on innovative financing for energy efficiency programs under funds from the US Department of Energy. He continues to write about local development issues and conflicts.

ISIS NUNEZ FERRERA

Isis is a Honduran architect specializing in urban planning, design and international development. She holds an MSc in Urban Design for Development from University College London and is currently a PhD researcher at the University of Westminster as part of the international HERA funded project on Scarcity and Creativity in the Built Environment (SCIBE). Her experience includes over 5 years of research and fieldwork on the urban dimensions of chronic poverty, diversity in the built environment, urban transport, citizen participation, slum upgrading and community-led development in Honduras, Brazil, India, Turkey, Kenya and the UK. She has collaborated on issues of housing rights and inclusive approaches with UN-HABITAT, Practical Action-UK, Overseas Development Institute (ODI), Development Planning Unit (DPU) at University College London, local government agencies in Honduras and various grassroots organizations. She is currently an associate of Architecture Sans Frontieres - UK, working in coordinating and developing the Change-by-Design international workshops undertaken in Salvador da Bahia, Brazil and Nairobi, Kenya.

MAT PROCTOR

Mathieu has qualifications and experience in architecture, urban design and spatial planning, and has worked in both the public and private sectors in the UK and Australia. Currently advising local authorities on the spatial design content of their statutory planning documents on behalf of the Design Council, amongst other projects Mathieu has worked on master plans in Western Sydney, urban design frameworks for expanding English New Towns, and advised state government on the development of large-scale strategic development sites in New South Wales. Sustainable communities in the broadest sense, encompassing architectural design, infrastructure provision, and employment opportunities within actual 'places' is Mathieu's core pursuit.

AGATINO RIZZO

Agatino Rizzo works as a lecturer of urban planning and design in the School of Architecture and Planning of the National Institute of Creative Arts and Industries at The University of Auckland. Between 2007 and 2008 Dr Rizzo worked as a post-graduate researcher at the Bauhaus Dessau Foundation. Since 2009 dr. Rizzo has worked as a faculty in the urban planning programs at University Technology Malaysia, Qatar University and the University of Auckland. His main research interests include topics such as mega-urbanisation and strategic urban planning in the developed and developing worlds.

JUDITH RYSER

Qualified as an architect and urbanist with an MSc in Social Sciences, Judith Ryser is dedicating her cosmopolitan professional life to the built environment, its sustainability and its contribution to the knowledge society. Her research activities in Paris, Berlin, Stockholm, Geneva (United Nations), Brussels (EU), Madrid and London in public sector posts, private practice and universities focused on cities and development strategies with emphasis on Europe. Based in London, she researches, edits and writes books, articles and reviews, produces reports for international organisations, guest lectures and works with community groups. She speaks at international professional conferences and carries out consultancies. She was invited to write an official blog towards the Open Cities project by the British Council. She is a member of the International Advisory Council of the FundacionMetropoli with which she engages in projects, is writing and editing books and plans an outreach in London. She was Vice-President of ISOCARP for which she led an Urban Advisory Planning Team, served on the editorial board and an award jury, wrote and edited many books and articles, and is joint editor of the International Manual of Planning Practice. She is a member of the Chartered Institute of Journalists serving on the International Committee, a member of the Urban Design Group and its editorial board.

RUI SANTOS

Rui Santos is an architect and a doctoral student of Urban Studies based in Lisbon. He concluded his Degree in Architecture at the Oporto University in 2007 and since then has been researching on eco-friendly architecture(s). In 2011, and after finishing his internship at UDLE-Nepal, he presented his Master thesis on 'Community-level Participatory Planning in Developing Countries' at the TU Berlin. For long interested in the discourses and practices linking architecture(s) to sustainability concerns, he currently aims at exploring the attachments between the production of space(s) and post-growth ideas.

CHEMA SEGOVIA

Architect from EscuelaTécnica Superior de Arquitectura of the University of Sevilla. He was a student of Elena Turetti at the Politecnico di Milano, where he became interested in theoretical research. His work since then has led him to understand reflection as being a purposeful exercise that leads to action. He is focused on observing sensitively the close urban environment and the ways cities are built. Among his works are 'Habitar entre líneas', a look from the present towards the planning and development perspectives of La Costa del Sol in Málaga, and 'Contravalación', which documents and explores the inner rhythms of the frontier between Spain and Gibraltar from a landscape point of view. Furthermore, he is a member of the contents coordination team of AulaCiutat and a developer of the theoretical frame of La Ciudad Construida together with Ramon Marrades and David Estal.

ULYSSES SENGUPTA

Ulysses Sengupta is Senior Lecturer in Architecture at the Manchester Metropolitan University and Director of SoftGrid Limited, an Architecture & Urban Design focused internationally networked office. Practitioners in the SoftGrid Network have been involved in some of the largest urban regeneration projects in the U.K. and are currently involved in large urban scale projects in China. Ulysses was Design Unit Leader at the University of Nottingham and Lecturer at the University of East London. He attempts to progress a parallel discourse between practice and theory on the subjects of architecture and urban design through teaching and research in the U.K. and abroad. His research attempts to address planning for currently unplannable topographies and methods of speculative design for alternative futures incorporating constant change, by inventing new theoretical approaches and implementable tools.

SEBASTIAN SEYFARTH

From 2005 until 2008 Sebastian studied Architecture at Brandenburg University of Technology Cottbus Germany. In 2008 he received the STUDEXA scholarship, an exchange grant which enabled him to study 2 trimester World Heritage studies at the 'University of Tsukuba' in Japan.

This experience was followed by an Internship at the architecture office Shigeru Ban Architects in Tokyo. Back in Germany in 2009 he worked at the architecture office Graft in Berlin. 2010 he started studying the international architectural generalist Master study course Architektur. Studium.Generale which allowed him to study in eight different universities. He is the recipient of various scholarships and is fluent in German and English and conversant in Japanese.

NICK WOLFF

Nick Wolff has an MSc from UCL in Building & Urban Design in Development. He has over 10 years of experience in urban regeneration and has worked extensively on a range of successful economic development projects in the most deprived parts of inner London. He is also on the board of an NGO working on slum development programmes in Africa.

PARTICIPANTS AND TUTORS

Alessandra Lualdi, Alex Bax, Alexandros Gasparatos, Anita Brechbühl, Anna Bocian, Anna Háblová, Annalisa Lodigiani, Assemble Studio, Barbara Elisabeth Ascher, BjörnBracke, Bodhisattva Chattopadhyay, Carlos Manns, Christine Oluwole, Claire Harper, Claudia Piscitelli, Clenn Kustermans, David Knight, Deljana Iossifova, Derek Martin, DominikaDudek, Duncan Bowie, Eoghan-Conor O'Shea, Eric Cheung, Farinaz Falaki Moghadam, Fotis Grammatikopoulos, Gary Grant, Giulia Maci, Henk van der Kamp, Huan-Qing Li, Isis Nunez Ferrera, Izabela Mironowicz, James Warne, Jeremy Till, Joel Abumere Idaye, Jon Goodbun, Judith Ryser, Kathryn Firth, Katia Pimenova, Lauri Lihtmaa, Marina Sapunova, Mat Proctor, Mateus Lira da Matta Machado, Matteo Basso, Michael Casey, Michael Klein, Mike Whitehurst, Naznin Chowdhury, Nick Wolff, Nikolay Zalesskiy, Nuala Flood, Peter B. Meyer, PiotrLorens, Ramon Marrades, Robert Tensen, Rony Hobeika, Rui Santos, Sebastian Seyfarth, Seppe de Blust, Serena Maioli, Silvio Caputo, Stefan Webb, Stella Okeahialam, Steve Tomlinson, Steven Chodoriwsky, Teresa Franchini, Tuba Dogu, Tuba Kolat, Ulysses Sengupta, Victoria Fierro, Vincent Goodstadt

PARTNERS

The Third European Urban Summer School (EUSS) – Times of Scarcity: reclaiming the possibility of making – was hosted in London by the University of Westminster, School of Architecture and the Built Environment, in collaboration with the Association of European Schools of Planning (AESOP), the International Federation for Housing and Planning (IFHP), the European Council of Spatial Planners (ECTP-CEU) and the International Society for City and Regional Planners (ISOCARP). The main partner in facilitating the EUSS was the team behind the project Scarcity and Creativity in the Built Environment (SCIBE) at the University of Westminster. Architecture collective Assemble generously provided working space at Sugarhouse Studios for the duration of the Summer School.

THE ASSOCIATION OF EUROPEAN SCHOOLS OF PLANNING (AESOP)

The Association of European Schools of Planning (AESOP), established in 1987, is an international association of universities teaching and researching in the field of spatial planning.

AESOP has the aims of:
* promoting within Europe the development of teaching and research in the field of planning;
* instigating cooperation and exchange between planning schools in Europe, and encouraging the harmonisation and equivalence of degrees which they award;
* coordinating initiatives which include other stakeholders in planning and
* representing the interests of European planning schools, particularly within Europe, at national and international level, and before both public and private institutions.

In 2012, more than 150 institutions, mainly European universities, were AESOP members. Current President (2012-

2014) is Gert de Roo (University of Groningen) and Secretary General (2011-2015) is Izabela Mironowicz. AESOP Secretariat General is located (2011-2015) in Poland, at the Wrocław University of Technology. More about AESOP activities can be found at www.aesop-planning.eu.

THE INTERNATIONAL FEDERATION FOR HOUSING AND PLANNING (IFHP)

The International Federation for Housing and Planning (IFHP) is a worldwide network of professionals representing the broad field of housing and planning. The Federation organizes a wide range of activities across the globe creating opportunities for an international exchange of knowledge and experience in these professional fields. The aim of such activities is to instigate positive change in urban environments towards an improved quality of life.

IFHP is a communication platform and network, promoting mutual learning and inspiration, and generating new ideas amongst professionals in order to equip them to find the best local solutions to the global challenges facing housing and planning today.

Since the summer of 2013, IFHP is based in Copenhagen, Denmark.

EUROPEAN COUNCIL OF SPATIAL PLANNERS -CONSEIL EUROPÉEN DES URBANISTES (ECRP-CEU)

Founded in 1985, ECTP-CEU brings together 25 professional town planning associations and institutes from 23 European countries as well as corresponding members. It is an umbrella association providing its members with a common framework to promote the visibility, recognition of the important societal role and practice of planning and urban development in Europe and its teaching, continuing professional development and the definition of professional responsibilities.

ECTP-CEU sets standards of education and conduct for the planning profession; engages in dialogue with local, national and European government; and identifies, and rewards examples of good planning all over Europe in particular through its awards.

Creating our futures

ECTP-CEU
European Council of Spatial Planners
Conseil européen des urbanistes

THE INTERNATIONAL SOCIETY OF CITY AND REGIONAL PLANNERS (ISOCARP)

The International Society of City and Regional Planners (ISOCARP) is a global association of experienced professional

planners. It was founded in 1965 in a bid to bring together recognised and qualified planners in an international network, which now covers some 80 countries worldwide.

ISOCARP aims to improve planning practice, encourage the exchange of professional knowledge between planners, promote the planning profession in all its forms, stimulate and improve planning research, training and education and enhance public awareness and understanding of major planning issues at a global level.

It organises an annual congress, seminars, working groups, awards and advisory teams. Its activities are covered in publications such as the ISOCARP Review, the International Manual of Planning Practice (IMPP), Congress proceedings etc.

SCARCITY AND CREATIVITY IN THE BUILT ENVIRONMENT (SCIBE)

SCARCITY AND CREATIVITY IN THE BUILT ENVIRONMENT

EUROPEAN COMMISSION
European Research Area

SEVENTH FRAMEWORK
PROGRAMME

Funded under Socio-economic Sciences & Humanities

SCIBE explored the relationship between scarcity and creativity in the context of the built environment by investigating how conditions of scarcity might affect the creativity of the different actors involved in the production of architecture and urban design, and how design-led actions might improve the built environment in the future. Research was based on the analysis of processes in four European cities: London, Oslo, Reykjavik, and Vienna.

The project was financially supported by the HERA Joint Research Programme which is co-funded by AHRC, AKA, DASTI, ETF, FNR, FWF, HAZU, IRCHSS, MHEST, NWO, RANNIS, RCN, VR and The European Community FP7 2007-2013, under the Socio-economic Sciences and Humanities programme. For more information, see www.scibe.eu and www.scarcity.is